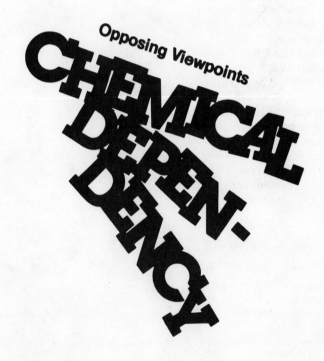

Opposing Viewpoints

CHEMICAL DEPEN- DENCY

Other Books of Related Interest in the Opposing Viewpoints Series:

American Values
Censorship
Crime & Criminals
Criminal Justice
Death & Dying

Other Books in the Opposing Viewpoints Series:

America's Prisons
American Foreign Policy
The American Military
The Arms Race
Central America
Constructing a Life Philosophy
The Ecology Controversy
The Energy Crisis
Male/Female Roles
The Middle East
Nuclear War
The Political Spectrum
Problems of Death
Religion and Human Experience
Science and Religion
Sexual Values
Social Justice
The Vietnam War
War & Human Nature
The Welfare State

Opposing Viewpoints

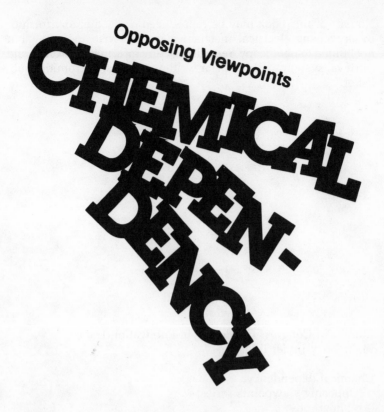

CHEMICAL DEPEN-DENCY

David L. Bender & Bruno Leone, Series Editors

Claudia Bialke Debner, Book Editor

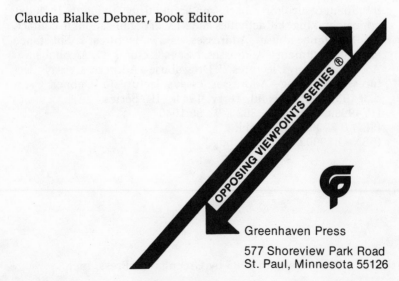

OPPOSING VIEWPOINTS SERIES ®

Greenhaven Press

577 Shoreview Park Road
St. Paul, Minnesota 55126

Library of Congress Cataloging-in-Publication Data
Main entry under title:

Chemical dependency.
   (Opposing viewpoints series)
   Bibliography: p.
   Includes index.
   Summary: Presents opposing viewpoints about the causes and treatment of alcohol, tobacco, and other drug addiction. Includes critical thinking skill activities and a list of organizations to contact.
   1. Substance abuse—Addresses, essays, lectures. 2. Substance abuse—Treatment—Addresses, essays, lectures. [1. Alcoholism—Addresses, essays, lectures. 2. Drug abuse—Addresses, essays, lectures. 3. Smoking—Addresses, essays, lectures] I. Debner, Claudia, 1951- .II. O'Neill, Terry, 1944- III. Series.
HV4998.C44 1985   362.2 9   85-16404
ISBN 0-89908-351-X (pbk.)
ISBN O-89908-376-5 (lib. bdg.)

"Congress shall make no law . . .
abridging the freedom of speech,
or of the press."

First Amendment to the US Constitution

The basic foundation of our democracy is the first amendment
guarantee of freedom of expression. The *Opposing Viewpoints
Series* is dedicated to the concept of this basic freedom and the
idea that it is more important to practice it than to enshrine it.

Contents

Chapter 3: How Harmful Is Tobacco?

Chapter 4: Should Drug-Related Laws Be Reformed?

Chapter 5: Is Drug Addiction Exaggerated?

Why Consider Opposing Viewpoints?

"It is better to debate a question without settling it than to settle a question without debating it."

Joseph Joubert (1754-1824)

The Importance of Examining Opposing Viewpoints

The purpose of the Opposing Viewpoints Series, and this book in particular, is to present balanced, and often difficult to find, opposing points of view on complex and sensitive issues.

Probably the best way to become informed is to analyze the positions of those who are regarded as experts and well studied on issues. It is important to consider every variety of opinion in an attempt to determine the truth. Opinions from the mainstream of society should be examined. But also important are opinions that are considered radical, reactionary, or minority as well as those stigmatized by some other uncomplimentary label. An important lesson of history is the eventual acceptance of many unpopular and even despised opinions. The ideas of Socrates, Jesus, and Galileo are good examples of this.

Readers will approach this book with their own opinions on the issues debated within it. However, to have a good grasp of one's own viewpoint, it is necessary to understand the arguments of those with whom one disagrees. It can be said that those who do not completely understand their adversary's point of view do not fully understand their own.

9

A persuasive case for considering opposing viewpoints has been presented by John Stuart Mill in his work *On Liberty*. When examining controversial issues it may be helpful to reflect on this suggestion:

> The only way in which a human being can make some approach to knowing the whole of a subject, is by hearing what can be said about it by persons of every variety of opinion, and studying all modes in which it can be looked at by every character of mind. No wise man ever acquired his wisdom in any mode but this.

Analyzing Sources of Information

The Opposing Viewpoints Series includes diverse materials taken from magazines, journals, books, and newspapers, as well as statements and position papers from a wide range of individuals, organizations and governments. This broad spectrum of sources helps to develop patterns of thinking which are open to the consideration of a variety of opinions.

Pitfalls to Avoid

A pitfall to avoid in considering opposing points of view is that of regarding one's own opinion as being common sense and the most rational stance and the point of view of others as being only opinion and naturally wrong. It may be that another's opinion is correct and one's own is in error.

Another pitfall to avoid is that of closing one's mind to the opinions of those with whom one disagrees. The best way to approach a dialogue is to make one's primary purpose that of understanding the mind and arguments of the other person and not that of enlightening him or her with one's own solutions. More can be learned by listening than speaking.

It is my hope that after reading this book the reader will have a deeper understanding of the issues debated and will appreciate the complexity of even seemingly simple issues on which good and honest people disagree. This awareness is particularly important in a democratic society such as ours where people enter into public debate to determine the common good. Those with whom one disagrees should not necessarily be regarded as enemies, but perhaps simply as people who suggest different paths to a common goal.

Developing Basic Reading and Thinking Skills

In this book, carefully edited opposing viewpoints are purposely placed back to back to create a running debate; each viewpoint is preceded by a short quotation that best expresses the author's main argument. This format instantly plunges the reader into the midst of a controversial issue and greatly aids that reader in mastering the basic skill of recognizing an author's point of view.

A number of basic skills for critical thinking are practiced in the activities that appear throughout the books in the series. Some of the skills are:

Evaluating Sources of Information The ability to choose from among alternative sources the most reliable and accurate source in relation to a given subject.

Separating Fact from Opinion The ability to make the basic distinction between factual statements (those that can be demonstrated or verified empirically) and statements of opinion (those that are beliefs or attitudes that cannot be proved).

Identifying Stereotypes The ability to identify oversimplified, exaggerated descriptions (favorable or unfavorable) about people and insulting statements about racial, religious or national groups, based upon misinformation or lack of information.

Recognizing Ethnocentrism The ability to recognize attitudes or opinions that express the view that one's own race, culture, or group is inherently superior, or those attitudes that judge another culture or group in terms of one's own.

It is important to consider opposing viewpoints and equally important to be able to critically analyze those viewpoints. The activities in this book are designed to help the reader master these thinking skills. Statements are taken from the book's viewpoints and the reader is asked to analyze them. This technique aids the reader in developing skills that not only can be applied to the viewpoints in this book, but also to situations where opinionated spokespersons comment on controversial issues. Although the activities are helpful to the solitary reader, they are most useful when the reader can benefit from the interaction of group discussion.

Using this book and others in the series should help readers develop basic reading and thinking skills. These skills should improve the reader's ability to understand what they read. Readers should be better able to separate fact from opinion, substance from rhetoric and become better consumers of information in our media-centered culture.

This volume of the Opposing Viewpoints Series does not advocate a particular point of view. Quite the contrary! The very nature of the book leaves it to the reader to formulate the opinions he or she finds most suitable. My purpose as publisher is to see that this is made possible by offering a wide range of viewpoints which are fairly presented.

David L. Bender
Publisher

Introduction

"Neither the overwhelming evidence of drug addiction's horrible cost, nor the lessons of history have had an appreciable impact on the misuse of drugs."

Millions of Americans are dependent on mood-altering chemicals ranging from nicotine to cocaine. Although not all drug usage ends in addiction, many studies link the chemically addicted to a higher rate of debilitating illness, crime, and even death. Virtually all sociologists would agree that drug addiction is one of America's serious endemic problems.

Neither the overwhelming evidence of drug addiction's horrible cost, nor the lessons of history have had an appreciable impact on the misuse of drugs. In the late 1700's, Thomas Jefferson estimated that "one-third of the people in the United States are killing themselves with whiskey." Last year, the National Institute on Alcohol Abuse and Alcoholism reported that alcohol was a factor in nearly 55 percent of fatal automobile accidents, and 60 percent of violent crimes; it was the most often cited contributing factor in divorce. According to the American Heart Association, tobacco is a contributing cause of 325,000 deaths annually. And in a recent issue of *Communication World,* estimates put the annual cost of illegal addictive drugs at 38 to 100 billion dollars. Much of this cost is linked to the rising drug-related crime rate.

The drug dependency problem facing the U.S. shows no signs of disappearing. Cocaine use rose an estimated 12 percent last year. Even heroin consumption increased slightly, due somewhat to the number of cocaine users who sought it for modifying "cocaine anxiety." Marijuana traffic rose approximately 5 percent. Alcohol and tobacco, in part because they are legal for adults, remained the pervasive drugs of choice.

The most popular method for reducing addiction has always been prohibition. For the first fifty years after America's first imported cigarettes arrived in the 1850's, state and federal legislatures alternately legislated and later repealed laws banning the cigarette. The movement to eradicate alcoholism culminated in 1919 with the 18th Amendment, commencing the Era of Prohibition. Passage of the 21st Amendment in 1933

13

ultimately repealed Prohibition.

Prevailing opinion now seems to favor attempting to halt the influx of illegal drugs in the foreign countries where they are produced. This has meant funneling millions of dollars into law enforcement narcotics operations and border patrols to slow the steady flow of cocaine, heroin, and marijuana into the U.S. Moreover, the U.S. government is politically pressuring drug-producing countries with threats to cut off aid if illegal drug production continues. As Edward I. Koch, mayor of New York, said, "Heroin and cocaine do not originate here, but have penetrated our borders with the impact and misery of a foreign invasion."

Another popular strategy for fighting drug use is to stress prevention, thereby stemming first use of drugs. William French Smith, U.S. attorney general, emphasized the need for this approach when he said, "The unpleasant fact is that unless you can eliminate the demand for drugs, the amount of money is so large that the dealers will continue to take whatever risk is necessary." One proposal for reducing chemical dependency is more programs to educate Americans on the addictiveness of alcohol, tobacco, and illegal drugs. Existing programs have not been measureably successful, but a 1984 Rand Corporation study concluded that comprehensive drug education programs offer the best approach to reducing drug abuse. The Rand study recommended that schools instigate preventive programs aimed at one of the most frequently cited causes of drug use among the young—peer pressure.

The overall scenario seems to reduce to this pivotal and complex question: Can America's problem of chemical dependency best be solved by eliminating the supply of drugs or by working toward reduction in the demand for drugs? *Chemical Dependency: Opposing Viewpoints* does not attempt to provide solutions to this multifaceted issue. Rather, it is intended to provide readers with information to aid them in reaching their own conclusions. The viewpoints are drawn from a broad spectrum of topical opinion on drug addiction, ranging from prevention to treatment. The sources include the varied opinions of senators, doctors, psychologists, sociologists, and numerous others including those personally affected by drug addiction. The questions debated are, What Are the Causes of Drug Abuse? How Serious a Problem is Alcoholism? How Harmful Is Tobacco? Should Drug Abuse Laws Be Reformed? Is Drug Addiction Exaggerated? and How Should Drug Addiction Be Treated? As with all books in this series, it is left to the reader to decide: Who is right?

What Are the Causes of Drug Abuse?

"The desire for high states is at the root of drug-taking in both children and grownups."

Pleasure-Seeking Causes Drug Dependency

Andrew Weil and Winifred Rosen

Andrew Weil is a research associate in ethnopharmacology at the Harvard Botanical Museum and is an adjunct professor of addiction studies at the University of Arizona. Dr. Weil received an A.B. degree cum laude in biology from Harvard and an M.D. degree from Harvard Medical School. Winifred Rosen, a New York writer, was a high school teacher for several years before she began writing books for young people. In the following viewpoint, the authors describe the innate need for humans to alter their level of consciousness and seek pleasure through drug use.

As you read, consider the following questions:

1. What are some of the other methods besides drugs that the authors suggest for varying conscious experience?
2. According to the authors, what are three ways in which drugs are used in various societies?
3. The authors list several historical figures who experimented with psychoactive substances. Do you think that this experimentation should be limited to adults who are aware of the risks? Why or why not?

The basic reason people take drugs is to vary their conscious experience. Of course there are many other ways to alter consciousness, such as listening to music, making music, dancing, fasting, chanting, exercising, surfing, meditating, falling in love, hiking in the wilderness (if you live in a city), visiting a city (if you live in the wilderness), having sex, daydreaming, watching fireworks, going to a movie or play, jumping into cold water after taking a hot sauna, participating in religious rituals. The list is probably endless, and includes nearly all the activities that people put most of their time, energy, and hard-earned money into. This suggests that changing consciousness is something people like to do.

Human beings, it seems, are born with a need for periodic variations in consciousness. The behavior of young children supports this idea. Infants rock themselves into blissful states; many children discover that whirling, or spinning, is a powerful technique to change awareness; some also experiment with hyperventilation (rapid, deep breathing) followed by mutual chest-squeezing or choking, and tickling to produce paralyzing laughter. Even though these practices may produce some uncomfortable results, such as dizziness or nausea, the whole experience is so reinforcing that children do it again and again, often despite parental objections. Since children all over the world engage in these activities, the desire to change consciousness does not seem to be a product of a particular culture but rather to arise from something basically human. As children grow older they find that certain available substances put them in similar states. The attractiveness of drugs is that they provide an easy, quick route to these experiences.

Many drug users talk about getting high. Highs are states of consciousness marked by feelings of euphoria, lightness, self-transcendence, concentration, and energy. People who never take drugs also seek out highs. In fact, having high experiences from time to time may be necessary to our physical and mental health, just as dreaming at night seems to be vital to our well-being. Perhaps that is why a desire to alter normal consciousness exists in everyone and why people pursue the experiences even though there are sometimes uncomfortable side effects.

Although the desire for high states is at the root of drug-taking in both children and grownups, people also take drugs for other, more practical reasons. These include:

To Aid Religious Practices

Throughout history, people have used drug-induced states to transcend their sense of separateness and feel more at one with nature, God, and the supernatural. Marijuana was used for this purpose in ancient India, and many psychedelic plants are still so used today by Indians in North and South America. Alcohol has been used for religious purposes in many parts of the world; the role of wine in Roman Catholic and Judaic rites persists as an example. Among primitive people, psychoactive plants are often considered sacred—gifts from gods and spirits to unite people with the higher realms.

To Explore the Self

Curious individuals throughout history have taken psychoactive substances to explore and investigate parts of their own minds not ordinarily accessible. One of the most famous modern examples was the British writer and philosopher Aldous Huxley, who experimented extensively with mescaline in the 1950s. He left us a record of his investigations in a book called *The Doors of Perception.* Some other well-known "explorers" are Oliver Wendell Holmes, the nineteenth-century American physician, poet, and author, who experimented with ether; William James, the Harvard psychologist and philosopher of the late nineteenth century, who used nitrous oxide; Sigmund Freud, the father of psychoanalysis, who took cocaine; William S. Burroughs, a contemporary American novelist and user of opiates; Richard Alpert (Ram Dass), a psychologist and guru, who has extensive experience with LSD and other psychedelics; and John Lilly, a medical researcher and philsopher, who has experimented with ketamine. Many others who have followed this path have done so privately, keeping their experiences to themselves, or sharing them only with intimate companions.

Chemical Balance Affects Feelings

By the early seventies, a handful of researchers scattered around the world had come to a startling conclusion: opium, and a wide variety of other drugs from LSD to aspirin, worked by mimicking endogenous chemicals—*substances already in the body.* Tiny shifts in the balances of these molecular human components govern not only how we feel physically, but also our mental state—who we are—at any given moment. And since the balance of chemicals inside the body can vary from moment to moment and person to person, drugs which mimic them naturally may produce widely variant experiences.

Dean Latimer and Jeff Goldberg, *Flowers in the Blood,* 1981.

"Let's have a drink" is one of the most frequent phrases in use today. It is an invitation to share time and communication around the consumption of a psychoactive drug. Like sharing food, taking drugs together is a ritual excuse for intimacy; coffee breaks and cocktail ("happy") hours are examples of the way approved drugs are used for this purpose. Disapproved drugs may draw people together even more strongly by establishing a bond of common defiance of authority. At the big rock concerts and Vietnam War protests of the 1960s, strangers often became instant comrades simply by passing a joint back and forth.

In different cultures other drugs perform the same function. For example, South American Indians take coca breaks together, much as we take coffee breaks, and chewing coca leaves with a friend establishes an important social bond. For South Sea Islanders, drinking kava in groups at night is the equivalent of an American cocktail party.

Aside from the ritual significance with which drugs are invested, their pharmacological effects may also enhance social interaction. Because alcohol lowers inhibitions in most people, businessmen and women have drinks at lunch to encourage openness and congeniality. Similarly, on dates people often drink to reduce anxiety and feelings of awkwardness. By producing alertness and euphoria, stimulants, such as cocaine, promote easy conversation, even among strangers.

So important is this function of psychoactive drugs that many people would find it difficult to relate to others if deprived of them.

To Enhance Pleasure

Human beings are pleasure-seeking animals who are very inventive when it comes to finding ways to excite their senses and gratify their appetites. One of the characteristics of sensory pleasure is that it becomes dulled with repetition, and there are only so many ways of achieving pleasure. As much time, thought, and energy have gone into sex as into any human activity, but the possibilities of sexual positions and techniques are limited. By making people feel different, psychoactive drugs can make familiar experiences new and interesting again. The use of drugs in combination with sex is as old as the hills, as is drug use with such activities as dancing, eating, and listening to or playing music. Drinking wine with meals is an example of this behavior that dates back to prehistory and is still encouraged by society. Some men say that a good cigar and a glass of brandy make a fine meal complete. Pot lovers say that turning on is the perfect way for a fine meal to begin. Psychedelic drugs, especially, are intensifiers of experience and can make a sunset more fascinating than a movie. (Of course, psychedelics can also turn an unpleasant situation into a living nightmare.) Because drugs can, temporarily at least, make the ordinary extraordinary, many people seek them out and consume them in an effort to get more enjoyment out of life.

> "Not only through advertising, but in the feverish emphasis on success, on winning at all costs, on being the center of attention through one kind of performance or another. . . We are an addictive society."

Society's Pressure Causes Drug Dependency

Philip Slater

Philip Slater, a well-known writer on psychological topics, is the author of *Pursuit of Loneliness* and *Wealth Addiction*. In the following viewpoint, Mr. Slater claims that American culture and its pervasive advertising generate unrealistic pressure on individuals to succeed. He insists that this pressure then causes many individuals to use drugs to relieve anxiety.

As you read, consider the following questions:
1. How does the author link noise pollution to drug addiction?
2. What does Mr. Slater see as the inevitable outcome of drug abuse?
3. According to the author, how do corporations fuel Americans' chemical addictiveness?

Philip Slater, "Want-creation Fuels Americans' Addictiveness," *St. Paul Dispatch,* September 6, 1984. Reprinted with the author's permission.

Imagine what life in America would be like today if the surgeon general convinced Congress that cigarettes, as America's most lethal drug, should be made illegal.

The cost of tobacco would increase 5,000 percent. Law enforcement budgets would quadruple but still be hopelessly inadequate to the task. The tobacco industry would become mob-controlled, and large quantities of Turkish tobacco would be smuggled into the country through New York and Miami.

Politicans would get themselves elected by inveighing against tobacco abuse. Some would argue shrewdly that the best enforcement strategy was to go after the growers and advertisers—making it a capital offense to raise or sell tobacco. And a great many Americans would try smoking for the first time.

Americans are individualists. We like to express our opinions much more than we like to work together. Passing laws is one of the most popular pastimes, and enforcing them one of the least. We make laws like we make New Year's resolutions—the impulse often exhausted by giving voice to it. Who but Americans would have their food grown and harvested by people who were legally forbidden to be in the country?

We are a restless, inventive, dissatisifed people. We like novelty. We like to try new things. We may not want to change in any basic sense, any more than other people, but we like the illusion of movement.

We Love Quick Fixes

We like anything that looks like a quick fix—a new law, a new road, a new pill. We like immediate solutions. We want the pain to stop, the dull mood to pass, the problem to go away. The quicker the action, the better we like it. We like confrontation better than negotiation, antibiotics better than slow healing, majority rule better than community consensus, demolition better than renovation.

When we want something we want it fast and we want it cheap. Obstacles and complications annoy us. We don't want to stop to think about side effects, the Big Picture, or how it's going to make things worse in the long run. We aren't too interested in the long run, as long as something brings more money, a promotion or a new status symbol in the short.

Our model for problem-solving is the 30-second TV commercial, in which change is produced instantaneously and there is always a happy ending. The side effects, the pollution, the wasting diseases, the slow poisoning—all these unhappy complications fall into the great void outside that 30-second frame.

Nothing fits this scenario better than drugs—legal and illegal. The same impatience that sees an environmental impact report as an annoying bit of red tape makes us highly susceptible to any substance that can make us feel better within minutes after ingesting

21

it—whose immediate effects are more or less predictable and whose negative aspects are generally much slower to appear.

People take drugs everywhere, of course, and there is no sure way of knowing if the United States has more drug abusers than other countries. The term "abuse" itself is socially defined.

Family Doctor Helped

The typical suburban alcoholic of the '40s and '50s and the wealthy drunks glamorized in Hollywood movies of that period were not considered "drug abusers." Nor is the ex-heroin addict who has been weaned to a lifetime addiction to Methadone.

In the 19th century, morphine addicts (who were largely middle-aged, middle-class women) maintained their genteel but often heavy addictions quite legally, with the aid of the family doctor and local druggist. Morphine only became illegal when its use spread to young, poor, black males. (This transition created some embarrassment for political and medical commentators, who argued that a distinction had to be made between "drug addicts" and "dope fiends".)

A Changing Society Linked to Addiction

According to the head of the National Institute on Drug Abuse, alcohol and drug abuse among young Americans is epidemic. What might cause a whole society to move in this direction? The typical addict feels that he has little control over what happens to him in life. If many people in a culture feel this way, rates of addiction will increase culturewide. The young person in America today faces an overwhelmingly complex society, and one in which opportunities for achievement are daily more limited. This alone should not cause a jump in addiction. In addition, however, people no longer seem to have confidence in their ability to handle deviations from familiar patterns. Somehow our basic institutions—family, school, work, and love relationships—are not giving us the security and sense of competence we need to proceed in a world that has become less orderly.

Stanton Peele, *How Much Is Too Much?* 1981.

Yet addiction can be defined in a way that overrides these biases. Anyone who cannot or will not let a day pass without ingesting a substance should be considered addicted to it, and by this definition Americans are certainly addiction-prone.

It would be hard to find a society in which so great a variety of different substances have been "abused" by so many different kinds of people. There are drugs for every group, philosophy and social class: marijuana and psychedelics for the '60s counterculture, heroin for the hopeless of all periods, PCP for the angry and desperate, and cocaine for modern Yuppies and Yumpies.

Drugs do, after all, have different effects, and people select the effects they want. At the lower end of the social scale people want a peaceful escape from a hopeless and depressing existence, and for this heroin is the drug of choice. Cocaine, on the other hand, with its energized euphoria and illusion of competence is particularly appealing to affluent achievers—those both obsessed and acquainted with success.

Paradoxical Addiction

Addiction among the affluent seems paradoxical to outsiders. From the viewpoint of most people in the world an American man or woman making over $50,000 a year has everything a human being could dream of. Yet very few such people—even those with hundreds of millions of dollars—feel this way themselves. While they may not suffer the despair of the very poor, there seems to be a kind of frustration and hopelessness that seeps into all social strata in our society. The affluent may have acquired a great deal, but they seem not to have acquired what they wanted.

Most drugs—heroin, alcohol, cocaine, speed, tranquilizers, barbiturates—virtually all of them except the psychedelics and to some extent marijuana—have a numbing effect. We might then ask: Why do so many Americans need to numb themselves?

Life in modern society is admittedly harsh and confusing considering the pace for which our bodies were designed. Noise pollution alone might justify turning down our sensory volume: It's hard today even in a quiet suburb or rural setting to find respite from the harsh sound of "labor-saving" machines.

But it would be absurd to blame noise pollution for drug addiction. This rasping clamor that grates daily on our ears is only a symptom—one tangible consequence of our peculiar lifestyle. For each of us wants to be able to exert his or her will and control without having to negotiate with anyone else.

"I have a right to run my machine and do my work" even if it makes your rest impossible. "I have a right to hear my music" even if this makes it impossible to hear your music, or better yet, enjoy that most rare and precious of modern commodities: silence. "I have a right to make a profit" even if it means poisoning you, your children and your children's children. "I have a right to have a drink when I want to and drive my car when I want to" even if it means totaling your car and crippling your life.

Rich in Aggravation

This intolerance of any constraint or obstacle makes our lives rich in conflict and aggravation. Each day we encounter the noise, distress and lethal fallout of the dilemmas we brushed aside so impatiently the day before. Each day the postponed problems multiply, proliferate, metastasize—but this only makes us more aggravated and impatient than we were before. And since we're unwilling to change our ways it becomes more and more necessary to anesthetize ourselves to the havoc we've wrought.

We don't like the thought of attuning ourselves to nature or to a group or community. We like to fantasize having control over our lives, and drugs seem to make this possible. With drugs you are not only master of your fate and captain of your soul, you are dictator of your body as well.

Unwilling to respond to its own needs and wants, you goad it into activity with caffeine in the morning and slow it down with alcohol at night. If the day goes poorly, a little cocaine will set it right, and if quiet relaxation and sensual enjoyment is called for, marijuana.

Cocaine or alcohol makes a party or a performance go well. Nothing is left to chance. The quality of experience is measured by how many drugs or drinks were consumed rather than by the experience itself. Most of us are unwilling to accept the fact that life has good days and bad days. We attempt—unsuccessfully but

These kids and their drugs nowadays—don't
they know it's just a form of escapism?''

© Uluschak/Rothco

24

valiantly—to postpone all the bad days until that fateful moment when the body presents us with all our IOUs, tied up in a neat bundle called cancer, heart disease, cirrhosis or whatever.

Every great sage and spiritual leader throughout history has emphasized that happiness comes not from getting more but from learning to want less. Clearly this is a hard lesson for humans, since so few have learned it.

Billions Creating Want

But in our society we spend billions each year creating want. Covetousness, discontent and greed are taught to our children, drummed into them—they are bombarded with it. Not only through advertising, but in the feverish emphasis on success, on winning at all costs, on being the center of attention through one kind of performance or another, on being the first at something— no matter how silly or stupid ("The Guinness Book of Records"). We are an addictive society.

Addiction is a state of wanting. It is a condition in which the individual feels he or she is incomplete, inadequate, lacking, not whole, and can only be made whole by the addition of something external.

This need not be a drug. It can be money, food, fame, sex, responsibility, power, good deeds, possessions, cleaning—the addictive impulse can attach itself to anything, real or symbolic. You're addicted to something whenever you feel it completes you—that you wouldn't be a whole person without it. When you try to make sure it's always there, that there's always a good supply on hand.

Most of us are a little proud of the supposed personality defects that make addiction "necessary"—the "I can't...," "I have to...," "I always...," "I never..." But such "lacks" are all delusional. It's fun to brag about not being able to live without something but it's just pomposity. We are all human, and given water, a little food, and a little warmth, we'll survive.

But it's very hard to hang onto this humanity when we're told every day that we're ignorant, misguided, inadequate, incompetent and undesirable and that we will emerge from this terrible condition only if we eat or drink or buy something, at which point we'll magically and instantly feel better.

Purchases Make Whole?

We may be smart enough not to believe the silly claims of the individual ad, but can we escape the underlying message on which all of them agree? That you can only be made whole and healthy by buying or ingesting something? Can we reasonably complain about the amount of addiction in our society when we teach it every day?

A Caribbean worker once said, apropos of the increasing role of

25

Western products in the economy of his country: "Your corporations are like mosquitoes. I don't so much mind their taking a little of my blood, but why do they have to leave that nasty itch in its place?"

It seems futile to spend hundreds of billions of dollars trying to intercept the flow of drugs—arresting and imprisoning those who meet the demand for them, when we activate and nourish that demand every day. Until we get tired of encouraging the pursuit of illusory fixes and begin to celebrate and refine what we already are and have, addictive substances will always proliferate faster than we can control them.

"The youngster who tried drugs in response to peer pressure, then continued because of pleasurable effect, may turn to chemicals in times of stress."

Peer Pressure Causes Drug Dependency

Donald Ian Macdonald

Donald Ian Macdonald is a well-known speaker and consultant on drug abuse. A pediatrician, he is also clinical associate professor of pediatrics at the University of South Florida Medical School and is president of the Florida Pediatric Association. He is president of the Scientific Advisory Council of the American Council on Drug Education and is director of clinical research of STRAIGHT, Inc., an adolescent treatment program. In the following viewpoint, he explains why teenagers are at high risk for drug dependency.

As you read, consider the following questions:

1. What are the reasons the author gives for the susceptibility of teenagers to abuse drugs?
2. Does Dr. Macdonald believe that all teenagers who try drugs will become addicted to them?
3. What are the four options that Dr. Macdonald cites as available to advanced drug abusers?

"Drugs, Drinking and Adolescents," by Dr. Donald Ian Macdonald. Reprinted courtesy of Committees of Correspondence, Inc. and Dr. Donald Ian Macdonald.

How serious are adolescent keg parties, media popularization of marijuana and cocaine, alcohol advertisements aimed at youth, the question of legal drinking age, and the management of youthful drug offenders? The answer depends on one's understanding of the increased susceptibility of the adolescent to chemical dependency and the tendency of drug use to progressively increase.

Normal adolescents are at high risk because of their curiosity, their love of risk-taking and excitement, their tendency to rebel, their need to prove themselves grown up, and most of all because of their desire to be accepted by their peers.

They are at increased risk because they begin adolescence as dependent persons lacking mature coping systems. The developmental status of the early adolescent, described so well by the psychologists Sigmund Freud and Jean Piaget, does not include the ability to adopt truly adult ethical and moral behavior.

Beginning Experiments

Drug use begins as an experiment. Most children refuse marijuana the first time it is offered, but more than 60 percent eventually try it. The first experience may produce no euphoria, but with subsequent exposure and practice the child learns to feel good chemically. Alcohol may be his first drug, and his first experience with intoxication is often at home.

The main risks of psychoactive drugs are their ability to distort sensual perception, alter response, and produce pleasure. This pleasure, so easily obtained, becomes a strong inducement to continued use. Another incentive is the pressure exerted by drug-using peers who welcome the newcomer into membership in their illicit, and, at first, exciting society.

The pursuit of pleasure is an essential human drive associated with vital functions of nourishment, reproduction, and relaxation. All pleasure, however, is strongly reinforcing. It can become habit-forming and dangerous. Pleasure that has no purpose other than the pleasure itself is particularly risky.

Parents, asked what they want their children to be when they grow up, frequently respond, "I don't care what Charley becomes as long as he's happy." This well-meaning but dangerous answer may add to our society's general hedonism, which says, "If it feels good, do it."

In the Long Run

A better answer might be, "I want Charley to grow up feeling good about himself," "living up to his potential," "having spiritual awareness," or "making a contribution to his society." These answers imply some deferment of gratification. In the long run, they are the most likely to produce satisfaction and stable happiness.

For most, experimentation with drugs leads to "moderate" or

"recreational" use. The user perceives few, if any, consequences of his drug use. He begins to look forward to weekend parties and the opportunity to get high. Each month, 70 percent of high school seniors drink alcohol and 30 percent smoke marijuana.

For many, "moderate" use gives way to "immoderate" use. Twenty-six percent of all male high school seniors drink intoxicating amounts of alcohol three or more times in each two week period. Seniors, remember, are the survivors. The dropouts are already gone.

Progression of Use

Progression of use continues. The youngster who tried drugs in response to peer pressure, then continued because of pleasurable effect, may turn to chemicals in times of stress. Adolescents worry about their changing bodies, dating, competing for positions on teams, acne, looming career choices, fears of nuclear war and military draft, and concerns about separating from parents and becoming independent.

Friends Influence Drug Use

"There really are developmental stages in drug involvement," says Dr. Denise Kandel, a professor of psychiatry at Columbia University's College of Physicians and Surgeons and co-author of . . . a 13-year continuing study of 10th- and 11th-graders.

The study suggests parents may be right to be concerned about whom their children choose as friends. "Marijuana use by one's friends in adolescence is an important predictor of marijuana initiation," the study says.

Sally Squires, *St. Paul Dispatch,* July 28, 1984.

The youngster who has his own supply of drugs gains status in the drug society as a potential supplier to others. He is able to get high during the week. As his drug use escalates, behavior changes. Straight friends, who become less interesting or who induce guilt, may be replaced by drug users, often older, who are drifting from traditional standards and goals. School performance may suffer as hangover, marijuana-induced memory loss, sleeping in class, truancy, and general lack of motivation increase.

At home this child, who is less inclined to do chores, finds himself increasingly restricted by house rules. Violent mood swings may be common in this child who treats home as a "pit stop" in which to be fed and financed. He prefers the solitary comforts of his room and blaring stereo system to any family interaction.

Immoderate drug use leads to dependency. Drugs taken to deal with problems begin to cause problems, which the teenager deals with by escalated drug use. In this stage of drug use, the adolescent becomes preoccupied with easily gained pleasure. Thrill-seeking may extend to sexual experimentation, which is often bizarre and/or homosexual.

Alcohol and marijuana, mistakenly called "soft" drugs by some, remain the major offenders. The most dangerous psychoactive drugs for children are the two they most frequently put into their bodies.

Daily drug use begins to exert its toll. It costs $50-$60 per week to support the average habit. To meet this need, the child may divert his allowance, hold a job, steal, sell drugs to others, or provide sexual favors to a drug supplier. Financial costs are not as great, however, as the emotional costs borne by children who become involved in increasingly shameful and illicit activities.

No child wants to be in trouble with the law, his school, or his family. The eyes of a child in trouble with drugs give him away. Expressions of pain, sadness, and death replace normal adolescent sparkle. Drug dependency hurts. When not high, these children feel increasingly cut off from others and increasingly doubt their own value.

Drugs and Suicide

Suicide becomes an option for many. Adolescent suicide rates have tripled in the last 20 years. This year more than 5,000 young people will take their own lives. The great majority will have drug or alcohol problems.

As drug problems mount, the user's ability to get high decreases and the "burned out" child turns to more frequent use of stronger and more costly chemicals. Blackouts and flashbacks may increase. Physical problems such as sore throat, cough, fatigue, and headache are common. At this stage, the child has usually been expelled from school and perhaps his family. He may be in trouble with the law and has great difficulty finding and keeping jobs.

The options available to the advanced drug users are (1) recovery through abstinence and acquisition of coping skills, (2) death by highway accident, suicide, or homicide, (3) progression to dependence on stronger and more costly drugs, and (4) "drifting." "New drifters" are the millions of Americans between the ages of 20 and 40 who have not progressed beyond the developmental age at which they become independent. They lack the skills and attitudes necessary for functional adult life.

Self-Induced Failures

There are few neighborhoods in the country that don't have at least one person whose history may include attempts at college, failed job opportunities, failed marriages, and a host of self-induced disappointments and "bad luck." They may leave home to escape parental rules and anger, but most will return again and again to live in a hostile-dependent relationship with parents who have little comprehension of the basic cause of their child's inability to take root.

Drug use is a progressive and dangerous societal problem. Those parents and professionals who remain ambivalent or silent, or who choose debate at the expense of action, do little for the millions of American youngsters who are in deep trouble with alcohol and other drugs. The burden is on those who claim that experimentation is expected, moderation is possible, and reponsible use is acceptable.

The burden of proof should not fall on those who disagree and believe that all adolescent drug use is abuse. Insistence that drug-free adolescence is a desirable and possible goal provides the most consistent and potentially effective framework on which to focus prevention, intervention, and treatment efforts.

"Some people inherit a behavioral propensity that heightens their risk for becoming sociopathic or alcoholic."

Alcoholism Is Hereditary

Constance Holden

Constance Holden is a staff member of *Science* magazine. In the following viewpoint, which she wrote for *Psychology Today*, Ms. Holden claims that there is a link between heredity and alcoholism. She describes several studies which she believes confirm that alcoholics have a brain "defect" making them susceptible to the addictive effects of alcohol.

As you read, consider the following questions:

1. According to the author, what is the link between antisocial personalities and alcoholism?
2. What were the results of the adoption studies cited in the viewpoint?
3. What brain wave has been found to be deficient in the alcoholics tested?

Constance Holden, "Genes, Personality and Alcoholism," *Psychology Today*, January 1985.
REPRINTED WITH PERMISSION FROM PSYCHOLOGY TODAY MAGAZINE.
Copyright © 1985 American Psychological Association.

Dipsomaniacs come in all shapes and sizes, from the classic skid-row bum to the wealthy senator's wife, from the addicted high school student to the bored housewife, from the happy-go-lucky tippler to the raving drunk maniac. Because alcoholism shows up in such a seemingly arbitrary fashion, researchers have been stymied in their attempts to understand the underlying biological or psychological factors that lead to alcoholism. But now some researchers are beginning to think there may be at least one definable segment of the alcoholic population—those with the character disorder called antisocial personality (ASP).

Antisocial personalities (previously known as sociopaths) tend to be charming, manipulative, attention-seeking, rebellious, impulsive, egocentric and ready abusers of drugs, other people and themselves. Antisocial personalities make up perhaps 25 percent of the total alcoholic population, an extraordinary ratio considering that the prevalence of ASP in the general population is only about 3 percent.

Psychologist Ralph Tarter of the University of Pittsburgh believes that ASP may prove to be a key in the search for genetic "markers" for alcoholism. The traits typical of ASP, he contends, may be a "behavioral manifestation of a genetic vulnerability" to both alcoholism and ASP. "In other words," he says, "some people inherit a behavioral propensity that heightens their risk for becoming sociopathic or alcoholic."

Adopted Children of Alcoholics

A decade ago such a theory would have been dismissed out of hand. But the search for genetic indicators of susceptibility to alcoholism has been galvanized by findings from adoption studies conducted in Denmark and Sweden in the early 1970s. These studies showed that when sons of alcoholics are adopted by other families, they are just as likely to become alcoholic as are those reared by their biological families. In other words, nature is stronger than nurture in determining whether these boys become alcoholics. A recent adoption study in Iowa confirmed that the greatest single predictor of alcoholism in a son is alcoholism in a father. While 10 percent of the general population is alcoholic, 25 percent of the sons of alcoholic fathers are alcoholic.

Research on the genetics of alcoholism has led to the revival of a category proposed in the 1940s by E.M. Jellinek, who distinguished between "familial" and "nonfamilial" alcoholism. Familial alcoholism, which means that a person has a close relative (parent or sibling) who is alcoholic, afflicts about half the alcoholic population, and some researchers believe that three-fourths or more of alcoholics have the disease in the immediate family. Nonfamilial alcoholism is assumed to be more dependent on environmental circumstances.

33

Researchers are now focusing on the families of alcoholics, particularly on the population most susceptible to the disease—young sons of alcoholics—in an attempt to pinpoint biological indicators of vulnerability. Some scientists are looking for differences in alcohol metabolism and blood chemistry. There is also increasing interest in brain function. Examinations of those who are especially vulnerable to the disease, for example, have shown that some changes in cognitive and motor function formerly attributed to alcoholism exist in some people before the onset of the disease.

Brain Waves of Alcoholics

A number of electroencephalogram (EEG) studies have found differences between the brain waves of alcoholics and nonalcoholics as well as between those of children of alcoholics and children of nonalcoholics. But EEG's are limited because they measure total brain activity and offer no clues to specific anomalies. Floyd Bloom of Scripps Institute compares EEG work with "looking at a crowded football stadium from an airplane."

The Genetic Factor

Alcoholism is analogous to diabetes or hay fever. Some people are born at risk. But such genetic vulnerability unfolds in specific environmental contexts. As always, nature and nurture interact.

Of the nation's 10 million alcoholics, half are now thought to be genetically predisposed and, as a group, develop the disease early in life, many by their mid-20s.

Minneapolis Star and Tribune, October 21, 1984.

A more precise way to look at the brain is receiving a great deal of attention right now: work with evoked potential—measuring a single brain wave in response to a stimulus. Last summer, for example, Henri Begleiter of the State University of New York Downstate Medical Center found that some sons of alcoholics have a specific brain anomaly that is characteristic of alcoholics.

Begleiter's subjects were 7- to 13-year-old sons of alcoholic fathers. These boys, who had never had alcohol (according to their mothers), were hooked up to electrodes and asked to make simple decisions about a picture of a head displayed at various angles. As they pushed buttons indicating their decisions, Begleiter measured the voltage of the P3 wave, a well-studied brain wave related to attention and learning. This wave is deficient in most chronic alcoholics, indicating a mild cognitive impairment. Thirty-five percent of Begleiter's high-risk subjects showed a similar P3 deficiency; it exists in very few children in general. These P3 experiments provided the first neurological evidence that a specific, genetically determined anomaly exists in both alcoholics and their non-drinking offspring.

Neurological Deficits

Meanwhile, other researchers have been finding indirect evidence for neurological deficits in high-risk subjects (the sons of alcoholic parents). This evidence comes from neuropsychological studies that attempt to infer deficits in brain functions through tests of motor and spatial abilities and problem-solving.

Psychologist Oscar Parsons of the University of Oklahoma examined four types of drinkers: familial alcoholics, nonfamilial alcoholics and social drinkers with and without family histories of alcoholism. He tested them for verbal abilities, learning and memory, abstracting and problem-solving and perceptual-motor skills. Not surprisingly, the alcoholics performed more poorly than did the social drinkers on all the tests. But within these two groups, those with a family history of alcoholism performed worse than did those without. The difference was especially striking in the more complex problem-solving tests and the perceptual-motor tests. Parsons concludes that familial alcoholism has an independent effect on test performance, and that it probably deserves to be regarded as "a distinct subcategory of alcoholism."

The finding that many persons who seem to be genetically predisposed to alcoholism have mild neurological deficits does not explain why they would be particularly vulnerable to compulsive and ultimately addictive drinking. Are the neurological deficits linked to chemical abnormalities that generate alcohol craving? Or are they associated with emotional or behavioral problems that lead to compulsive drinking?

Antisocial Personality

One behavioral problem that stands out in any group of male alcoholics is antisocial personality, a disorder that shows up in childhood and is characterized by impulsivity, egocentricity, short attention span, sensation-seeking, aggressiveness and poor socialization. There is increasing evidence that ASP ranks almost as high as family history as a predictor of alcoholism in men. Victor M. Hesselbrock of the University of Connecticut, for instance, has conducted psychoneurological tests with alcoholics and found that "family history of alcoholism per se doesn't influence tests but family history plus antisocial personality does." Fifty-two percent of the alcoholic subjects were antisocial; among those who had two alcoholic parents, the rate was 71 percent.

Our researchers have come up with similar numbers. Thomas Babor, a social psychologist at the University of Connecticut, found that 40 percent of the people he studied in alcoholism clinics were antisocial personalities, and that the two major precursors of alcoholism were family history and ASP. Furthermore, those with ASP had more alcoholism among their relatives and had a more severe form of the disease. They started earlier, drank more and sought help at an earlier age (33), on the average, than did the other alcoholics, who didn't seek help until the age of 39 years....

'Dad!' . . . 'Son!' . . .

ROTHCO

© Liederman/Rothco

What makes the correlation between ASP and alcoholism significant for studying the genetics of alcoholism is that there appears to be a component of heritability to ASP. Remi Cadoret of the University of Iowa conducted an adoption study to look at both alcoholism and ASP. He found that each disorder clustered in families, although environmental influences play a stronger role in the development of ASP. Other researchers have found that identical twins (who share all their genes in common) are much more likely to both have or both not have ASP than are fraternal twins (who have a genetic overlap of about 50 percent).

Genetic Link

More support for a possible genetic link between ASP and alcoholism is provided by the fact that certain childhood disorders often precede the development of ASP, alcoholism or both. One is attention deficit disorder, a catchall diagnosis for traits including short attention span, impulsivity and hyperactivity. The other is childhood conduct disorder, a kind of junior antisocial personality. Several studies have shown that severe alcoholics are more likely than nonalcoholics to have childhood histories marked by these symptoms. And one study by Hesselbrock found that even among social drinkers, those with a history of childhood attention disorders started drinking at an earlier age.

As the evidence for a genetic component becomes stronger, researchers may take another look at long-term studies that show a preponderance of certain personality traits among alcoholics. A group of children seen at a child-guidance clinic in St. Louis in the 1920s, for example, was followed up in the 1960s. The alcoholism rate in this group was seven times as high as among members of a similar group of adults who had not been referred to clinics as children. In addition, the alcoholics had shown more antisocial symptoms in these childhood tests than had the nonalcoholics.

Another study, by researchers Helmut Hoffman and colleagues at the University of Minnesota, went back and examined the Minnesota Multiphasic Personality Inventory (MMPI) scores of a group of male Minnesota graduates who later ended up in alcoholism centers. Their MMPI scores were significantly higher than normal on three scales: the masculinity-femininity index (indicating sex-role conflict, psychopathic deviance and hypomania (hyperactivity), indicating that they were more impulsive, nonconforming, gregarious and self-preoccupied than their peers.

Personality Characteristics

These personality findings are suggestive, but they would have more meaning if they could be correlated with biological findings. One study that may provide such information is under way at Rutgers University Center of Alcohol Studies. Biochemist David Lester explains that researchers there are tracking the progress of New Jersey teenagers who have recently started drinking, using chemical and physiological measures as well as psychological tests and interviews.

The families of alcoholics are another major area of interest as reseachers look for biological and behavioral clues to alcoholic susceptibility. Depression, for example, is a very common early psychopathology for female alcoholics, and George Winokur of the University of Iowa has found a high incidence of depression among the female family members of male alcoholics. Whether this indicates a genetic link will be addressed in Winokur's next study. Using an inherited blood factor as a marker, he hopes to see if siblings who share this marker can also be paired for alcoholism and depression.

Possible Brain Defect

Although the puzzle of alcoholism is now being worked on from a number of angles, few investigators are ready to say what makes an alcoholic. Tarter is an exception. Afer an extensive survey of the data on alcohol metabolism, blood chemistry and neurological, psychophysiological and behavioral research, he has concluded that there is a severe form of alcoholism, linked with behavioral tendencies, that may be associated with a brain defect occurring in the areas of the brain that control temperament and behavior.

A Physical Difference

Dr. James W. Smith, Medical Director of the Schick-Shadel Hospital in Seattle, which has a 40-year record of successfully treating alcoholics, contends that the incidence of color-blindness in alcoholics is greater than in the general population; that blood group "A" is found in alcoholics more often than in the general population; that a disproportionately high percentage of alcoholics are unable to taste the chemical phenolthiocarbimide; that alcoholics in contrast to non-alcoholics show abnormalities in adrenal gland function, regulation of blood pressure, metabolism of glucose; that two enzymes produced in the liver have been found to be at different levels in the case of alcoholics in contrast to non-alcoholics; and that alcoholics break down one amino acid to one abnormal end product while non-alcholics break the acid down to a normal end product.

All this points to the possibility, if not probability, that those who become "hooked" on alcohol may be physically different from those who do not.

William Plymat Sr., "The Addictive Nature of Alcohol," The American Council on Alcohol Problems.

Tarter and his colleagues, Arthur Alterman and Kathleen Edwards, base their argument on the apparent heritability of temperament. Individual pacing, rhythm and activity level seem to be remarkably stable throughout life, with some people being predominantly sedate and emotionally controlled while others tend to be consistently hyperactive and mercurial. Tarter explains that alcoholics with typically hyperactive temperaments drink to change or moderate their moods, are likely to abuse substances other than alcohol and are more egocentric and emotionally demanding than most people. In other words, they have much in common with antisocial personalities. Tarter also agrees with Robert Cloninger, a Washington psychiatrist, that women with hysterical or borderline personalities and such things as anorexia or bulimia may be manifesting socially conditioned versions of the same genetic patterns as male alcoholics. The hallmark, he says, is emotionally and behavorial undercontrol.

Tarter says that electrophysiological tests have confirmed that many of the alcoholic's traits have a physiological basis. On tests, such as those for electrical skin conductance, alcoholics are slow in returning to baseline levels, which Tarter says indicates "autonomic instability." He has found a high correlation between these results and the cognitive and motor deficits identified in sons of alcoholics.

Need for Mood Alteration

Unusually reactive autonomic nervous systems may help explain why alcoholics enjoy booze more than most people do. As both sedative and a stimulant, alcohol is particularly rewarding to alcoholics in terms of hyping themselves up or calming themselves down. Most alcoholics also have trouble with "downers" and abuse amphetamines. In Tarter's view, these findings support the notion that an alcoholic's primary aim in drinking (except in the late stages) is not so much relief of physical craving as it is mood alteration.

An impulsive, hedonistic personality is not enough by itself to cause the compulsive, desperate and literally suicidal behavior that marks the fullblown alcoholic, Tarter says. But these traits may activate a dormant biological susceptibility. Alcoholism and ASP might be likened to two adjacent weeds that quickly become tightly and inextricably entwined, each nourishing the growth of the other.

A possible implication of Tarter's theory is that many alcoholics may have no specific vulnerability to substance abuse. Thus, the currently ill-defined concept of a "vulnerable personality" could reappear in biological trappings.

Behavioral, biochemical and genetics researchers may eventually arrive at a "biobehavioral" explanation of alcoholism. But it will take a while. There is scarcely a finding by one person or group that is not questioned by another. In the meantime, increasing recognition of the many facets of alcoholism should spur more innovative approaches to prevention and more individually tailored treatment for a disease from which only one sufferer in 35 now successfully recovers.

"(Intervention) is essential if there is to be any hope of breaking the intergenerational linkages within families where there is alcohol abuse or child abuse and neglect."

Alcoholism Is Caused by Child Neglect

Children of Alcoholics Foundation

The Children of Alcoholics Foundation is a voluntary, nonprofit organization created to assist children of alcoholic parents. The following viewpoint is excerpted from the foundation's testimony and recommendations submitted to the US Attorney General's Task Force on Family Violence. The authors plead for societal intervention to protect children of alcoholic parents from the neglect and abuse that they claim leads children eventually into alcoholism.

As you read, consider the following questions:
1. What does the author believe is the primary cause of alcoholism linking one generation to the next?
2. List some of the adverse conditions that a child might expect in an alcoholic home.
3. Do you think these conditions might produce an "alcoholic personality"? Why?

Testimony presented by the Children of Alcoholics Foundation to the Attorney General's Task Force on Family Violence, February 16, 1984.

The Children of Alcoholics Foundation, Inc. is a voluntary, non-profit, public organization created to assist children of alcoholic parents—a silent but troubled group whose problems have been largely neglected. The work of the Foundation initiates an effort to make Americans aware of the intergenerational link in the disease of alcoholism and provides a means to help prevent the suffering and anguish borne by so many children of alcoholic parents. The major thrust of the Foundation is to focus attention on problems parental alcoholism causes for youngsters and to seek solutions.

Family violence is certainly a problem in alcoholic family systems. Indeed, families where there is alcohol abuse share similar dynamics with those in which there is family violence. There is, for example, isolation, an intergenerational history of the alcohol abuse or the violence, parental personality characteristics inlcuding but not limited to low frustration tolerance, low self-esteem, impulsivity, dependency, and lack of understanding of the needs and abilities of youngsters. The Children of Alcoholics Foundation is particularly concerned with combatting the range of emotional, physical and sexual child neglect and abuse that can occur in alcoholic families. . . .

Emotional neglect by alcoholic parents is a major and almost inevitable theme of life for children in alcoholic homes. Neglect and the lack of "quality love" defies quantitative measurement but is nonetheless overwhelmingly real to the growing child. Neglect occurs because the active alcoholic parent experiences family life through a fog, unaware of children's needs and problems. Generally the sober spouse is also too involved with the drinking parent to be aware of youngsters, and they are generally ignored. To the child, neglect may be experienced as an absence of intimacy, of love or warm involvement with parents. It may mean a lack of attention or the neglect may be of physical needs such as being properly fed, bathed, or clothed. Or, it may mean that an older child is expected to assume responsibilities for younger siblings or the home. Inconsistency of emotional and physical caring are the norm. In most alcoholic families, as in other neglectful families, the neglect can be characterized as an act of omission rather than an act of commission that occurs because the parents' functioning is impaired by alcoholism or alcohol abuse. The pain, isolation and conflicted or suppressed feelings these youngsters experience is directly related to fluctuations in their parents' blood alcohol levels.

Kinds of Abuse

Abuse by alcoholic parents may be verbal, physical, or sexual. It takes many forms. An alcoholic parent verbally abuses a youngster when he or she accuses the child of being the cause of the parent's drinking and tells the child the drinking is the child's fault.

All too often, the non-alcoholic parent reinforces this destructive notion by siding with the alcohol abuser. Physical abuse, too, takes place, and there are often instances of violence, of beating, of battering, and of incest. Alcoholism treatment agencies have reported beatings with hangers, children being locked in a closet and children being sent to their room for a couple of days without eating. In families where children are not being physically abused but there is violence between parents, youngsters will be deeply affected by it. Domestic violence is played out on the entire family and children in alcoholic homes are witnesses. A survey by the Hotline operated by Abused Women's Aid in Crisis (AWAIC) from November 1980 - January 1981 showed that of 800 callers, 73%

Emotional Neglect

Alcoholism programs identify emotional neglect by parents as a major theme of life for children in alcoholic homes. For the active alcoholic, family life may be experienced through a fog. For the sober spouse, family life revolves around the alcoholic's needs and behaviour; the children are generally ignored. "It's a neglect of omission rather than commission. Since birth, the kids know they will never be as important in the house as the alcoholic. There's an absence of intimacy, and they learn to accept rejection and suppress their own feelings. Emotional neglect and the lack of quality of love is part of their upbringing. That's what doesn't come through in statistics." . . . You see a lot of cases where responsibility is given to the adolescents to stay home, clean, watch your brother and sisters. Many children have far more responsibilities than they can handle at that age which of course leads them to increase their own drinking."

Migs Woodside, *Children of Alcoholics,* July 1982.

had husbands who were abusing alcohol; 40% of the women were also drinking and 90% of the women had an average of 3-4 children. The fact that the children have witnessed violence is revealed in play therapy when toys are used to reenact the violence. Programs for youngsters from alcoholic homes also note they are seeing cases of incest, generally between fathers and daughters or mother's boyfriend. They are also hearing about childhood incest from adult alcoholic patients who are themselves children of alcoholics. These adults report that there were sexual relations, not in high number, but in some amount between parent and child and even siblings. Similar findings of incest in alcoholic homes were indicated in recent studies of 200 adult children of alcoholics, of which 62% were female and 38% were male. The incestual acts consisted of fondling, oral sex, or intercourse.

A problem of major proportions for children in alcohol-related child abuse and neglect cases is the total lack of recognition of the relationship between alcohol and violence. Alcohol treatment programs and child abuse workers tend to be poorly informed about each other's fields. Traditionally, alcoholism programs have worked exclusively with alcoholic adults, and occasionally nondrinking spouses are included in counseling. Rarely, however, are children brought in as part of the therapeutic group. While those few programs working with children from alcoholic homes are sensitive to abuse and neglect, most alcoholism treatment programs working primarily with alcoholic adults need to be more aware of these issues. The consequence of this lack of awareness is that oftentimes cases of child abuse and neglect go undetected. It is of paramount importance that alcoholism counselors be trained not only to ask about child abuse, but to appropriately report and learn techniques to deal with child abuse to avoid its tragic consequences for children and their families.

Similarly, child abuse workers need to have much better information about the disease of alcoholism. They need to know the physical, social, and emotional characteristics of alcohol abuse. They need to be trained to look for alcoholism in families. Too often, child abuse workers overlook alcohol abuse or regard it as yet another symptom of an underlying problem. They need the information and education that alcoholism is not a symptom of family dysfunction; it is itself the problem....

Research on Neglect Needed

Underlying the difficulties in identification and treatment of child abuse and neglect, is a lack of research about the needs of children in alcoholic families. Although there are 7 million children of alcoholic parents under the age of 20 in the United States and many millions of adults who have grown up in alcoholic families, interest in the special needs and characteristics of this group has been a very recent development. There have been numerous reports on the association of child abuse and alcohol abuse. Many of the findings linking parental drinking with child abuse are based on clinical and personal observation of incidence, similarity of situational and structural factors and clinical profiles of child abusers and alcohol abusers. Because of its stigma, there is even less data available on linkages of sexual abuse of children and alcohol abuse. Material is generally based on case narrative, descriptions of home environments, or limited to cases involving adult daughters and incestuous fathers.

There is a large gap in knowledge about relationships of alcohol abuse, child abuse and incest which calls for investigations beyond exploring linkages and begins to examine cause and effect. These gaps in knowledge hamper the development of effective prevention programs tailored to the needs of children of alcoholics who are over-represented in caseloads of medical, psychiatric and child guidance clinics, the criminal and juvenile justice systems, as well as child abuse registries. Research on this group, therefore, has the potential along with more adequate professional training based on greater knowledge to improve prevention and treatment techniques.

Need for Intervention

There are other aspects of the problem that do not easily fall into the areas of research or professional training. Traditional ways that family violence is identified are not sufficient to combat child abuse and neglect. While a battered spouse can come forward to seek help, most often a child cannot. In alcoholic families where denial of the problem is a most significant aspect of the disease, children operate in isolation with a strong taboo against revealing the family's secret and their own suffering. Ways must be found and provided that help children of their parents identify themselves as needing help. Once identified as needing help, innovative ways must be found to motivate and keep under supervision and in treatment members of what are often society's most difficult to reach families. This is essential if there is to be any hope of breaking the intergenerational linkages within families where there is alcohol abuse or child abuse and neglect.

Ranking the Causes of Drug Abuse

Reprinted with the permission of King Features Syndicate, Inc.

Many experts have presented provocative arguments debating the causes of drug abuse. One of the arguments, illustrated in the cartoon above, is that life's pressures are a primary cause of drug use. The following exercise gives you an opportunity to discuss the reasons for drug abuse and debate your opinion with others in a group.

Instructions:

Step 1. Working in groups of four to six students, and using the viewpoints in this chapter as a resource, rank the causes of drug abuse in the order the group thinks is the most important: 1 for most important, 10 for least important.

_____ Many adolescents start using drugs because of peer pressure and then continue to use drugs because they become addicted.

_____ Drug abuse is a hereditary condition that makes drug use almost uncontrollable in these more susceptible individuals.

_____ Many people simply have addictive personalities. Those who are addicted to chocolate bars as adolescents become hard drug users as adults.

_____ People take drugs to feel the temporary pleasure that drugs provide.

_____ People need intimacy and, like sharing food, taking drugs together is a ritual excuse for social interaction.

_____ Life in modern society is harsh. People use drugs to escape from society's pressures.

_____ Drug addicted parents provide a role model after which children pattern themselves. Drug addiction is taught.

_____ Drug pushers lure young adults into using drugs.

_____ Using any kind of drugs at all, even aspirin, can lead to uncontrollable addiction in many people.

_____ Some people can't cope with everyday disappointment. Some adolescents will become hooked on drugs to ease the pain of a failed test.

Step 2. Each group should compare its ranking with others in the class in a class-wide discussion. Prepare to defend your group's ranking. After discussing the causes of drug abuse, individual class members may want to share their reasons for personally choosing to use or not use drugs.

Periodical Bibliography

The following list of periodical articles deals with the subject matter of this chapter.

A. Adams — "Bloody Streets: Only Hope Is to Escape," *U.S. News & World Report,* November 19, 1984.

Maureen Dowd — "Prep Schools in a Struggle To Curb Spread of Cocaine," *The New York Times,* May 27, 1984.

Joshua Fischman — "Where There's Smoke . . .," *Psychology Today,* April 1985.

Signe Hammer and Lesley Hazleton — "Cocaine and the Chemical Brain," *Science Digest,* October 1984.

John Hughes — "Why Cocaine?" *The Christian Science Monitor,* April 5, 1985.

Jet — "Former Star Doc Ellis Says Fear of Success Drove Him to Use Drugs," April 30, 1984.

Peter Kihss — "Alcoholism Called a Family Trait," *The New York Times,* July 21, 1982.

N. Langer — "Do Sex and Drugs Mix?" *Ms.,* May 1984.

Dean Latimer — "The Test That Failed," *Inquiry,* May 1984.

Joyce Lewis — "Alcoholism: First Drink to Last," *Consumer's Research Magazine,* March 1982.

William A. Nolen — "Doctor's Orders: Why Patients Should Never Ignore Them," *50 Plus,* April 1984.

Prevention — "Alcohol and Aging: Double Trouble," June 1984.

Science News — "Going to Pot: Peer Group Connection," February 18, 1984.

U.S. News & World Report — "Death of a Kennedy—A Grim Reminder," May 7, 1984.

How Serious a Problem Is Alcoholism?

"The present deplorable trend in America toward more and more consumption of liquor will be halted only by those who refuse to be intimidated."

The Case for Abstinence

Glenn D. Everett

Much of the controversy surrounding prevention of alcoholism is centered on the public's attitude toward teetotalers. Glenn D. Everett, who was a correspondent for the Religious News Service at the time he wrote the following viewpoint, was told that he would have to drink alcoholic beverages to be accepted in Washington. Mr. Everett explains how he overcame society's prejudice and used his status as a non-drinker to his professional advantage. Although the following viewpoint was written several years ago, Mr. Everett presents a timeless argument that society's prejudice against the teetotaler can be overcome.

As you read, consider the following questions:

1. How did the author resist the social pressure on him to drink alcohol?
2. In what ways does Mr. Everett think his abstinence helped him?
3. What examples does the author give of people who let liquor control them?

Glenn D. Everett, "You Don't Have to Drink!", published by the Preferred Risk Mutual Insurance Company, 1965.

I'm a non-drinking member of a profession in which social drinking is demanded. I am a Washington newspaperman, covering a political and diplomatic beat.

When I first came to the capital at 23, a decade ago, I was told I'd have to learn to drink, at least enough to be sociable. The cocktail party is Washington's greatest social institution, and newsmen have to attend hundreds of them in the process of cultivating news contacts and making acquaintances among public officials.

Back in the old saloon days and during prohibition, drinking had a social stigma attached to it. Today the situation is reversed. The drinking of whiskey and gin cocktails is not only socially acceptable, it's socially demanded. In some small towns the drinker may still be frowned on, but not here in the city. Drinking is considered smart.

How can a non-drinker justify his principles in a society where drinking has become so widely accepted? How can he resist social pressure? Let's face it. It isn't easy to refuse. I had lots of uncomfortable moments till I got my social bearings sufficiently to know how to cope with the problem.

Facing the Problem

I wish our churches would be franker with young people. I wish they would tell any young man entering a profession calling for social contacts that he's going to face the problem, that many of his associates will drink and that drinking will be expected of him—unless he makes up his mind that he's going to refuse flatly. I wish they'd tell the girl who's going to marry a young man entering the business world that as the wife of an aspiring professional man she's going to have to face the problem of liquor and help her husband meet it.

I wish our pastors and youth counselors would deal with this problem more realistically, because unless we really let young people know what they're going to face in the way of social pressure and give them good, concrete reasons for resisting it, we're going to leave our youth unprepared.

I can understand well how many of our youth, who would really prefer not to drink, become convinced they must for social reasons. After 10 years of bucking the cocktail circuit in our nation's capital and drinking ginger ale and cokes, maybe I can give some advice on how to refuse a drink when it's pressed on you.

In the first place you have to decide whether you're going to drink or not drink. I made up my mind rather strongly on that when I was going to college. I knew a couple guys who were expelled from a small church college for drunkenness. They didn't look very good the night they tore up the library on what was supposed to be a hilarious spree. For one, it meant the ruin of what could have been a promising law career. He never went back to college.

50

While in graduate school at a Big Ten university I saw a lot more students drinking. It was more common on the big campus. I saw some coeds when they were so tipsy that the way they behaved left me with no respect for them or the men they were with. They were paying a mighty high price for a good time.

I knew a congressman's son, a brilliant boy, who first flunked law school, then was court-martialed as an army officer simply because he couldn't stay away from beer. He caused his father terrible anguish and finally woke up to the fact that he was ruining his life.

Damage Caused by Alcohol

The litany of alcohol-related harm is becoming alarmingly familiar. Alcohol is linked to:

- The deaths of more than 20,000 drunk drivers and their innocent victims annually.

- A high percentage of child abuse, spouse abuse, homicides and suicides.

- Thousands of cases of cancer, heart disease, cirrhosis of the liver and birth defects.

All told, alcohol is a factor in more than 100,000 deaths. Upwards of 10 million Americans are alcoholics or problem drinkers, including 3.3 million under the age of 18. The other costs to society—occurring from property damage, hospitalization and incarceration—are nearly $120 billion each year.

Michael F. Jacobson and Ronald Collins, *The Los Angeles Times*, March 10, 1985.

The ones who wake up, painful as the experience is and humiliated as they feel when they realize how they've behaved, are the lucky ones. Lots of young men and women don't wake up until they're too far down the road to alcoholism to stop.

So, from what I could see in college, drinking didn't look too smart. My parents were opposed to liquor, I heard many a sermon against it in church, and what I saw it doing to some of my young friends convinced me it was a good thing to avoid.

Liquor and the American Way

For awhile after graduation I was breaking my way into journalism as a general assignments reporter; and as city editor of a small Minnesota paper, I had to cover police court. There I really saw the cost to our society of letting beer and liquor become a controlling part of the American way.

I would see not only those whose lives had been sacrificed on alcohol's altar—the white-pallored, trembling stumblebums and floozy, unkempt women—but also those who travel in the more respectable circles of society. They're the ones who never get their names in the papers because they're too influential with the editor. They presented a pathetic sight as they paid fines for "speeding," "disorderly conduct," or some other minor charge a friendly prosecutor would agree to put on the books.

But the police officers and reporters present knew what really happened, the drunken brawl, the wild orgy that went on until police were finally called to break it up. Hollow laughs couldn't hide the sordid truth of what police had seen.

A Shaken Man

I remember seeing a man who had murdered his wife in a drunken rage, seeing him the morning after when he realized the gravity of the charge he faced and comprehended what he had done to the one who entrusted her life to him at the marriage altar. He was a shaken man.

There were girls from respectable families who'd been pulled in at 3 a.m. when police investigated a drinking and petting party in parked cars. I'd seen them when through the fog of morning-after hangover they'd meet their parents and realize the situation in which police had found them. It wasn't pleasant to witness. The mother always had the same stunned look of disbelief. It haunts you.

Worst were the accident cases. They'd come in from the hospital in bandages and splints to be arraigned for drunken driving or manslaughter. You'd hear the widow of the man who'd been killed tell through puffed lips of that last terrible moment when the other car veered across the center line.

In the courtroom you'd see her young son and daughter, still mourning their father, straining forward to catch words of testimony. You'd try not to look at them, until suddenly there'd be a stir and the daughter would be carried out in a faint.

And worst of all you ever see is the salesman who had run down two young boys on a bicycle . . . one dead, the other crippled by spinal injury . . . drunkometer test positive . . . car off the road when it hit them . . . manslaughter . . . defendant pleads guilty, brokenly tells judge how sorry he is . . . judge stern . . . 10 years in state penitentiary . . . the man sobs. And you aren't surprised when he commits suicide at the pen six months later.

Not everyone gets indoctrination into the costs of alcohol via the public court, though our courts are open any morning you care to go and see the sordid story. It's a good antidote to the "men of distinction" ads.

No, not everyone who drinks is going to end up in police court, but none of them who do ever thought they were going to.

The ironic fact that really becomes apparent after you have

"Hey, what is this stuff? It makes everything I think seem profound."

learned to refuse liquor at any and all occasions including White House dinners, is that you don't have to drink to be sociable after all. You can, if pressed, explain with just enough obvious irritation to cause the host to drop the subject, that you simply don't like to drink. Ask for ginger ale. They always have it—for chasers.

Nobody shuns you. You don't lose friends—and you definitely gain influence. I don't care what the drinker says to cover up. He has an inner respect for the man who doesn't drink and won't compromise on the issue. The man who won't yield to pressure on that issue isn't likely to yield to temptation or mob pressure on others, and people know it.

The young professional or business man, no matter what field he's in, can build respect and prestige faster by refusing to drink than through all the sociable cocktails he can possibly imbibe. And young wives when entertaining need make no apology for refusing to serve alcohol. You make a fatal mistake the minute you apologize for taking the abstinence stand.

The present deplorable trend in America toward more and more consumption of liquor will be halted only by those who refuse to be intimidated. I'll never forget the day Premier Mendes-France of France raised his glass of milk in a toast at the National Press Club. It took nerve to do that, but he saw alcohol eating the heart out of his country. And he gained stature by his bold act of fighting it.

"Moderate alcohol consumption. . . may reduce the risk of heart attacks, lessen symptoms of exhaustion and discomfort, and encourage healthy psychosocial attitudes and desirable social interaction."

The Case Against Abstinence

William J. Darby

William J. Darby is president of the Nutrition Foundation in New York and is an emeritus professor of biochemistry at the Vanderbilt University School of Medicine. With his colleagues at Vanderbilt University, Dr. Darby has made several notable scientific discoveries. In the following viewpoint, he claims that alcohol in moderation not only makes life pleasant but also reduces the threat of heart attacks and may promote healthy social attitudes.

As you read, consider the following questions:

1. According to the author, drinkers of alcohol live longer than people who abstain. Why?
2. Is alcohol a stimulant or depressant?
3. Do you agree with the author that drinking in moderation is healthy? Why or why not?

William J. Darby, "The Benefits of Drink," *Human Nature*, November 1978. © 1978 by Human Nature, Inc. Reprinted by permission of the publisher.

Most people like to have a few drinks during the course of a day. The American businessman enjoys his martini or highball at lunch; the Frenchman considers his bottle of wine an essential part of his meal. In nearly every country of the world alcoholic beverages serve important social functions. It is also true, however, that people often feel guilty or concerned about drinking, believing—incorrectly—that the effect of even moderate use of alcohol is harmful and equating its consequences with the serious health problems that arise from excessive drinking.

Until recently, little effort was made to investigate whether benefits to health might result from drinking in moderation—a term I will define more precisely later on. In the case of Americans, reluctance to confront the possibility of any desirable effects of alcoholic beverages may stem, in part, from puritanical feelings of guilt about "demon rum." The American attitude toward drinking tradionally has wavered between two extremes: the alcohol-is-sinful school on the one hand, and the image of the brawling boozer, as exemplified by the hard-drinking "private eye" or the barroom character of Western movies, on the other. The middle ground generally has been neglected.

Studies now indicate that moderate alcohol consumption—which we can tentatively define as three drinks or less per day—may reduce the risk of heart attacks, lessen symptoms of exhaustion and discomfort, and encourage healthy psychosocial attitudes and desirable social interaction. (A drink is the quantity of beverage that contains approximately 12 ml of alcohol [ethanol]: a 1-oz. jigger of 80 proof spirits, a 3.5-oz. glass of table wine, a 12-oz. glass of light beer, or a 10-oz. glass of ordinary American beer.

Drinkers Live Longer

Statistics published by the United States government in its *Second Report on Alcohol and Health* (1974) reveal that moderate drinkers are likely to live longer than teetotalers, ex-drinkers, and people who drink to excess. Part of the reason for the moderate drinkers' longevity may lie in the fact that they are usually individuals who lead active social lives and who have life-sustaining interests that enhance their vitality. But, as investigations of alcohol and heart disease begin to suggest, there may be physiological effects involved as well.

A recent study by Arthur L. Klatsky and his colleagues at the Kaiser-Permanente Medical Center in Oakland, California, offers new evidence that moderate drinking may serve as a deterrent to heart attacks. They studied 464 patients who had been hospitalized with a first myocardial infarction (heart attack) and discovered that an unusually large proportion were teetotalers. Their curiosity aroused, Klatsky and his colleagues evaluated the medical histories of 120,000 patients and found that moderate alcohol users were 30 percent less likely to have heart attacks than were non-drinking patients or matched controls or so-called risk controls—people who suffer from diabetes, hypertension, obesity, high serum cholesterol, or who smoke. (All of these factors are associated with increased risk of heart attacks.)

Health Hazards of Abstinence

It was found that nondrinkers run a significantly greater risk of myocardial infarction than do users of alcohol. This finding was independent of age, sex, or prior related disease. In each of the groups of drinkers—those who drank up to two drinks daily, those who drank three or more drinks daily, and even those who drank six or more drinks per day—fewer heart attacks occurred than among the abstainers. The investigators concluded that "abstinence from alcohol may be a new risk factor." In a subsequent report from Massachusetts, where investigators studied 399 cases of infarction and evaluated 2,486 case histories, evidence persisted of a lower rate of heart attacks in subjects who consumed six or more drinks per day.

Less Heart Disease

Moderate drinkers tend to have less heart disease than teetotalers, according to a new study.... The study, by Dr. Arthur Klatsky, a cardiologist at the Kaiser Permanente Medical Center in Oakland, found that nondrinkers were more likely to be hospitalized for coronary artery-related heart disease than people who had one or two drinks a day.

Even patients who took three or more drinks a day were less likely to have that type of heart disease than nondrinkers or people who drank less than one drink a month, Klatsky reported at a meeting of the American College of Cardiology in Anaheim.

Klatsky's findings were based on an examination of the records of 100,000 people who had physical examinations at the Kaiser facility between 1978 and 1982. During that period, 756 of the patients subsequently were hospitalized for conditions related to coronary artery disease.

Harry Nelson, *Los Angeles Times*, April 7, 1985.

In another analysis of blood-pressure findings involving almost 84,000 men and women, Klatsky and his colleagues found that individuals taking two or fewer drinks per day had similar or slightly lower blood pressures than did teetotalers or persons taking larger quantities of alcohol. More than three drinks daily was progressively associated with increases in average blood pressure, and the prevalence of hypertension was approximately doubled among whites who took six or more drinks per day and 50 percent greater among blacks. These findings are all in keeping with the interpretation that *moderate* use of alcohol may have a favorable effect on cardiovascular disease.

Equally significant are the findings of the Honolulu heart study conducted by Katsuhiko Yano and his fellow researchers, who examined the relation of alcohol and coffee consumption to the risk of coronary heart disease. In this prospective six-year study, the investigators analyzed the incidence of coronary heart disease among 7,705 Japanese men living in Hawaii. The men ranged in age from 45 to 68 at the time the study began, and 56 percent of them were younger than 55. During the six-year period of observation, which followed a comprehensive medical examination of each man, 294 new cases of coronary heart disease developed.

Wine and Beer

The researchers divided the men into three basic groups: lifetime teetotalers, ex-drinkers, and current drinkers. They found that ex-drinkers had the highest incidence of heart attacks, about 56 cases per 1,000 men; for teetotalers these figures were roughly 44 cases per 1,000 men; and drinkers had the lowest incidence of all—30 cases per 1,000 men. The difference in incidence between drinkers and nondrinkers was statistically significant. In order to determine the effect, if any, of different alcoholic beverages, the researchers compared the incidence of heart disease with the amount of wine, beer, and hard liquor consumed per day, adjusting their figures to take account of the patients' ages. No matter which beverage the men drank, drinkers consistently had fewer heart attacks than nondrinkers. The trend was most evident in the case of beer drinkers, and beer was the most popular beverage, accounting for about two thirds of the total alcohol consumed.

In terms of total alcohol consumption, Yano and his colleagues found that nondrinkers or light drinkers (those who consumed beverages containing no more than 15 ml or about ½ oz. of pure alcohol per day) suffered more heart attacks than those who drank moderately (the equivalent of 16 to 60 ml, or 2 oz., of pure alcohol per day). Furthermore, there were a greater number of deaths from coronary heart disease among nondrinkers than among drinkers. In an accompanying editorial in the prestigious *New England Journal of Medicine*, William B. Kannel concludes, "It is encouraging to note that not everything one enjoys in life predisposes to cardiovascular disease. There is nothing to suggest, for the present, that we must give up either coffee or alcohol in moderation to avoid a heart attack."

Psychological Factors

One might argue that the lower frequency of heart attacks among drinkers was due not to the protective effects of alcohol, but to psychological or behavioral factors. However, Yano and his colleagues found that the incidence of heart disease was not only lower in drinkers than in nondrinkers, but also that the incidence decreased as individual consumption of alcohol increased up to 60 ml (2 oz.) of alcohol per day. This led them to observe that alcohol consumption seems to be directly related to a reduction in the risk of coronary heart disease. There is growing evidence that moderate alcohol intake may elevate the amount of a fatty substance in the blood known as high-density lipoprotein (HDL). Several recent reports, including the Kaiser-Permanente study, have concluded that the presence of HDL is related to a lower risk of heart attack. By contrast, low-density lipoprotein (LDL) has been linked to a higher risk of heart attack. A hypothesis now being investigated is that alcohol consumption may influence the form of cholesterol—containing lipoprotein in the blood.. . .

The Benefits of Drinking

Most drinking customs in America evolved as a means of reducing the tensions of modern life, stimulating communication between people and giving people a pleasant ritual with which to mark special occasions. Along the way, society found that it could simultaneously and somewhat painlessly raise billions of tax dollars to fund programs that benefit drinkers and nondrinkers alike while providing gainful employment and an important market for perishable agricultural products.

Several studies, including one at Kaiser Permanente in Los Angeles, revealed that regular moderate drinkers live longer and have a substantially reduced rate of heart disease (the No. 1 killer of Americans) than do nondrinkers.

F.A. Meister, *The Los Angeles Times*, March 10, 1985.

A comparison of beverages on the basis of equivalent quantities of alcohol would show that four 1-oz. jiggers of 80 proof whiskey are roughly equivalent to four 10-oz. glasses of ordinary American beer (4.5 percent), four 12-oz. glasses of light beer (3.2 percent), or half a bottle (four 3.5-oz. glasses) of table wine. These each contain 40 to 48 ml of alcohol—amounts that are now widely accepted as safe daily levels of consumption—and are equivalent to the standard of 1.5 oz. of alcohol that was put forth in 1862 by Sir Francis Anstie, a British doctor, as "Anstie's law of safe drinking." However, there is no consensus that Anstie's recommendation represents the maximum safe alcohol intake for all people, nor is it possible to save one day's ration and add it to another's. There is mounting evidence indicating that the majority of healthy, normal adults may safely consume considerably more than Anstie's limit without impairment of health. . . .

But then how does one define moderation? There is evidence that a daily intake of around 56 g of alcohol—which translates into 6 oz. of 80 proof spirits, 20 oz. of table wine, or four and one half 12-oz. bottles of beer—causes little, if any, damage to health. Available evidence suggests that, on balance, it may even be beneficial. On theoretical and experimental grounds, intermittent or weekend drinking would appear to carry less risk of liver damage than daily drinking, but there are no clinical studies that permit a definite conclusion. Weekend drinking in this case means drinking only the stated amount each day, not saving the entire week's allotment for a Saturday-night party. Until more evidence is available, the limit of 44 ml, or 35 g of alcohol a day (the equivalent of three 1-oz. jiggers of 100 proof spirits or about four jiggers of 80 proof spirits) established by Anstie over a century ago could be used as a measure of certain healthful moderate consumption by today's drinkers. But there is evidence to support more liberal levels for most persons. . . .

There are traditional folk uses of alcohol. For centuries a stiff shot of whiskey or other distilled spirits has been recommended as a cure for the common cold. According to an old English remedy, the thing to do at the first sign of a cold is to hang your hat on the bedpost, drink freely from a good bottle of whiskey until you see *two* hats, and then get into bed and stay there. Neither of these remedies has merit.

A Depressant, Not Stimulant

Although alcohol is often thought of as a stimulant, it is actually a depressant. Alcoholic beverages appear to stimulate because they reduce or anesthetize feelings of exhaustion or discomfort that stem from the portion of the brain that is responsible for judgment and social control. Drinking breaks down inhibitions and, for this reason, promotes social interaction.

This quality of promoting social intercourse accounts in large measure for the recently reported beneficial effects of alcoholic beverage consumption by residents of homes for the aged. During the late 1960s a series of studies was conducted by Robert Kastenbaum, a psychologist at Cushing Hospital, in institutions for the aging near Boston.

In one study, for example, beer, cheese, and crackers were served six afternoons a week. When the study began, 76 percent of the male patients were incontinent and required safety restraints. Within two months the rate of incontinence had dropped to 27 percent and restraints were necessary in only 12 percent of the cases. A the same time, the percentage of ambulatory patients increased from 21 percent to 74 percent. Group activity more than tripled, moving progressively upward to 71 percent by the second month.

A substantial reduction in the prescription of psychotropic drugs was also recorded by Kastenbaum. At the beginning of the study, three fourths of the group was receiving Thorazine. By the second month, no Thorazine was required by any of the patients. A similar reduction occurred in the numbers and dosages of another prescription drug that was being administered. An unexpected development during this period was that ward personnel gave up their normal lunch break, which permitted them to leave the unit, and instead remained to eat and socialize with the patients.

Similar improvements in socialization and patient status have been observed in other investigations in which moderate amounts of alcoholic beverages have been made available. It should be noted, however, that the use of alcohol in one of Kastenbaum's studies was accompanied by other changes in the environment, such as the use of a larger ward that had additional entertainment facilities. Thus, improved patient and staff relationships cannot be attributed solely to the effects of alcohol. Nevertheless, the patients' preference for beer or wine over nonalcoholic beverages when they were given a choice indicates that the "socializing" influence of alcohol was a factor. Although Kastenbaum reported no negative effects on the patients, it is evident that persons who may have been dependent on alcohol in their younger years should be continuously supervised in any resumption of alcohol intake.

On the basis of current evidence we may conclude that the moderate use of alcoholic beverages is safe, that it contributes to our supply of energy, to our enjoyment of life, and in some instances, to our health. So it would seem that there may be a profound truth underlying the traditional French toast, *à votre santé*—"to your health." And as some people might say, I'll drink to that.

"Heavier penalties for drunk driving are a must."

Drunk Driving:
A Victim's Story

Micki Peluso

Micki Peluso's thirteen-year-old daughter was run over and killed by a drunk driver who was on parole at the time for a previous drunk driving offense. Mrs. Peluso, who lives in Staten Island, New York, is the mother of six children. In the following viewpoint, she shares the story of her child's death and makes an urgent plea that tougher laws be implemented to jail drunk drivers.

As you read, consider the following questions:

1. What was the court's judgment against the drunk driver?
2. What was the father's reaction to the accident?
3. How did the community respond to the sentence handed down to the driver?

Excerpted from "Death Toll" by Micki Peluso which first appeared in *Victimology: An International Journal,* 9 (1984) 2:186-190. © 1985 Victimology Inc. All rights reserved.

That day started out as any other, better, in fact than most. For the intense heat wave that permeated the Northeast had broken, and the crisp, cool dryness that foretells the coming of fall, was in the air.

Noelle, high-spirited and full of mischief as usual, bounced into the living room that afternoon and announced that she was bored. How she could have been was beyond me, for life with her was anything but boring. Her crazy antics and off-beat sense of humor made our family life uncertain, at best. . . .

At seven thirty that evening Noelle had the misfortune of walking down our country road at the same time a drunk driver, with a notorious past record of drunk driving offenses, was speeding down it inebriated, and out of control. As a result, Noelle's life was destroyed and her family's lives destroyed as well.

Shortly after she left, I planned to go bike riding, but something on television caught my eye and I lingered awhile. Had I but left when I'd planned, perhaps her fate might have been altered. Perhaps not.

I was just leaving when a neighbor came running to my door, screaming my name.

"Noelle's been in an accident," she said.

"How bad?" I asked.

"Pretty bad," she said.

"Take me to her!" I cried.

My ten-year old daughter started screaming hysterically.

Running in Fear

The accident was about a quarter of a mile from my home. I could only be driven part way because of all the cars blocking the road. I ran the rest of the way with fear pulsing through my veins.

When I reached her she was lying face down, swollen and blue. "She has no pulse!" I screamed to a friend who was kneeling by her side. "Yes she does," he said, "but it's very faint."

The wait for the ambulance seemed endless. I wanted to turn her over and try to resuscitate her but my neighbors stopped me. "Give her oxygen!" I screamed when the paramedics arrived. "She's not breathing!" They gave her oxygen and had to restart her heart. I stood there watching and shaking and praying. God had always answered my prayers and kept all six of my children safe. Surely he would do so again.

My eighteen-year old son came up the road and stood trembling by my side. I made him go and look for his sister, who was seventeen and due to walk up that very road on her way home from work. I couldn't let Kelly find her sister like this and it gave Dante something to keep his mind occupied.

Riding to the hospital in the ambulance seemed to take forever even though it was only blocks away. Everything seemed to be

moving in slow motion, and I was an observer, not a participant.

The wait in the emergency room was shared by neighbors and friends. It was a nightmare. Kelly and Dante were with me, Nicole, the youngest, was at the home of a friend, and I couldn't find my oldest daughter, Kim, who was out on a date, or my oldest son Michael, who was on an Army Reserve trip.

My husband, out of town on business, had been called and faced a five-hour trip of agonizing worry and heartache.

The wait went on. I knew from listening to the paramedics talk among themselves that Noelle was in a coma and that her neck was broken. I was sure she would be all right. I would will her to be all right.

The doctors strode into the waiting room like omens of death. They asked to speak to me alone. I shook with dread. I felt suffocated by their aura of hopelessness.

"She can't live," they said. "She is only alive because of the respirator." "Her spinal cord is severed." "You may as well disconnect her now, because she can't be saved." "No!" I said. "I want her kept on the life support system." They looked at me as though I didn't understand. I understood perfectly, but I refused to take their word as final. I asked to see her. . . .

A World of Unreality

When I reached her, I entered a world of unreality. This could not be my child, not my beautiful, lively girl, who had left me not more than an hour ago. What I saw was some stranger, swollen and bloodied beyond belief. My daughter was somewhere beneath this mass of human destruction. Her jaw was shattered and her nose and collarbone were broken. She was in a deep coma. My tears mingled with the blood that steadily trickled down her face, an alien face that did not even vaguely resemble my child. "Please God," I prayed. "Just let her live."

She was soon moved to the Intensive Care Unit and I followed her. Kelly and Dante had run out of the hospital in shock and hysteria, while I was in with Noelle, and were brought back by my friends.

My daughter Kim had been found and ran into my arms, sobbing, "Not Noelle!" "Not my sister!" The rest of the night is a blur in my memory. My priest was there and supported my refusal to take her off the life support systems. My husband came sometime during the night and cried out, "Oh, my baby!" I remember nothing more.

The next morning she seemed so much better. She was still in a coma, but the swelling had gone down and her color was better. We allowed hope to set in.

The following day she began opening her eyes. I talked to her and she responded by blinking her eyes. The doctors refused to believe this until they examined her and saw for themselves, that she could both hear and communicate.

Fighting to Live

She fought to live. She blinked that she was not in pain. Her eyes darted about trying to find me and she could follow my voice. I don't think she could see me, at least not clearly, but I'll never know for sure. Tears would trickle down her cheeks and although the nurses assured me that it was due to the medication they were giving her to keep her eyes moist, they haunted me.

My husband called specialists from all over the country. One of the best, from Philadelphia, was flown in by private jet. He arrived

64

on Thursday. I dreaded his arrival, because I feared he would tell us what we most dreaded to hear.

"She can't be saved," he said, and tears were in his eyes. "Don't let her awaken from the coma into a world where she will never speak, move, swallow, or breathe on her own. She will deteriorate slowly, a horror for all of you but more so for her." We cried, but we could not let her go. "You must," he said, "for she will have a perfectly sound mind, a pair of eyes and ears, and nothing more. Don't do that to her." He returned to Philadelphia and we sat together, stunned and unable to make any kind of decision.

Five Days

It was now five days since Noelle had been hit. Her bruises healed in a miraculously short time, her blood pressure stabilized and the swelling receded. She seemed to be trying to heal her broken body, but she could not heal her severed spinal cord. She suffered the most severe spinal cord damage possible. After the doctor went back to Philadelphia, Noelle slipped back into a deep coma and no longer communicated with anyone. Sometimes I wonder if she heard his prognosis. There was no hope.

Meanwhile, we were torn. To let her live was cruel beyond belief. To let her die was an abomination we could not conceive of. Yet we were pressured daily by the doctors and nurses to do just that. Days passed in desperation before the yoke of indecision was lifted from us at last. One of the doctors came in to see us.

Drunk Drivers As Criminals

We Americans have little difficulty in labeling the burglar who kills during the commission of his crime as a "murderer." The same applies to the rapist or armed robber who kills while committing his crime. However, as a nation we are not yet prepared to swallow the bitter and truthful fact that the drunk driver who kills at the wheel of his automobile has equal disregard for his victim as do these other criminals. Our past and present DWI laws stand as testimonial representation to our refusal to apply the label of "criminal" to those who are arrested and convicted of Driving While Intoxicated.

Rodney F. Buck, *The Angolite*, January/February 1985.

"We can't go on like this," he said. "Not you, not me, not the nurses caring for her. It's too big for any of us to handle. I go home at night and hug my children. We've got to let her be. Whatever happens must happen of its own accord."

Relief overwhelmed us. This was the only solution we could abide by. We all felt strongly that she could not hold on much longer. He spoke to us on a Sunday, one week after the accident.

By Monday she started to go rapidly downhill. She was running a high temperature and by Tuesday I didn't think she would make it through the night.

The Tears Are Real

Late Tuesday evening I was visiting her one last time before going home to get some sleep, leaving my husband and Kim to sleep in the waiting room next to her. The male nurse attending her assured me that her condition remained unchanged. "Except for the tears," he said. "What tears?" I asked. "Why, she's crying." he said. "But the nurses told me it was just eye fluids dripping down from her medication," I answered. "No," he said, "She's crying. The tears are real."

I suppose he meant well, but I was shattered. I had half-heartedly allowed myself to believe that the large tears that occasionally rolled down her face were due to the coma. Now this well-meaning nurse confirmed my worst fears. My daughter was crying. I went home and drank an unknown quantity of some kind of alcohol and went to bed and wept.

The next morning she started to fade away from us. We still prayed for a miracle, a miracle that would not come. God was determined to have her. On Wednesday afternoon at three-twenty, she left us forever. Although we had prepared ourselves for this moment, the reality of her death threw us all into deep despair....

Unspoken Blame

My husband lost the love of his life, the daughter whose sardonic wit kept him going in the worst of times. They had a very special rapport between them. He was inconsolable. He rejected her death and blamed himself. He also blamed me for not seeing to her safety in his absence. The blame was never spoken, only felt. He retreated into the only oblivion he knew; long, hard hours of work. God, for him, ceased to exist.

Guilt weighed heavily on me, for I had suggested she go on that last walk. Later I refused to accept the guilt. It was too much to bear and fate had a greater hand in causing her death than I. I went through the full scope of emotions, from despair to anger, and then devastating depression. Had I not a responsibility to my husband and children, I would not have functioned at all....

The drunk driver that struck Noelle down that fateful August evening was on parole at the time for a previous drunk driving offense. He was a known alcoholic and had been cited several times for public drunkenness.

At the time of the accident, he was unlicensed. He was seen by witnesses driving at a high rate of speed and very erratically. After he hit Noelle, he left the scene of the accident and continued down the road where he finally stopped and switched places with the passenger in his car.

When the police arrived, he was given a breath test and told to walk a straight line. He failed both. He was nonetheless released. During the six months preceding his trial, he was arrested three more times for public drunkenness while on bail.

At his trial, he pleaded guilty to charges of drunk driving, driving without a license, manslaughter and leaving the scene of an accident. He was sentenced to two and a half to six years in a state prison.

While this seems very lenient, and it most certainly is, it was the highest sentence given out in this area for drunk driving and the first time a drunk driver had been sentenced to a state prison.

Letters, petitions and phone calls assailed the judge's office, showing how outraged the community was over another drunk driving death in the area. Outrage is good and heavier penalties for drunk driving offenses are a must, but neither of these can ease the pain of losing a child or loved one. Statistically, thousands are killed or injured each day by drunk drivers. This doesn't really strike home until it's one of yours. Even as you read this somewhere a child is lying shattered, on the road, by the mindless act of drunk driving. Don't let it be your child.

For yet a thousand years won't wash away
the stains,
Or ease the pain that sears my broken
heart's remains.

> *"I was the drunk driver. I caused one of those twenty-six thousand deaths. And, I can tell you, that's not an easy thing to live with."*

Drunk Driving: A Driver's Story

Kevin Tunell

Kevin Tunell of Fairfax, Virginia was driving home from a high school drinking party when his car edged over the center line, hit an oncoming vehicle, and killed a teenage girl. He was charged and found guilty of driving while intoxicated. His sentence required that for one year he retell his story to groups of high school students. In the following viewpoint, he describes the pain resulting from his mistake and explains why he hopes that his message may reduce future drunk driving deaths.

As you read, consider the following questions:

1. What was Kevin's reaction when he found out he had killed Susan Marie Herzog?
2. What was the reaction of his family? His friends?
3. Do you think that the judge's sentence for Kevin was fair?

I spent 1982 and part of this year talking to teenagers in school auditoriums. I had to do this for at least 40 hours every week. It was either that or go to jail.

At the start of my senior year at Fairfax High School a year and a half ago, I was not unlike your usual grade-conscious, wanting-to-be-popular 17-year-old. I played on the rugby team and hung out with my friends on weekends. My grades were pretty good, and I was looking forward to college.

Then one night my life changed drastically. New Year's Eve. A night full of excitement and good times. My girlfriend Ginny and I had plans to celebrate at a friend's home with six other couples.

On the way to the party, we stopped off to visit a guy in our class, Steve, who had broken his leg and wouldn't be able to get out that night. We drank a bottle of champagne with him, and left another bottle behind to keep him supplied for the rest of the evening.

Then Ginny and I drove to the party, where we danced and drank and talked and joked until midnight. The parents upstairs didn't know that we were drinking. We weren't rowdy; we were just a bunch of high school seniors having a good time.

Don't Try to Drive

At the door, as Ginny and I were leaving, two friends came up and held out their hands: "Hey, Kevin, don't try to drive tonight. Give us your keys. We'll get you home."

"No, s'okay," I said. "I'm all right. I can handle it."

I was feeling warm, elated inside. It had been a great party, and I had handled myself well, I thought. I felt *good,* even a little powerful.

I dropped Ginny at her house. It was already 1:00 a.m., the time I was supposed to be home, so we talked only a few minutes, then said good-night.

"Be careful, Kevin," she called after me. "Listen, I care a lot about you, so get home safely."

"I will. G'night," I called back.

Starting my father's silver Aspen station wagon, I headed home. It had been one of the nicest New Year's Eves ever.

I was still feeling that warm glow, so terrific, as I breezed effortlessly down Commonwealth Boulevard. I didn't notice my speedometer, or the 30-mile-an-hour sign, or that I was three feet over the double yellow line rounding a curve.

Then it was too late to notice, because that's when I plowed into Susan Marie Herzog's Volkswagen.

A Hazy Nightmare

The memories of that evening meld into a hazy nightmare. I don't remember climbing out of my car through the window or seeing Susan Herzog's car, a crumpled mass of metal. I do remember riding in the police car with Officers Kolodziej and Petracca.

"Was anyone in the other car hurt?" I asked. "Did they get out okay?"

"Don't worry, Kevin, everything is okay," they reassured me.

It was at the police station at about 3:00 a.m. that I learned that everything was *not* okay. A police chaplain, the Reverend Gary Martin, told me. Susan Herzog in the other car hadn't made it. She had been a senior at Robinson High School. Bright and well-liked. Vice-president of her class. And I had killed her. He didn't say it that way. My head was so fuzzy I can't recall just how he said it; but that's what it boiled down to.

My senior-year-big-man-on-the-rugby-team-and-I-can-handle-it-at-drinking-and-driving image came crashing down around me. I didn't feel so powerful anymore. I felt sick, and scared.

Shame & Guilt

When Pastor Martin told me that my parents were at the police station, I groaned, "I *can't* see them. *Please!*" Shame and guilt welled up inside me. I'd done the worst thing a person can do—taken another life. How could I possibly face my *parents?* I put my head down into my hands and wished that the floor would swallow me up.

Jails Cannot Cure Alcoholism

As a recovered alcoholic myself, I am as anxious as you (more so, I dare say) to keep intoxicated drivers off the streets and highways of our state for their own safety and that of others.

However, . . . the alcoholic needs treatment (hospitalization or attendance at AA meetings) in order to recover and lead a happy, fulfilled life of sobriety and service. It can be achieved, as thousands of us grateful recovering alcoholics can attest. But no number of jail sentences or DWI's will effect recovery.

Catholic Bulletin, December 25, 1981.

But Mom and Dad came in, and they hugged me and said, "Kevin, we love you, and we want you to know that we're going to stick with you through this."

There were times after that when I got so depressed I felt the walls were going to close in on me. The next day was one of those times. All through the day, every newscast reported the crash: "A drunken youth driving on the wrong side of the road . . . collided into her car. . . . His name is being withheld due to his age. . . . Funeral services. . . ."

I didn't want to go out that day. My older brother Keith came over, and we talked, but I felt miserable. I couldn't forget that I'd bought two bottles of champagne using my other brother Kent's old driver's license. I couldn't forget that I'd risked Ginny's life, my life, the life of everybody I'd passed on the road. I couldn't forget that I'd *killed* someone.

Drinking and Driving Don't Mix

I had known the danger. Who hasn't heard over and over: Drinking and driving don't mix!

Afterward people wrote letters to the newspaper editor. They were angry and demanded that this unidentified teenager go to jail for what he'd done.

My best friend Carl came up to me at school in disbelief. "Kevin, I'm hearing an incredible story about you—that you ran into some girl and killed her. That's not true, is it?"

"Yeah, Carl," I gulped, not wanting to look at him. "I'm afraid it is true."

Susan Herzog's parents filed a $1.5 million suit against me. The police left a warrant for my arrest, and one day in February, we gathered for a trial at the Municipal Court Building. There was a wait, seemingly endless. I watched the clock for four hours, and nervously wondered what was going to happen to me.

Then the proceedings finally began. Mom and Dad and Keith and a couple of neighbors had come to lend moral support. And the Herzogs were there, sitting directly behind me. I didn't want to look to the left or to the right, feeling that they were staring right through me, feeling their bitterness, how much they must hate me.

The Sentencing

The judge sentenced me to a year of telling my story about the crash to groups of school kids, wherever I was asked to speak. I had to work at that full time. School had to come second. If I passed, fine; if I failed, tough.

At the end of the hearing, Mr. Herzog stood up and read a statement about his daughter. I remember his saying: "If it had been Susan who caused the accident, if she had been the drunk one behind the wheel, I would have *expected* her to serve time in jail!" That's the way a lot of people felt. Some still do.

Others have reached out in many ways, with cards and letters; my minister and my friends have talked with me. My family got me through the depressing times, through the horrible nightmares when I'd wake up in a sweat.

But what has helped me most has been standing in front of kids like me, sometimes feeling nervous or close to tears, with a message that might influence someone not to repeat my mistake.

"Did you know," I ask them, "that *twenty-six thousand* people die every year because of drunken drivers, and that *five thousand* of them are our age? Think of it! That's seventy people dying every day out on the roadways. An accident occurs every minute!

71

Did you know that half of you sitting here will at some time in your life be in an accident caused by a drunk driver?

The Drunk Driver

"You don't think it's going to happen to you. I didn't think it would happen to me, but it did. I was the drunk driver. I caused one of those twenty-six thousand deaths. And, I can tell you, that's not an easy thing to live with."

Sometimes somebody will laugh, will make fun of what I'm saying, probably because he thinks getting drunk is the "in" thing to do. But I keep on talking until I know he's gotten the message. At the end I ask the audience to try to stop drinking; and some of them get together and organize school campaigns against drunk driving.

The Herzogs eventually dropped the suit against me. I have talked with Mrs. Herzog a few times. And one of those times, I told her about squeezing in classes and labs and exams so that I was able to graduate with my class, about giving talks during the school year and working with handicapped kids in the summer. I told her that I would be on probation until I was 21, that I would not be driving until the court allowed me, that I wanted to go to college.

But Mr. Herzog has never spoken with me; and I understand how hard it must be to talk to someone who has caused you so much hurt.

I've asked God's forgiveness, and I've managed to accept that. Now it is up to me to do the rest. I have to do the best with the sentence the judge gave me.

I've learned a lot about people's feelings and how important it is to reach out to one another. I'll continue telling people about the 26,000 deaths caused by drunk drivers. And I hope that somewhere along the way someone will be saved from the tragedy and pain that the Herzogs and my family and thousands of other families are living through.

"What liquor advertising in America sells is euphoria: the camaraderie of ex-football players downing lite beer after lite beer."

Liquor Advertising Promotes Alcoholism

Frank McConnell

Frank McConnell is a member of the English Department at the University of California, Santa Barbara. As a recovering alcoholic, he has a unique perspective on how liquor advertisements entice those prone to alcohol abuse. In the following viewpoint, Mr. McConnell claims that the marketing of alcohol as a cure-all for life's dissatisfactions promotes an image that is false but difficult for some to resist.

As you read, consider the following questions:

1. Why does the author believe that beer advertisements "always" include a group?
2. What does Mr. McConnell think the liquor advertisements *should* include?
3. What does the author suggest as a first step toward coping with alcohol addiction?

Frank McConnell, "Ads and Addictions," *Commonweal*, December 1983. Reprinted with permission.

"Don't take the car, you'll kill yourself!" Who hasn't seen that commercial by the National Council on Alcoholism—the drunk husband lurching toward his car and the panicked wife shouting from the porch? And who does not know that it has become virtually a standard punch-line for every standup comic on the circuit? When in trouble, play with that line, and the audience roars (one reason, of course, being that probably half of them are snockered, so the joke becomes self-defense: that poor boob, thank God we're not like *him*, we can handle the stuff, can't we?)

But: "If you've got the time, we've got the beer." A group of healthy, shiny-faced American males go out for a day's Marlin fishing (Hemingway sport), or mountain climbing, or hang-glider flying, just all buddies together and having a *heck* of a good, invigorating time. And, inevitably, what do you do at the end of a great day like that? Why, you gather at your favorite bar, and you start calling for the beer, probably with that most *macho* of American phrases, "Run a tab, Rosie."

As a slogan, it's about as broad and silly as "Don't take the car, etc." So why isn't anybody laughing?

Sanctioned by Society

Any recovering alcoholic (and yes, I'm a member of the club) can tell you. It's because the use—and abuse—of alcohol is so deeply ingrained in, and sanctioned by, our culture that *not* drinking is perceived as the abnormal, and of course only the abnormal, the outsider, can be the clown or the fool and get a laugh.

I am concerned with the ways media reflect both the national self-image and the national self-delusions: I am not, fear not, about to preach you a sermon on the evil of demon rum. But this time around, my subject is liquor and anti-liquor advertising in America, which is to say the ways we try to come to terms with (or don't try to come to terms with) a disease which is among the major causes of death in this country. If statistics mean anything, three out of ten of you reading this piece will contract or have contracted the sickness. In fact, given the demographics of *Commonweal's* readership—heavily Irish and German—it is probably more like four or five in ten, since the evidence is that a predisposition, at least, to the sickness is genetically transmitted, sorry. And ten out of every ten will find themselves, their lives, their loves, affected and probably affected severely, by someone who *has* the sickness. Now *that's* what I call a disease.

A Curious Disease

It is a curious disease, moreover. Like tooth decay and hypertension, it is a disease of civilization; only when men have become civilized enough to ferment grain, precipitate sugar from cane, or evolve the profession of insurance salesmen do these ailments become possible.

It is also a disease one of whose prime constituents is secrecy. *No* drinker wants to admit that he (or she) drinks too much, so the heavy drinker goes to elaborate, and sometimes rather brilliant, lengths to invent proofs that he (or she) doesn't drink too much. I have sometimes thought, indeed, that as much intellectual energy has been expended by drinkers demonstrating that they don't drink as was expended by Scholastic theologians demonstrating the existence of God.

Not that everyone is fooled, of course. In adultery, runs the cliche, the wife (or husband) is always the last one to know. But alcoholism is a disease, not a sin, and in that condition it is the victim who is always the last to know—if, that is, he is lucky enough to find out.

Pressured to Drink

In a society that blatantly promotes—through the mass media and intense social pressure—the consumption of alcoholic beverages as a source of pleasure, a way to relieve tension, even an antidote to aging, limits on alcohol consumption are . . . for some people, completely unacceptable.

Stephanie Brown, *The Stanford Magazine*, Summer 1982.

Do you know a beer commercial that *doesn't* include a group? Do you know a brandy or bourbon ad that shows one person alone drinking? I'll answer for you: you don't, and the reason you don't is that the people who sell us our booze are smart enough to realize that it is a private addiction sanctioned by public, social acceptability. Imagine the commercials if heroin (an equivalently dangerous drug) were legal: four old pals, sitting around the apartment, setting up their gimmicks, spoon, match, hypodermic: "This skin-pop's for you."

Writing the Ads

Not that the people who run the distilleries or write the liquor ads are vampires sucking self-respect and productivity out of the soul of the Republic. They are, like the rest of us, poor souls struggling between heaven and earth and trying to make a buck on route. But the way they write the ads reflects a great deal about the way we think about alcohol abuse, and the ways we invent to convince ourselves—actually, to con ourselves—to believe there really is no such thing.

Think about booze as a metaphor for social and sexual roles. In a very serious way, we use liquor not only as social lubricant ("Ice is nice, but liquor is quicker"—Ogden Nash), but as a way of *validating* ourselves socially. James Bond—the last public school gentleman or the first punk rocker—can consume infinite vodka martinis per diem and still be razor-sharp when he confronts the vile machinations of SPECTRE. "I'll drink till I drop down, with one eye on my clothes," sings Roger Daltrey in the Who's brilliant punk-opera, *Quadrophenia*. And no American private eye would be worth his salt (and his lime and tequila?) if he did not keep a bottle of something in his lower desk drawer.

The Fiction of Alcohol

We are always in control: that is the message of the fictions of alcohol, and of the advertisements for alcohol. It is, I am convinced, the real root of the disease—the desire for total control of the environment, and the denial that there are things that can happen to us over which we have *no* control. "You have the *right* to feel rotten," said my alcohol counselor, and it was an insight and a revelation of some cultural as well as personal import. Because the liberal myth of American society is precisely that you *needn't* feel rotten: and if you do, if you happen to be black in a white world or female in a male world or chemically addicted in a "normal" world, then there must be something wrong with you. How to fix it? Well you know, you can always have a drink.

Booze—since it tried so hard to kill me, I enjoy calling it by its vulgarest name—is a kind of inverted sacrament. It is a chemically-authenticated denial of the Fall (after the third beer, do you feel that anything is *wrong* with you?) and it is marketed as such. Lately I understand why bread and wine are the materials of the Eucharist—as opposed, say, to water and roast beef; because bread and wine *are* products of civilization, unimaginable to pre-Neolithic, which is to say, pre-urban man, and the Eucharist is a blessing, a *baruch*, on the chances for urban man to exchange his urbanity for something like transcendence. But Eucharist is not euphoria, and what liquor advertising in America sells is euphoria: the camaraderie of ex-football players downing lite beer after lite beer, the romanticism of a man in a tuxedo and a woman in an evening dress sharing a snifter of brandy, or the pure success—myth of a wealthy entertainer and businesswoman extolling the virtues of her favorite brand of vodka. The point of this sacrament is not that it conduces toward transcendence, but precisely that it reintroduces us into the secular city where, already, we felt so hopeless and alone. The real horror of alcoholism, said Malcolm Lowry, a great novelist *(Under the Volcano)* and a drunk of Olympic-class proportions, is the terrible sterility of existence as *sold* to you.

Females in Ads

And sold to whom? we might ask. Very few liquor ads involve women alone (except for sherry, which, as we all know, is "downright upright," right?). But the percentage of female alcoholism is—again, if statistics mean anything—rather rapidly approaching fifty percent of the total addicted population. Why the reticence, then? Just because, I think, we find the image of a woman drunk still more offensive than the image of a man drunk: sexist perhaps, but also an index of the degree to which we remain faintly embarrassed about using our drug of choice. And it is also significant, surely, that the most powerful of anti-alcohol ads on television are those which show us the suburban housewife asleep at noon on the sofa, with an empty bottle overturned at her feet and a cigarette smoldering in the ashtray. It is melodramatic stuff, to be sure; a second-rate Dickens couldn't have done worse. But it is also supremely

DUNAGIN'S PEOPLE

U.S. SENATE

1985 The Orlando Sentinel
News America Syndicate

"WHEW! DEBATING BEER AND WINE ADVERTISING IS EXHAUSTING! THANK GOODNESS IT'S MILLER TIME!"

DUNAGIN'S PEOPLE by Ralph Dunagin © by and permission of News American Syndicate.

intelligent, since, for a number of people, this is really what the specious glamour of the liquor ads comes down to.

Mack Sennett, the master of silent slapstick comedy, said that he always wanted to make a film where the Keystone Kops would, predictably, drive their car into a ditch, and then leave the camera rolling, so that the audience could—*would have to*— watch the cops crawl, bloody and broken, out of that terrible accident. They never let him do it. I, for one, would like to see one of those brandy or sherry commercials where the elegant man and woman congregate over their bottle and glasses, with a slow dissolve to the next morning: sprawled on the bed, hair dishevelled and sweaty, dry mouth, and unable to get up before noon.

I try not to be a moralist in these columns and I am not—repeat *not*—advocating a new prohibition or a ban on liquor advertising. But I am saying that a great deal of national distress is attributable to the way in which we market and mythicize this *very* dangerous substance. I am also, I suppose, suggesting that a large part of our natural and national growing-up process might be to realize that we *are* an addicted society, and that at least the first step toward a greater sanity might be facing up to that addiction. At the very least, we ought to be able to train ourselves to laugh as hard at "If you've got the time, we've got the beer" as we do at "Don't take the car, you'll kill yourself." The first one, after all, *is* the sillier line.

"The answer to responsible drinking is not found in banning or censoring advertising."

Liquor Advertising Does Not Promote Alcoholism

Clifford R. Williams

Clifford R. Williams is director of government affairs for the Miller Brewing Company. He believes the answer to drinking problems in the US lies in educating the public to make responsible drinking decisions. In the following viewpoint, Mr. Williams claims that censoring liquor advertising would be a direct attack on the first amendment and concludes that it would not solve the alcoholism problem.

As you read, consider the following questions:

1. How does the author justify his stance that liquor advertisements are protected by the First Amendment?
2. Is there any scientific evidence to prove that alcohol advertising has any impact on alcoholism?
3. According to the author, what is the role of education in the prevention of alcohol abuse?

Clifford R. Williams, "Direct Attack on the First Amendment," *engage/social action*, January 1985. Reprinted with permission.

America is a land rich in diversity, envied by many around the world. The primary reasons for this diversity are the freedoms enjoyed by every American citizen. Freedom to think, freedom to speak, freedom to worship...that is America.

For more than two centuries, millions have migrated to this country to live in the land of freedoms. Many left their native lands because of religious persecution. Those millions came here to have the right to practice their beliefs without fear of interference or reprisal. In essence, their convictions were protected by the First Amendment to the Constitution, an amendment guaranteeing freedom of religion, freedom of speech and freedom of the press. To this day, the First Amendment, although challenged, remains the foundation of our diverse democracy.

Challenges are a natural part of a democratic society. Challenge to a myriad of beliefs makes our society a rich tapestry of varied and sometimes conflicting viewpoints. Those conflicting viewpoints are a natural and integral part of democracy. It is when challenges threaten to *limit* our inherent freedoms that the rich tapestry threatens to unravel.

Threat to First Amendment

One example of a threat to the First Amendment is the increased pressure by lobbying groups and allies, such as the United Methodist Church, to enact laws or regulations restricting beer and wine advertising on the broadcast media. This effort has resulted in a polarization of viewpoints.

Anti-alcohol spokespersons say that beer and wine advertising is the root of drinking problems in this country; so they propose to take their case to Congress and federal agencies. Others see such lobbying efforts as a direct attack on the First Amendment freedom of speech, including commercial speech, and totally without merit to prevent alcohol abuse.

Miller Brewing Company believes that the answer to responsible drinking is not found in banning or censoring advertising. We firmly believe that the answer is in effective education about the product. Education is the stepping stone to an informed consumer. A consumer who understands the product will use it responsibly, or choose not to use it at all.

Educational Programs Needed

Currently, Miller Brewing Company and other alcohol beverage producers are major sponsors of educational and research programs to reduce alcohol abuse and alcoholism. Miller educational programs are offered to the public, as well as to our employees. Our booklet, "Somebody Do Something," details our actions and is available at no cost from the Consumer Affairs Department, Miller Brewing Company, 3933 West Highland Boulevard, Milwaukee, WI 53201.

The National Beer Wholesalers Association, located in Falls Church, Virginia, has a massive and outstanding kindergarten-through-twelfth-grade alcohol education program being offered throughout the United States. Individually and collectively, members of the alcohol beverage industry are cooperating in a great effort with federal, state and local programs to develop an intelligent, mature consensus about the use or non-use of alcohol beverages in this country.

Advertising Does Not Create Alcoholics

Common sense tells us that advertising on radio and TV doesn't create an alcoholic. Drinking behavior is influenced by a variety of psychological and physiological factors, the most important being family example, followed by peer pressure.

There is not one recognized study linking broadcast advertising of beer and wine with overindulgence. What advertising does is play a fundamental role in influencing which brand a beer or wine drinker chooses to buy.

Edward O. Fritts, *The Los Angeles Times,* March 10, 1985.

But beyond the educational programs, films and literature loom the simplistic efforts to ban advertising on broadcast media. Many feel education is not enough. They seem to believe that only through bans on beer and wine broadcast advertising will the root of drinking problems be eliminated.

No Scientific Proof

There is no scientific evidence that beverage alcohol advertising has any significant impact on the rate of alcohol abuse and alcoholism in America today. *No scientific proof.* This fact was determined in a study by David J. Pittman, Ph.D., and M. Dow Lambert, Ph.D., of Washington University, St. Louis, Missouri.

There *is* proof that alcohol problems are related to a complex interaction of biological, cultural and psychological factors acting on individuals. Other countries of the world, such as the Scandinavian countries and the Soviet Union, prohibit or restrict alcohol beverage advertising. Yet their people have far greater alcohol abuse problems than Americans have.

Miller television advertising depicts adults in pleasant and often humorous settings. Popular Lite celebrities average nearly 50 years of age—hardly role models for children or teenagers. Some are former athletes and others have no association with sports whatsoever. In public appearances, Lite celebrities take the opportunity to stress individual responsibility in the use of our products.

Personal care is necessary whether one drives, flies or performs the many other common tasks that include an element of potential danger.

Freedom of Information

Censoring beer and wine advertising on broadcast media represents a direct attack on the inherent rights of all Americans who enjoy freedoms guaranteed by the First Amendment. Citizens of this country have the freedom to be exposed to a variety of viewpoints, beliefs and products.

Justice Harry Blackmun of the United States Supreme Court wrote that "people perceive their own best interests only if they are well enough informed." The *New York University Law Review* concurs with Justice Blackmun, and says, "The state can ensure that the dangers of alcohol are disclosed to the public, but the First Amendment prevents the government from making the paternalistic assumption that the less people know about alcohol, the better off they will be."

Churches are granted tax-exempt status and their leaders are free to criticize anything they choose, based on their moral judgments. However, in joining a lobbying campaign, such as that being conducted by the Center for Science in the Public Interest (Project SMART), a church threatens the freedom of others to speak and the freedom of millions of citizens to hear all sides and judge for themselves.

Access to information and the right to provide that information is the foundation of our democracy. The United Methodist Church has traditionally opposed drinking, but it recognized in the late 1960s that personal conscience, not a winking "abstinence," was at the heart of preventing alcohol abuse. It still is, and abridging someone else's freedom will come home to haunt all of us.

Recognizing Statements That Are Provable

From various sources of information we are constantly confronted with statements and generalizations about social and moral problems. In order to think clearly about these problems, it is useful if one can make a basic distinction between statements for which evidence can be found and other statements which cannot be verified or proved because evidence is not available, or the issue is so controversial that it cannot be definitely proved.

Readers should constantly be aware that magazines, newspapers and other sources often contain statements of a controversial nature. The following activity is designed to allow experimentation with statements that are provable and those that are not.

Most of the following statements are taken from the viewpoints in this chapter. Consider each statement carefully. *Mark P for any statement you believe is provable. Mark U for any statement you feel is unprovable because of the lack of evidence. Mark C for statements you think are too controversial to be proved to everyone's satisfaction.*

If you are doing this activity as a member of a class or group, compare your answers with those of other class or group members. Be able to defend your answers. You may discover that others will come to different conclusions than you. Listening to the reasons others present for their answers may give you valuable insights in recognizing statements that are provable.

If you are reading this book alone, ask others if they agree with your answers. You too will find this interaction very valuable.

P = *provable*
U = *unprovable*
C = *too controversial*

1. The present deplorable trend in America toward more and more consumption of liquor will be halted only by those who refuse to be intimidated.

2. Many of our youth, who would really prefer not to drink, become convinced they must for social reasons.

3. You don't have to drink to be sociable.

4. Studies now indicate that moderate alcohol consumption may reduce the risk of heart attacks, lessen symptoms of exhaustion and discomfort, and encourage desirable interaction.

5. Most people like to have a few drinks during the day.

6. Intermittent or weekend drinking would appear to carry less risk of liver damage than daily drinking.

7. To let a totally paralyzed patient live is cruel beyond belief.

8. Twenty-six thousand people die every year because of drunken drivers.

9. Drinking while driving may affect a person's reaction time.

10. The use—and abuse— of alcohol is so deeply ingrained in, and sanctioned by, our culture that *not* drinking is perceived as the abnormal.

11. Three out of ten of you reading this will contract alcoholism.

12. We still find the image of a woman drunk more offensive than the image of a man drunk.

13. A great deal of national distress is attributable to the way in which we market and mythicize liquor.

14. The First Amendment, although challenged, remains the foundation of our diverse democracy.

15. A consumer who is knowledgeable about the effects of liquor will use it responsibly, or choose not to use it at all.

16. Not everyone who drinks is going to end up in police court.

17. A comparison of beverages on the basis of equivalent quantities of alcohol would show that four 1-oz. jiggers of 80 proof whiskey are roughly equivalent to four 10-oz glasses of American beer.

18. No drinker wants to admit that he or she drinks too much.

19. Alcoholism is a disease, not a sin.

20. Challenges are a natural part of a democratic society.

Periodical Bibliography

The following list of periodical articles deals with the subject matter of this chapter.

Business Week	"Stiffer Warnings May Mean Less Risk For Cigarette Makers," October 15, 1984.
William G. Cahan	"Abusing Children by Smoking," *The New York Times,* March 3, 1985.
Harry S. Casey	"Warning to a Teen-Age Girl," *Reader's Digest,* February 1985.
Ken Cummins	"The Cigarette Makers: How They Get Away with Murder," *The Washington Monthly,* April 1984.
Owen Edward	"What Every Man Should Know: How to Smoke," *Esquire,* May 1983.
Lindsey Gruson	"Employers Get Tough on Smoking at Work," *The New York Times,* March 14, 1985.
Russell King	"Should Smoking Restrictions Be Written into Law?" *The New York Times,* November 13, 1984.
David Margolick	"Antismoking Climate Inspires Suits by the Dying," *The New York Times,* March 15, 1985.
Erika Reider Mark	"Can Your Husband's Cigarette Give You Cancer?" *Good Housekeeping,* May 1981.
New York	"Out of the Ashes," October 22, 1984.
William J. O'Connor	"In Defense of Smokers," *Business and Health,* November 1984.
Stanley S. Scott	"Smokers Get a Raw Deal," *The New York Times,* December 29, 1984.
Anastasia Toufexis	"Report from the Surgeon General," *Time,* March 8, 1982.
Susan West	"Behind a Smoke Screen," *Science '84,* May 1984.
Elizabeth M. Whelan	"Big Business vs. Public Health: The Cigarette Dilemma," *USA Today,* May 1984.
World Health	"The Chronology of U.S. Warning Against Cigarettes," October 1984.

How Harmful Is Tobacco?

"A number of respected scientists do not believe a causal relationship between smoking and illness has been established."

The Link Between Smoking and Disease Is Questionable

Horace R. Kornegay

Horace R. Kornegay is president of the Tobacco Institute and is a former congressman from North Carolina. In the following viewpoint, he argues that the case against smoking is built on statistics that are not valid. One by one, Mr. Kornegay presents the most prominent research studies on tobacco and then contends that they are not totally valid.

As you read, consider the following questions:

1. How does Mr. Kornegay argue against the laboratory "proof" that smoking causes cancer?
2. How does the author refute the link between heart disease and smoking?
3. Do you agree with the author that the claim of "300,000 excess deaths" being caused by smoking is merely propaganda? Why or why not?

Horace R. Kornegay, "The Cigarette Controversy," *engage/social action,* September 1980. Reprinted with permission.

For many adults, cigarette smoking is one of life's pleasures. Does it cause illness—even death? No one knows.

The case against smoking is based almost entirely on inferences from statistics. The "conventional wisdom" about smoking came from judgments expressed by committees of doctors in England and the United States. In our country, anti-smoking organizations pressured the government to endorse these judgments. Never before (or since) had a committee "discovered" a single "cause" for so many diseases.

A number of respected scientists do not believe a causal relationship between smoking and illness has been established. Others believe that it has.

If smoking does cause disease, why, after years of intensive research, has it not been shown *how* this occurs? And why has no ingredient in smoke been identified as the causal factor?

Smoking: Health Statistics

Statistics are said to show that among the 60 million Americans who are smokers, some may fall victim sooner, or in greater number, than other people to three major types of ailments—cancer, diseases of the heart and circulatory system, and the pulmonary illnesses, emphysema and chronic bronchitis.

These happen to be our greatest medical problems, coming to the forefront as the major infectious diseases of the past were "conquered" through scientific research. There have been other coincidental trends, among them the growth in popularity of cigarettes.

Scientists call these heart and lung problems "degenerative" ailments, for they seem to develop very slowly, through some kind of distortion or breakdown of body mechanisms. Though each illness is very different, all three—and more—are blamed by some sources primarily on one factor—cigarettes.

Laboratory Work

We hear about laboratory "proof" that smoking causes cancer. Mice have been painted, hamsters swabbed, and rats injected with "tars" condensed from tobacco smoke in laboratories but not found in the smoke itself. Rabbits have been fed nicotine. Dogs have been forced to "smoke" through holes cut in their windpipes. Subsequent "changes" in various cells of these animals have been cited as evidence that cigarettes cause diseases, though production with smoke of human-type lung cancer—or heart disease or emphysema—has *never been verified* in laboratory experiments.

It is no wonder that an American Cancer Society official has said that "a clever enough researcher can make almost anything induce cancer in animals, *but his findings may have no relevance to human exposure.*"

Somehow it's possible, the argument goes, that direct exposure to tobacco smoke can damage cells in the respiratory tract. The human heart is not exposed to smoke, and so there is even greater guessing about how it might be affected.

The Problems of Guesswork

Simply blaming cigarettes for heart disease doesn't help. In some countries not even statistics fit that notion. The government's National Heart and Lung Institute points out that we've learned so much about how to treat heart ailments that we overlook how little we know about their *causes*. "We tend to obscure our ignorance," the Institute says, "by making it seem that a problem has been solved when it has, in fact, been only half solved."

Emphysema, which makes breathing difficult, is a kind of lung disease typically found in older persons. Doctors ponder whether, among other things, it might be caused by inhaling some substance or whether it might result from some blood circulation difficulty. In any event, and despite speculation that smoking has something to do with it, the official view of the government institute responsible for lung research remains candid: "We do not know the cause of pulmonary emphysema, how to stop its progress even if detected early, or how to prevent heart disease caused by emphysema."

Unproven Causes

There *is* a cigarette controversy. The *causal theory*— that cigarette smoking causes or is the cause of the various diseases with which it is reported to be related statistically—is just that, a theory.

That the cause or causes of lung cancer and other diseases has *not* been scientifically proved is supported in the almost 4,000 printed pages of testimony and evidence presented on the cigarette labeling bills of 1982 and 1983 by research workers, government officials, voluntary health association representatives and behavioral experts.

The Tobacco Institute, *The Cigarette Controversy: Why More Research Is Needed,* February 1984.

Those who consider smoking a menace, rather than an enjoyment, have acted as prosecutors, trying to convince the public they have an airtight case. But isn't the "jury" entitled to some serious doubts? For example:

• Statistics do not explain why the majority of smokers never develop the diseases "associated" with smoking.

• Smoking cannot be the *sole* cause of *illness, because in every* case nonsmokers are afflicted too. For example, a study published last year in the Journal of the National Cancer Institute reported that the incidence of lung cancer among nonsmokers doubled in the last decade.

- Research suggests that because a patient tells a doctor he or she smokes, that patient is more apt to be diagnosed with an ailment "associated" in the familiar statistics with smoking.
- At the same time that increases in lung cancer have been reported, new techniques and equipment have made it possible to identify more cases with certainty.
- Too many conflicting reports are ignored in the anti-smoking messages from "authorities." For instance, the American Heart Association warns about tobacco but doesn't remind us that in Japan, where the smoking rate is much *higher* among men than in the United States, the heart disease death rate is far *lower*. Or that the US rate has been *falling* for the past fifteen years in the face of *increasing* smoking.
- We are told that more people have been smoking at younger ages, which suggests to some that illnesses associated with smoking should appear sooner. Yet the peak age for lung cancer stays right around sixty and, if anything, may be moving to *older* ages.

Such observations, needless to say, do not *exonerate* cigarettes. Yet, drawing conclusions *against* cigarettes is equally unjustified.

Deceptive Propaganda

No doubt you have heard or read that smoking is responsible for "300,000 excess deaths" in this country each year. Let's look at how this "fact" developed:

In 1964, the assistant surgeon general said that such an estimate would involve "making so many assumptions," that it might be "misleading." Yet a year later, a former advertising executive who just doesn't like smoking announced that cigarettes cause 125,000 to 300,000 deaths a year.

Another government official agreed, claiming smoking was responsible for *at least* 125,000 premature deaths a year. He acknowledged getting the figure from the advertising man.

So the advertising man was asked in a Congressional hearing where *he* got *his* estimate. His reply: From the government! The government man tried to justify it. He took some arbitrary percentages of the annual deaths from various ailments, including several *which were not even claimed by the Surgeon General to be causally related to smoking!*

Later the Surgeon General himself undertook to explain the 300,000 figure. He did this by:

- Taking as his basis the unsupported estimate above.
- Adding to it another unsupported 102,000 deaths—"from diseases where the relationship to cigarette smoke, while not so obvious, is nevertheless clearly indicated."
- Adding to *this* another unsupported but "reasonable estimate" of 60,000 excess deaths from smoking *women,* who had not been included in the earlier estimates.

Nobody took the trouble to expose this silly game, or to point out that the "authorities" considered *nothing but smoking* in comparing the longevity of one group of persons with another. But scientists, quietly studying twins, made a significant contribution. Let us see what happens, they reasoned, to people with *identitical genetics* and different smoking habits.

Experiment Failures

Experiments using air pollutants, such as sulfur oxides and oxides of nitrogen, have produced emphysema in laboratory animals. Yet many animal experiments have failed to induce emphysema with long-term exposure to cigarette smoke.

The Tobacco Institute, *Cigarette Smoking and Chronic Obstructive Lung Diseases: The Major Gaps in Knowledge,* 1984.

By 1970 a study appeared of Swedish identical twin pairs with differing smoking habits, including cases where one twin didn't smoke at all. There was no association between smoking and higher overall mortality. Later similar findings were reported among Danish twins. But tobacco's foes still repeat that number—300,000. A simple, rounded, large, impressive—and meaningless—statistic.

Many Contrasts

Smoking and health statistics have been built up by comparing smokers and nonsmokers. But when large numbers of people are sorted into two groups this way, are there *no other differences* between them? Differences which might account for contrasts in health patterns?

There are, indeed, say authorities who have studied such things. Some of them are surprising.

Smokers generally are more communicative. They are more creative, more energetic, drink more coffee and liquor, marry more often, prefer spicier and saltier food. They take part in more sports and change jobs more often. *They are more likely to have parents with heart disease and high blood pressure!*

These and other findings, accumulating in the medical literature, raise the question of whether smokers may have higher illness rates *because of the kind of people they happen to be.*

Science has learned that a blueprint of our constitutional, physical and chemical makeup is laid down at the moment of conception. This is genetics and, as the saying goes, we cannot choose our grandfathers. The blueprint is still fuzzy—we do *not* know, for example, the extent to which our genes may map our actual behavior and choice of lifestyle, and how these in turn may affect our relative well-being.

91

The Nonsmoker

Some persons who believe smoking is harmful to the smoker have also jumped to the conclusion that tobacco smoke harms the nonsmoker.

Scientists have conducted many experiments to test this hypothesis, carefully analyzing "smoke-filled rooms" and looking for "pollutants" under extreme conditions rarely, if ever, found in a normal social situation. Result: The preponderance of evidence simply does not support the health effect theory. As the scientific journal which published a controversial study by California researchers earlier this year, editorialized: "Generally speaking, the evidence that passive smoking in a general environment has health effects remains sparse, incomplete and sometimes unconvincing."

Yet some persons would like government bodies to adopt new laws or regulations to curb our right to make our own personal decisions about smoking.

In this case, the solution seems clear: Personal courtesy, thoughtfulness, and tolerance by both smokers and nonsmokers; a few simple, voluntary practices in special situations, and respect for individual freedom of choice.

Needed: Objective Research

It is human nature to want to assume some things we don't really *know*. Certainly that has been the case among many people who have had something to say about smoking and health.

But that is not the spirit of science. True scientists make assumptions *only* for the purpose of *testing* them, proving or disproving them.

In that spirit, notwithstanding the easy answers some people claim to have, scientists throughout the world continue to seek the *truth about smoking*.

"Smoking, in the words of the surgeon general, is the 'chief single avoidable cause of death in our society.'"

The Link Between Smoking and Disease Is Unquestionable

David Owen

David Owen is a New York writer whose latest book is *None of the Above: Behind the Myth of Scholastic Aptitude.* In the following viewpoint, he states that cigarettes are the cause of 300,000 deaths a year. However, Mr. Owen believes that many smokers do not accept this fact because tobacco companies run massive publicity campaigns rationalizing their products and effectively silencing their opponents.

As you read, consider the following questions:

1. According to Mr. Owen, why do smokers continue to smoke despite the health risks cited by doctors and scientists?
2. Does the author believe the advertisements claiming that cigarette companies are not after the teenage market? Do you agree?
3. Do you think smokers freely choose their addictions? Or, like the author, do you think the use of cigarettes is a response to a physical craving?

Three thousand Americans died of lung cancer in 1930. Today the disease kills that many every nine days. The reason for the increase is smoking. Cigarettes didn't begin to catch on in a big way until after World War I, and lung cancer has an incubation period of 20 to 30 years. In the United States, smoking now causes 85 percent of lung cancer cases, 30 percent of all cancer cases, and a total of 350,000 premature deaths every year, including deaths from emphysema, bronchitis, pneumonia, and heart disease (but not including 2,000 deaths from house fires caused by careless smoking or as many as 5,000 deaths among nonsmokers who breathe in smoke that others exhale). Smoking, in the words of the surgeon general, is the "chief single avoidable cause of death in our society."

Not so, claims the tobacco industry. For more than 20 years, in the face of overwhelming proof to the contrary, cigarette manufacturers have maintained that the link between smoking and "various health conditions and outcomes" (as an industry spokesman I interviewed recently referred to cancer and death) is entirely conjectural. If nothing else, the industry's claim is remarkable for its bravado. Creationists maintain an equally implausible position, but they can at least point to the Bible; cigarette companies can cite no authority higher than their own propagandists and a shrinking handful of medical flat-earth men.

War on Medical Fact

Despite this, the cigarette industry's 20-year war on medical fact has been remarkably successful. American tobacco companies sold 593.6 billion cigarettes in 1983, down slightly from the year before but up 20 percent from 1964, the year of the surgeon general's original report. When the dangers of smoking were first publicized, tobacco companies frantically diversified in hopes of offsetting the expected disintegration of their earnings. But America's cigarette addiction was stronger than the companies had dared to hope (48 percent of lung cancer victims who survive surgery begin smoking again, most within a year), and they were able to change their strategy. In 1981 R.J. Reynolds (Winston, Camel) bought $215 million worth of new cigarette-packing equipment and began a ten-year, $1 billion construction project at its main cigarette plant in North Carolina. Philip Morris (Marlboro, Merit), meanwhile, negotiated a $350 million merger with Rothmans International, the British cigarette giant, and undertook a $25 million plant expansion. In recent months, Reynolds has divested itself of three major non-tobacco subsidiaries.

The lung cancer industry's surprising health demonstrates the power of the unrelenting lie. Truth is no match for deceit that gives no quarter. Smoking causes cancer? "No conclusive medical or clinical proof has been discovered," deadpans Philip Morris. Plenty

'On the other hand, a large percentage of our best customers continue to experience premature terminal health difficulties ...'

of proof *has* been discovered? "We are medically unqualified to comment or make judgments," says the chairman of the British tobacco lobby. Why don't you ask someone who *is* qualified? "Rothmans never comments on opinions expressed by members of the medical profession." There's a dark genius to this tactic. By calmly, steadfastly refusing to acknowledge that the sun rises in the east and sets in the west, the tobacco industry makes its critics seem shrill and hysterical and provides smokers with the morsel of doubt they need to rationalize continuing to consume. The transcendent achievement of the cigarette lobby has been to establish the cancer issue as a "controversy" or a "debate" rather than as the clear-cut scientific case that it is.

Governments Support Tobacco

The tobacco industry maintains this deception with the aid of an enormous global network. Governments support cigarettes (and even subsidize their production) in order to reap the tax and export revenues they generate; politicians smile on the cigarette industry in return for the right to keep their hands in the deep pockets of the tobacco lobby; magazines and newspapers look the other way rather than lose their major advertisers; and of course smokers themselves keep the whole enterprise going by continuing to squander their money and their health.

Peter Taylor calls this vast and convoluted network the Smoke

Ring. His book *[The Smoke Ring]* is an examination of "why governments place wealth before health" and of "the political and economic mechanisms of the power of tobacco." Taylor has experienced these processes first-hand. He is a British television correspondent whose credits include "Death in the West," a powerful documentary that juxtaposes Marlboro commercials with footage of real-life American cowboys dying of lung cancer and emphysema. The film also contains an interview with a Dr. Helmut Wakeham, vice president for "science and technology" at Philip Morris. Wakeham is asked whether cigarettes are harmful. "Anything can be considered harmful," he replies. "Applesauce is harmful if you get too much of it." Interviewer: "I don't think many people are dying from applesauce." Wakeham: "They're not eating that much." . . .

Smoke and Mirrors

"I am convinced by the medical evidence and the unanimous verdict of the world's leading medical authorities that cigarettes disable and kill," Taylor writes in his preface; "but I also recognize that they bring economic benefits which, in purely financial terms, outweigh the cost of human suffering." Everyone has heard sentiments like this before. Health aside, he claims, smoking is healthy for the economy. Is this correct?

According to a pamphlet published by the Tobacco Institute, the industry's lobbying juggernaut, tobacco employs 393,000 Americans directly and 1.6 million indirectly ("such as matchbook makers and packaging suppliers, even flavoring formulators and public opinion surveyors"), for a total contribution to the work force of two millions jobs. If tobacco disappeared tomorrow, therefore, we would lose "2.5 percent of America's private sector labor force." According to an advertisement paid for by something called the Tobacco Industry Labor/Management Committee that has appeared in a number of magazines, these jobs are now "threatened . . . by well-meaning people who haven't stopped to consider" how their concern about smoking upsets "our brothers and sisters" in the tobacco industry, who, among other things, "marched in the Nation's Capital to support health care for the elderly." Can we possibly afford to warn school children about the dangers of cigarettes when so many benefits are at stake?

Weigh Both Sides

But the industry's specious "cost-benefit analysis" looks at only part of the equation. After all, smoking kills 350,000 Americans each year, just 43,000 fewer than it employs. As the tobacco industry likes to say, "weigh both sides before you take sides."

Another part of the equation is the jobs the Tobacco Institute didn't think to include on its list. Smoking indirectly provides livelihoods not only for "flavoring formulators and opinion surveyors" but also thoracic surgeons, funeral directors, florists, grave diggers, street sweepers, firemen, magazine editors, and a substantial fraction of the membership of both houses of Congress.

A Clear Case Against Tobacco

A great many things about cancer are debatable because of a lack of solid evidence and differing interpretations of the evidence that is available. But this is not so with regard to the impact of tobacco on health. "It would be hard to find another subject so thoroughly and extensively investigated during the last 25 years," notes Dr. E. Cuyler Hammond, special research consultant for the American Cancer Society. Indeed, it is remarkable how consistent all of the evidence indicting cigarette smoking as a health hazard has been.

If just a *fraction* of the evidence implicating cigarettes in cancer and other diseases were submitted in charges against any other substance, with the possible exception of alcohol, there would be no controversy at all. If, for instance, the leaf in question were spinach, there would be one less vegetable in our gardens.

American Council on Science and Health News & Views January/February 1981.

Smoking, it must be admitted, does generate enormous tax revenues. According to the Institute, tobacco is responsible for about $4.4 billion in federal taxes and $4.3 billion in state taxes each year (including, ludicrously, Social Security and personal income taxes paid by industry employees; would they stop paying taxes if they worked for someone else?). The industry also exports more tobacco and tobacco products than it imports, giving it an annual trade surplus of $1.7 billion.

Tobacco's Drain on Resources

But these benefits, large though they may be, don't begin to make up for tobacco's huge drain on public and private resources. According to the Department of Health and Human Services, smoking annually costs Americans $13 billion in medical bills, $25 billion in lost productivity, and $3.8 billion for Medicaid and Medicare. For nearly half a century, the federal government has subsidized tobacco growers through "commodity loans" that set a minimum market price for tobacco. Jesse Helms likes to claim that this welfare program pays for itself, but it has actually cost taxpayers $700 million in lost principal and interest alone. The program costs further millions each year to administer. The Department of Agriculture spends even more millions on research aimed at finding cheaper ways to grow tobacco, providing a free boost to the cigarette industry and effectively nullifying the surgeon general's efforts to discourage smoking. As Taylor would have discovered if he had looked a little deeper, the cigarette industry's arithmetic is highly deceptive.

The industry's deceptions don't end with arithmetic. "Do cigarette companies want kids to smoke?" asks an advertisement paid for by the Tobacco Institute. The answer, according to the ad, is, "No!" A photograph shows a kid's dresser drawer with a pack of cigarettes tucked in among some gym shorts and a scuffed-up baseball. "All of us need a time of 'growing up' to develop the mature judgment to do so many things," the text continues. "Like driving. Voting. Raising a family. . . . In our view, smoking is an adult custom and the decision to smoke should be based on mature and informed individual freedom of choice."

Kids Are Industry's Lifeblood

This is baloney. Kids who smoke are the lifeblood of the tobacco industry. "Smoking is a habit that begins in the young," a spokesman for the American Cancer Society told me, "and it is the young smoker who becomes the confirmed adult smoker. People who pick up this habit in their early twenties do not become confirmed smokers. It's the smoker who begins at the age of 11 and 12 who becomes the one-, two-, three-pack-a-day smoker in his twenties, thirties, and forties. If you're selling a product that requires frequent, continuous, and heavy usage, as a cigarette does, then you obviously have to keep in mind that unless you get the teenager to smoke, you really don't have a consumer out there." Indeed, 75 percent of all smokers are hooked before the age of 21. A report commissioned by the Tobacco Institute in 1978 documented the industry's cloudy outlook but identified as a "silver lining" the fact that "the percentage of smokers in the 17-24-year-old age group is up and the amount smoked per day per young smoker is also up." (More kids are also now using chewing tobacco.)

In 1975 Brown & Williamson (Kool, Raleigh) paid for a marketing study that suggested strategies for persuading "young starters" to smoke Viceroys, a popular high-tar brand. "Present the cigarette as one of a few initiations into the adult world," the study suggested. "In your ads create a situation taken from the day-to-day life of the young smoker but in an elegant manner have this situation touch on the basic symbols of the growing-up, maturing process. . . . *Don't* communicate health or health-related points." Brown & Williamson denies that it ever made use of this advice, but virtually all cigarette advertising is based on it. Even the Tobacco Institute's ad follows it precisely: "Driving. Voting. Raising a family." By arguing that smoking isn't kid stuff, the Institute deviously reinforces the same "initiation" image that the Brown & Williamson study recommended.

In 1964, in response to public criticism, the tobacco industry adopted nine "advertising principles" relating to young people:

"No advertising shall appear in publications directed primarily to those under 21 years of age.... No one depicted in cigarette advertising shall be or appear to be under 25 years of age.... Cigarette advertising shall not suggest that smoking is essential to social prominence, distinction, success or sexual attraction.... Cigarette advertising shall not...show any smoker participating in, or obviously just having participated in, a physical activity requiring stamina or athletic conditioning beyond that of normal recreation."

"All companies continue to observe the principles of this code," says the Tobacco Institute. But in fact all violate them flagrantly as a matter of course. *Rolling Stone* and *National Lampoon,* two publications aimed directly at young people, have a much higher density of cigarette ads than most magazines aimed at adults. That 14-year-old models aren't used in those ads is irrelevant; eighth-graders don't smoke cigarettes in order to look like eighth-graders.

"Social prominence, distinction, success, and sexual attraction," far from being proscribed, are virtually the *only* themes of tobacco advertising. One Lorillard ad shows a shirtless athlete in a locker room toweling himself off and enjoying a Kent after "obviously just having participated in" a game of tennis. In some versions of the ad, you can see his racket. (When I asked Lorillard's vice president for public relations whether this ad violated the industry's principles, she told me, "In our opinion it does not. It shows a confident, mature adult choosing to smoke Kent. He just happens to be in a locker room.") Recent ads for Camel and Winston (R.J. Rey-

Michael Keefe for the Denver Post, reprinted with permission.

nolds) show men climbing mountains, a sport that, because of the altitude, would make most smokers dizzy. (At summer camp in Colorado many years ago, my tent mates and I used to smoke cigarettes on mountains *in order* to get dizzy.)

Cigarette Companies' Principles

Magazine publishers know that cigarette companies don't pay attention to their "principles." Publications that depend on cigarette advertising bend over backward to be accommodating. *Mademoiselle* "used editorial ploys to de-emphasize smoking, gave misinformation, and excluded smoking from mention on relevant health topics altogether," according to a 1982 study by the American Council on Science and Health. In *Ms.*, a publication otherwise attentive to women's health, the Council found "a complete absence of articles on the hazards of smoking," even on the danger of smoking during pregnancy or while taking birth control pills.

The October 8, 1984 issues of *Time* contained an 18-page advertising supplement called "Lifestyle/Healthstyle: Strategies for a Healthier, Happier and Longer Life." According to the American Academy of Family Physicians, which *Time* identified as the source of the health advice in the supplement, the original version of the text contained "many strong statements" about the dangers of smoking. All were deleted by *Time*. As Elizabeth M. Whelan pointed out in *The Wall Street Journal*, the text made no mention of smoking except in a brief "lifestyle" quiz, which awarded two points to readers who were "almost always" careful not to smoke in bed and implied (incorrectly) that smoking only low-tar cigarettes, or fewer than ten high-tar cigarettes a day, is not unhealthy. The section's introduction noted "a rise in the incidence of cancer" but attributed this increase to "the chemicals we are exposed to in our foods, water, and the air we breathe" rather than to its principal cause, cigarettes. . . .

This article was originally commissioned by *The New Republic,* but Martin Peretz, the magazine's owner and editor-in-chief, killed it after it had been set in type. What was the basis for this decision? "Massive losses of advertising revenue," said Leon Wieseltier, the editor who had assigned it. Peretz told me that he thought smoking was not as dangerous as doctors made it out to be and that, therefore, "this is a costly crusade that I am willing to forgo." Although he wouldn't admit it to me, Peretz spiked the article after showing it to his publisher, Jeffrey L. Dearth, and his former publisher, James K. Glassman, now executive president of *U.S. News and World Report* and president of *The Atlantic,* and asking them if he should run it. "This is not our finest hour," Wieseltier said later. "Whereas in this case I think it's true that we buckled before an advertiser, I wouldn't make that a general rule about the magazine. The reason the cigarette companies have such a grip on us is because of the relative size of the account." . . .

Is it really true that smokers freely choose their addictions? Is their "decision" to ruin their health really based on "mature and informed individual freedom of choice"? More than half of all smokers either don't know or don't believe that smoking causes heart attacks; 40 percent don't know that it causes most lung cancer. Maintaining this ignorance has cost the tobacco industry hundreds of millions of dollars' worth of advertisements and public relations. The last thing it wants is a public (particularly a young public) that knows "both sides."

An Industry Hinges on Disproving the Evidence

Even though cigarettes, *when used as intended,* have killed millions of smokers during the 20th century, the tobacco industry has never been liable for one single death. Given the fact that evidence of the risks of cigarette smoking has been available to the industry since the 1930s and that other industries have often been held liable for unforeseeable injuries caused by otherwise useful products, this is truly amazing.

This sense of amazement vanishes, however, when one considers the time, money and legal expertise which have gone into the tobacco companies' defense. Fully cognizant of the fact that once held liable for causing the illness of one single smoker, the floodgates would be opened for literally thousands of similar suits, the industry has used all of its considerable resources to prevent such an occurrence. The industry's aggressive, united defense, which hinges on the assertion that cigarette smoking has not been proven to cause disease, has consistently overwhelmed the lone lung cancer victim or widow who has sought compensation for his or her suffering.

Cathy Becker Popescu, *ACSH News & Views,* March/April 1983.

Ninety percent of the nation's adult smokers tried to quit last year. If nicotine addiction were entirely psychological, the tobacco industry would go broke. The industry stays in business by entrapping its customers when they're too young to know any better and then keeping them confused until they're too old to do anything about it. Despite the industry's denials, a lot of cigarette advertising is aimed at young people. Older customers just aren't as important; they may switch brands, but they seldom defect entirely. Marlboro, the most heavily advertised brand in the world, is three times as popular among children and teenagers as it is among adults. If Philip Morris really doesn't want kids to smoke, why does it use cowboys in its advertising and plaster its logo on racing cars?

"The biggest factor in the growing tide of antismoking sentiment has been the increasing number of reports indicating direct, physical harm suffered by the nonsmoker in the smoker's environment."

Second-Hand Smoke Harms Nonsmokers

Philip R. Sullivan

One of the dilemmas regarding the link between smoking and non-smokers' health is determining which evidence to believe. Numerous studies have been conducted alleging that a correlation exists between second-hand smoke and the health of nonsmokers. Philip R. Sullivan, a practicing psychiatrist in Boston and an assistant clinical professor at Harvard Medical School, claims that the evidence is irrefutable. In the following viewpoint, Dr. Sullivan claims that nonsmokers are becoming less tolerant of smoking because of the effect it has on *their* health.

As you read, consider the following questions:

1. In what three ways does smoking harm the nonsmoker, according to Dr. Sullivan?
2. Do you agree with the author that nonsmokers are forced to underwrite smokers' health insurance losses?
3. The author explains several reports of second-hand smoke harming nonsmokers. Do you think these results are legitimate or are they merely coincidence?

I could hear the crinkling of cellophane from my car's back seat as Lisa wrenched the newly opened pack of cigarettes from her surprised companion and twisted its usefulness away. "If I'm going to invest in an older man," she exclaimed, "the least he can do is take care of his health!"

I glanced in my rearview mirror, as if to see the car behind, and tried to get a peek at my friend's reaction. Tom, a successful professional was in his later 40's at the time. Lisa, his beautiful steady date of six months, was still hanging on to her 20's.

I never did get to see his expression, priceless as it no doubt was, and his words were too low-toned to make their way forward over the din of snow tires. Since my age was getting up there, too, I was not thrilled with her appellation, and that distracted me at the time from a proper appreciation of the event's significance.

Now that six years have passed, along with Lisa and Tom's romance, I have a better perspective on at least one aspect of the event. Without fully grasping it, I had witnessed my first instance of a new attitude toward smoking: militant disapproval based on perceived injury to the nonsmoker.

No Longer Good Sports

Waftings of that blue-gray haze never thrilled nonsmokers, of course. But once the habit had gripped the Sophisticated Majority and when the celebrities punctuated their words with artistic mobiles of exuded fumes, nonsmokers were expected to be good sports about minor inconveniences like smarting eyes and irritated throats.

Scientific studies made the first inroads on established attitudes. First in a trickle, then in an avalanche, epidemiological data indicated beyond the shadow of a reasonable doubt that smoking was dangerous—to the smoker! So overwhelming did the evidence become, of increased heart disease, cancer, emphysema and so on that additional reports hardly qualify now as newsworthy.

The issue, in regard to smokers, has become not whether they should smoke but how to help them stop this psychologically addicting habit. Perhaps despairing of their ability to cease and desist, many smokers say, in the words of Billy Joel: "It's my life, leave me alone!"

But Lisa, of course, would not do that. She became one of a growing vanguard concerned about the adverse effects of smoking on nonsmokers like themselves. Her specific type of worry flowed from an inescapable logic: "If you care about somebody, you do not care to lose them prematurely."

Spiraling Costs of Medical Care

Another, less personal disadvantage to the nonsmoker became apparent as a spinoff finding in studies on the spiraling costs of medical care. For instance, in May 1980, *The New England Journal of Medicine* reported that "the high-cost 13 percent of patients consumed as many resources as the low-cost 87 percent." Harmful personal habits like smoking were found substantially more often in these high-cost patients. In other words, a significant portion of the nonsmoker's health insurance premium was being used to underwrite the increased medical expenses of smokers. That sort of finding hit some folks where it hurts them the most—in their checkbooks.

Reprinted with permission from the Minneapolis Star and Tribune.

No doubt the biggest factor in the growing tide of antismoking sentiment has been the increasing number of reports indicating direct, physical harm suffered by the nonsmoker in the smoker's environment. As early as 1980, *The New England Journal of Medicine* reported that the breathing capacity of nonsmokers chronically exposed to tobacco smoke showed detectable impairment. In the following year, the *British Medical Journal* reported the results of a Japanese study in which wives of heavy smokers were noted to have a higher risk of developing lung cancer, and the risk was greater in proportion to the amount their husbands smoked.

Reports also began to accumulate in regard to undesirable effects of parental smoking on children. In 1981, the *British Medical Journal* reported an inverse relationship between children's height and number of smokers in the home. (That finding of course refers to the statistical analysis of a population of children, not to an individual instance.) A study, reported in September 1983 in *The New*

England Journal, showed diminished growth of breathing capacity among children of smoking mothers. On the plus side, *The Journal of the American Medical Association* reported a study in 1984 that showed improved birth weight in a group of infants whose mothers had substantially decreased their smoking.

Passive Smoking

How were the harmful effects of smoking transmitted to the nonsmoker? Scientists believed the most likely explanation lay in passive absorption of the fumes, especially in closed places. An experiment, reported in *The New England Journal* on September 9, 1984, confirmed this hypothesis. Products of cigarette smoke were found at higher levels in the bodies of nonsmokers who lived with smokers, increasing with the daily cigarette consumption of the family. A similar increase occurred in nonsmokers who worked with smokers, also increasing with the number of smokers in the workroom.

As the evidence of direct harm to nonsmokers accumulates, so does the likelihood of direct confrontation between the two groups. The new warning, to be required by the Surgeon General on all cigarette advertising, ups the attack on smoking by a notch. But such caveats will do little to protect the nonsmoker right now.

Outlawing Smoking

What should be done? Some concerned citizens, perhaps recalling the famous motto that "evil has no rights," would outlaw smoking, at least in public places. Indeed, the now defunct Civil Aeronautics Board seriously considered a proposal this past year to ban all smoking on commercial airlines.

Wisely, I think, the board ultimately rejected the proposal. Given the current strength of the smoking compulsion and the large number of smokers involved, who would have enforced the ruling? Flight attendants, it seems, would need to have been reoutfitted with police uniforms. At the very least, advertising agencies would have had to scrap slogans about flying friendly skies.

Written Smoking Policies

Some municipalities have already shown a very creative approach to the problem. Newton, Massachusetts—despite its current proximity to one of those big-time football mills—cannot be all bad. I recently spoke to Bernice Joyal, the Health Commissioner, about her city's new smoking ordinance. She explained to me that all employers will be required to establish, in conjunction with their employees, a written policy governing smoking in their workplace.

"What difference will that make?" I asked. "After all, each workplace already has a smoking policy, at least implicitly!"

"Yes," she answered. "But this is going to make everyone think it out clearly. It's consciousness raising to begin with. Then, the written policy has to be posted on the wall. If employees think their rights are not being protected, there are a series of grievance steps they can follow, starting with the company, then through this office and eventually to the courts. . .if it needs to go that far."

I had to admit that the ordinance seems to make a great deal of sense. In dealing with a behavior that is both personal and public, the requirement of grassroots participation in the struggle toward a fair solution takes into account the psychological realities as well as the public-health needs. I will follow, with interest, the results of this experiment in human engineering.

"Some of tobacco's severest critics have acknowledged that smoking has not been established as a cause of disease in nonsmokers."

Second-Hand Smoke Does Not Harm Nonsmokers

Thomas E. Smith Jr.

Thomas E. Smith Jr., a US Senator from South Carolina, doubts the validity of studies linking second-hand smoke to nonsmokers' health. He represents one of the most important tobacco producing states in the US. In the following viewpoint, Senator Smith argues that all of the research linking smoke to disease in nonsmokers is refutable.

As you read, consider the following questions:

1. How might the senator's position to represent South Carolina, a tobacco-growing state, color his argument?
2. How does he refute the highly publicized Japanese study concerning nonsmokers? Is his argument effective?
3. Do you agree with Dr. Sherwin Feinhandler that "the smoker has become a ready target for general frustrations, anxiety and discontent"? Why or why not?

Thomas E. Smith, Jr., "Public Smoking Laws: Who Needs Them? Who Wants Them?" *Legislative Policy*, Volume 3, Number 2, 1982. Reprinted with permission from the National Center of Legislative Research.

Anti-smokers have seized upon certain research reports to try to link environmental tobacco smoke with cancer, lung problems and other diseases.

Two highly publicized 1981 population studies have been cited frequently to support the claim that environmental cigarette smoke increases the risk of lung cancer in nonsmokers. A Japanese study by Dr. Takeshi Hirayama and one by a Greek team headed by Dr. Dimitrios Trichopoulos both suggested that nonsmoking wives of smokers have a higher risk for lung cancer than nonsmoking women married to nonsmokers.

Shortly after the Japanese study appeared in the *British Medical Journal,* questions were raised by other scientists in the medical literature here and abroad about the design of the study and validity of Hirayama's conclusions. A number of highly critical letters in the *Journal* pointed out inadequacies and inconsistencies in the data.

Indoor Air Pollution

The study was faulted for not recording the cell types of the lung cancers found and not accounting for either the level of exposure to ambient cigarette smoke or to indoor air pollution from household heating and cooking equipment. Problems with the sample selection and statistical analysis were noted.

The authors of the Greek study conceded the limitations of their research. Trichopoulos and colleagues admitted that the number of cases studied was small, noting they presented their data "principally to suggest that further investigation of this issue should be pressed."

The authors offered little information about the population from which the sample was selected, nor did they indicate that they had considered factors such as diet, family history or occupational exposure in reaching their conclusions.

Under scientific scrutiny, both studies fall short of being the definitive studies the anti-smokers claim they are.. . .

Measuring Environmental Smoke

Some have claimed that reported levels of some tobacco smoke components in the atmosphere—CO, nicotine and particulates—are hazardous to nonsmokers' health. These claims overlook a number of important scientific factors. In fact, research has shown that the main sources of CO in the environment are motor vehicles and industrial operations. Indoor levels are affected by outside levels, by cooking and heating, even by the number of people around, because CO is generated by body metabolism. Still, environmental tobacco smoke often is blamed for contributing significant amounts of CO to the body, thereby endangering the health of nonsmokers.

Studies conducted under realistic conditions indicate that atmospheric CO from tobacco smoke rarely exceeds 10 parts per million (ppm) and is closer to 5 ppm in public places with normal ventilation. Both figures are well below the limit of 50 ppm recommended by various health agencies for workers exposed over an eight-hour period.

As Dr. Duncan Hutcheon, a professor of medicine who has reviewed the literature, testified before a New Jersey Public Health Council hearing on public smoking regulation in late 1978, "Environmental studies suggest that tobacco smoke has little impact on the CO content of room air except under highly artificial conditions."

Airborne Particulate Matters

Like CO, airborne particulate matter arises from many sources other than tobacco smoke. It can include everything from paper and textile lint to scurf, animal dander, even pollen and fuel residues. Yet a 1980 study involving measurement of particulates in public buildings around Washington, D.C., is cited frequently by advocates of public smoking restrictions. In those buildings where smoking was permitted, James Repace and Alfred Lowrey said, levels of particulate matter were far greater than in places where smoking was not permitted.

A Minor Annoyance

Cigarette smoke can be annoying at times to some people, but the majority of smokers are courteous enough to refrain—or douse smoking materials—when they might bother others.

It should be noted, moreover, that there is not sufficient evidence to conclude that other people's smoke causes disease in nonsmokers.

Two scientific workshops reached that conclusion independently in 1983. The more recent, convened by the U.S. Public Health Service, after examining all available research said that the effect of environmental tobacco smoke on the respiratory system varies from negligible to quite small.

The Tobacco Institute, *Regulation!*, April 1984.

Questioned from the floor by a consulting engineer, Repace admitted they had not measured the quantity of outdoor air introduced by ventilating systems. Another critic noted the team had also failed to measure particulate levels before smoking began, failed to present data on actual ventilation rates, and, most important, *failed to determine the specific contribution of tobacco smoke to particulate levels.* The commentator, Dr. Theodor Sterling, a Canadian expert on environmental contaminants, noted that his own analysis of Repace and Lowrey's earlier data suggested particulate levels were far more strongly related to the number of persons present than to the percent of them smoking. "The claim that smoking is responsible for indoor air pollution is," Sterling suggested, "an oversimplification of a complex, multi-source problem."

The Nicotine Factor

Dependence on measurements of CO or particulates to determine ambient smoke levels has been denounced repeatedly because both are produced by many sources. Nicotine is considered a much more reliable indicator, since it is produced almost exclusively by burning tobacco—and studies using nicotine as a smoke index suggest that the contribution of tobacco smoke to the atmosphere is minimal.

Drs. William Hinds and Melvin First, researchers from the Harvard School of Public Health, found only very small amounts of nicotine in the atmosphere of crowded bars, bus and airline terminals, restaurants and student lounges. Their data, published in 1975, indicated a nonsmoker would have to spend 100 hours straight in the smokiest bar to inhale the equivalent of a single filter-tip cigarette, a situation one observer noted might be harder on the liver than on the lungs.

Small Amount of Exposure

Further comment on the nicotine measurement study came from a colleague then at Harvard Medical School. Even under the most severe concentrations reported, that physician wrote in *New England Journal of Medicine,* the nonsmoker would be exposed to "an amount of tobacco so small that the risk of development of any adverse health effect would be non-existent, on the basis of any available data in the literature today."

Other researchers in Europe who used different methods to measure the presence of tobacco smoke in the atmosphere reported slightly higher nicotine concentrations than Hinds and First. But they, too, concluded, based on their measurements, that smoking does not represent a risk to nonsmokers.

Thus it is clear that a great deal of misinformation and numerous unsubstantiated allegations have distorted the nonsmoker health question. Claims that tobacco smoke causes disease in nonsmokers simply are not convincing. Undoubtedly, however, such claims will persist, but what is really needed is unbiased, scientific inquiry.

Emotional Reactions

The emotional and psychological reactions of some nonsmokers to smoking may, of course, simply reflect frustration with life in general. One researcher who has studied smoking customs in different societies told a Congressional hearing in 1978 he thinks that is the case. Dr. Sherwin Feinhandler, a lecturer in cultural anthropology at Harvard Medical School, said upheavals in society and overcrowding have made people supersensitive to other people's behavior. Because smoke is so visible, people have something positive to react against. "To some people," he said, "the smoker has become a ready target for general frustrations, anxiety and discontent."

Whatever the reason, anti-smoking groups would have you believe that annoyance with ambient cigarette smoke is widespread. Contrary to this claim, however, is a national survey reported by Response Analysis of Princeton, N.J., in 1978. It indicated that tobacco smoke is at most a minor annoyance. It found that when people are asked about the kinds of things that annoyed or irritated them in their everyday lives, only about two percent of the annoyances mentioned were related to smoking.

"The national trend is clearly for greater expanses of nonsmoking areas in our public life."

Public Smoking Laws are Desirable

Nick Thimmesch

In a country as committed to personal freedom as the US, it is no surprise that smokers are as adamant about their right to smoke as are nonsmokers increasingly committed to their right to breathe smokeless air. As nonsmokers lobby to ban public smoking, the tobacco lobby has fought back, resulting in a decade-long legal struggle. In the following viewpoint, Nick Thimmesch, a former writer and manager for *Time* and *Newsday* magazines, reports on what he believes to be the favorable reaction toward the antismoking movement's campaign to restrict smoking in public areas.

As you read, consider the following questions:

1. According to the author, nonsmokers have the right to eat in smokeless areas of restaurants and to sleep in smoke-free floors of hotels. Do you agree? Why or why not?
2. What has the antismoking organization ASH done to promote segregation of smokers and nonsmokers?
3. What does Mr. Thimmesch cite as the drawbacks to public smoking?

Nick Thimmesch, "No Smoking: No Ifs, Ands or Butts," *The Saturday Evening Post,* July/August 1983. Reprinted with permission from The Saturday Evening Post Society, a division of BFL&MS, Inc. © 1983.

The antismoking movement, that dedicated gang of activists determined to clean up the indoor air and also persuade people to quit smoking, is having a profound and even fascinating effect on nation's business. . . .

Increasing numbers of companies have greatly restricted smoking on their premises. Big corporations such as Mobil Oil, Sears, Johns-Manville, Xerox, the Bank of California, and Travelers Insurance took the lead in this category, ruffling some employees' feelings in the process.

Similarly, federal workers must now abide by smoking-zone regulations. A number of states have passed comprehensive bills affirming nonsmokers' rights, and some states greatly restrict smoking in public buildings. Minnesota's "Clean Indoor Air Act" requires no-smoking areas in all buildings open to the general public. Bars and tobacco stores are excepted.

The National Trend

The national trend is clearly for greater expanses of no-smoking areas in our public life. The residue of smoking costs big bucks in cleaning, maintenance, repair and replacement. The financial penalty in lowered productivity, absenteeism and health, disability and death benefits makes any corporate or government bottom-line specialist become a potential convert to the no-smoking cause. . . .

Hotel operators, who are traditionally willing to cater to the whims and variety of lifestyles of their guests, are now setting aside entire floors for clients who want a smoke-free environment. Many hostelries, including the luxurious sort in the Hyatt Regency, Radisson and Four Seasons chains, provide rooms reserved strictly for nonsmokers. At this writing, there is one motel operator bold enough to designate his entire establishment as no smoking: The "Non-Smokers Inn" in Dallas.

The entrepreneuers who felt the first pressure of the no-smoking movement are restaurant and cafeteria owners. For many diners there is nothing more obnoxious than smoke drifting into the nostrils and mouth while enjoying a meal.

Many restaurant operators have responded to the complaints by nonsmokers, and have tried to set aside nonsmoking sections and in some instances have even made sure that their establishments are entirely unpolluted by any pernicious smoke fumes. There is no official count available on the number of such dining places, but they're increasing at a rapid rate. . . .

Now, in the economic area, it is Muse Airlines, founded and run by Lamar Muse and his son, Michael, which has assumed the chore of coordinating the efforts to provide complete travel arrangements specifically designed for nonsmoking customers. . . .

Some crusaders against smoking are now suing to prohibit smoking in sport areas and domed stadiums. But realists in the move-ment admit that a total prohibition on smoking in these caverns makes the crowd laugh whenever such an announcement is made. It is more practical to establish smoking and nonsmoking sections in these huge facilities. . . .

The United States, more than any country in the world, is a na-tion where petitioners and activists can bring about great changes in the law and in society. Businessmen were reminded of this verity in the turbulent years of the '60s and '70s, when public interest groups of the Nader variety sprang up everywhere to challenge the status quo. The lesson was often painful.

Nonsmoking Commercials

No activist shook the tobacco industry, rattling vast areas of bus-iness in the process, more than John F. Banzhaf shook it. He found-ed ASH in March 1968, when he was only 27. The year before, Banzhaf had won fame when he single-handedly and successful-ly petitioned the Federal Communications Commission to require broadcasters to devote substantial time to nonsmoking messages (commercials).

The Right to Breathe

Smoking is being treated more and more like a social disease these days. As evidence of the harm of cigarette smoke to non-smokers continues to grow, the non-smoking majority is becoming increas-ingly vocal and aggressive in asserting its right to breathe smoke-free air.

Interestingly, even many smokers believe they should not be inflict-ing their emissions on others. A Gallup poll in April 1983 found 82 percent of non-smokers and 55 percent of smokers saying smokers should refrain in the presence of non-smokers, and varying propor-tions up to 30 percent of smokers said smoking should be prohibit-ed in such places as hotels, restaurants, workplaces, planes and trains.

Jane E. Brody, *St. Paul Pioneer Press*, November 11, 1984.

Since then, ASH has led the fight against the jeopardies of smok-ing on a score of fronts and helped bring about large smokefree areas in American life. One of the first was that rather confining space of an airliner that is known as the passenger section.

"In 1971, I phoned Edward E. Carlson, president of United Airlines," Banzhaf recalls, "and told him we had a sick guy, quite sensitive to smoke, who had to fly from Chicago to Florida, so what should we do?

"I didn't say ASH would go to court, but he understood. He took my suggestion of segregating the smokers and was so pleased with the results that he made it general policy."

Banzhaf and other activists hammered away at federal regulatory agencies and the airlines, causing them to shrink the smoking section to generally less than 30 percent of seats, to always guarantee passengers seats in nonsmoking and to virtually eliminate the problem of cigar and pipe smoking.

ASH's most recent victory was a ruling that the Civil Aeronautics Board must not rescind regulations providing that: Ventilation systems must be fully functioning when smoking is permitted; passengers in "no smoking" must not be "unreasonably burdened" by drifting smoke; pipe and cigar smokers must be "specially segregated."

"Now we're going after planes with fewer than 30 seats that are exempted," Banzhaf says. "We'd also like to ban all smoking on short flights."

Smokers to the Rear

Operators of bus lines and passenger trains didn't roll over and play dead for ASH either, but today only the rear 30 percent of buses are for smokers, and Amtrak has clearly delineated smoking and non-smoking cars.

"Nearly three-quarters of the states have now restricted smoking in public facilities," says Banzhaf, "and the federal government has extensive guidelines for its government-owned buildings."

"We're still having a major problem with smoking in hospitals, of all places. George Washington University right here in the District of Columbia was blatantly violating local laws. Smoking can cause fires in hospitals, especially when a groggy patient drops a cigarette on a bed. But if a doctor permits a patient to smoke, it's hard to make him stop."

The Offended Majority

Banzhaf says that business has really turned around on the smoking question, that it realizes that the majority, non-smoking public can be offended by employee smoke and that smoking in the everyday workplace costs big money.

"The government ruled there is no discrimination violation when an employer says he won't hire a smoker, and that's a plus," says Banzhaf. "Employers don't want to get hit up for big disability payments to workers who can prove that their health has been damaged from smoke."

He claims ASH is not against smokers, only against what they can do to nonsmokers. "The right of a nonsmoker to breathe clean air takes precedence," he says. Banzhaf has interdicted smokers on elevators and has even taken one to court and won his case.

"The future for smokers is in smoking lounges, private offices and the great outdoors," Banzhaf says. "If a smoker wants to close his office door, run around that office, sleep on the floor or smoke there, that's his or her business.

"The attitude toward smoking has really changed since we started ASH. Last year, we had the lowest per capita cigarette consumption since 1957. Total cigarette consumption has dipped for several years now. We're getting many more people to quit.

"Once, smoking made you socially acceptable. It was done everywhere; it was in every business and workplace. Now, you must go to the back of the bus to smoke. That's how much the tolerance of smoking has changed."

"Public smoking laws have been described as nuisance laws."

Public Smoking Laws Are a Nuisance

The Tobacco Institute

The Tobacco Institute's stated aim is "to promote better public understanding of the tobacco industry." It was founded in 1958 by manufacturers of smoking and chewing tobacco to promote tobacco products. The following viewpoint urges smokers and nonsmokers to settle their differences with "common courtesy" instead of with public smoking laws. It describes several instances of problems caused by antismoking legislation.

As you read, consider the following questions:

1. The Tobacco Institute says that "it is not the province of government, but of people, to work out solutions to problems of social behavior." Would you classify smoking as a social behavior problem? Why or why not?
2. How does the restauranteur in the article justify not separating smokers and nonsmokers?
3. How does the author defend the smokers' right to smoke cigarettes in public places?

"Public Smoking—Common Sense for the Common Good," published by the Tobacco Institute in 1983. Reprinted with permission.

Have you heard the one about the airline counter agent who asks the passenger whether he'd like a seat in the smoking section—or one *inside* the plane?

It may have been funny the first time a stand-up comedian told it. But it's really no joke. Restrictive smoking laws and regulations have sprouted up across the country for all sorts of places, from airplanes and jury rooms to restaurants and office buildings.

But how far should government go in controlling the personal behavior and restricting the freedom of choice of adults? Must common sense, good manners and mutual consideration be supplanted by statute? Need the freedoms of many be abridged by law to relieve the few of occasional minor annoyances? Let's take a look.

Those who argue for smoking laws often cite health fears to support their views. But these are theories only. The Surgeon General has said there is not sufficient evidence to conclude that other people's smoke causes disease in nonsmokers. The Surgeon General also says no tobacco smoke allergy has been demonstrated in humans. He says what response does occur in healthy nonsmokers may be due to psychological factors.

Not the Government's Business

So when the anti-smokers' health claims are shown to be unproved, the public smoking question boils down to this: Why should it be the business of government?

We think it is *not* the province of government, but of *people,* to work out solutions to problems of social behavior. State interference in such matters is neither effective nor appropriate.

Public smoking laws have been described as nuisance laws.

Dr. Theodore Gill, a dean of John Jay College of Criminal Justice, has written that nuisance laws are "inflicted" by single-minded persons who look to government to solve personal differences—with at least one result they do not anticipate.

"It would be inaccurate and foolish for me to suggest," said Dr. Gill, "that nuisance laws are primary causes for the (increasing) disrespect for the law. I think it accurate though to say such laws contribute to a general disrespect for all law."

He added that in touchy areas such as smoking, involving personal taste, the feelings of others and complex counterclaims of private and public space, "community acceptance and what we hope will be increasingly common courtesy should prevail."

Common Courtesy Should Prevail

Dr. Gill is right. Common courtesy *should* prevail. Do we really need policemen checking smoking compliance in restaurants, on airplanes, in our office buildings? Of course not.

Most businesses will see to the mutual comfort of smoking and nonsmoking patrons should they perceive the need. Their desire to maximize patronage and profits is the incentive. Proprietors don't need smoking laws. They don't need the police to enforce what they can work out for themselves.

In fact, some businessmen believe such laws could put them out of business. As a Santa Monica restauranteur put it, "If they came in and told me I could allow smoking in (only) one section, and nonsmoking in another...I couldn't operate. It wouldn't be economically feasible for me to run my restaurant."

The police don't want smoking laws either. "We've got enough problems catching holdup men and burglars," was the way Undersheriff Tom Rosa of Santa Clara, California, put it. He was echoed by Assistant Police Chief Michael Sgobba of San Diego, who said, "Unless an officer has absolutely nothing to do, he isn't going to go out and give someone a citation for smoking in an unauthorized zone."

But not just proprietors and law officers feel this way. Eight times in five years electorates—from tiny Zephyrhills, Florida, to San Francisco, *twice* statewide in California—have been able to vote on whether they wanted smoking laws.

16 Million Ballots Later...

Eight times average citizens weighed government intervention in public smoking against freedom and self-determination. In all, almost 16 million ballots. And the *vote was for freedom of choice*.

The lone exception was San Francisco. By less than 1 percent of votes cast, the City by the Bay affirmed an ordinance forcing all *private sector* employers to adopt smoking policies agreeable to

Reprinted with permission from the Gainesville Sun.

all *nonsmoking* employees. If a single nonsmoker objects to the policy, the employer must prohibit smoking or face up to $500 in fines daily.

"Municipal Nanny"

In San Francisco, columnist Herb Caen quoted one cigar-smoking boss' threat to hire only smokers from now on and the Sunday Examiner & Chronicle editorialized sadly about "the municipal nanny." USA Today wrote that "the emerging conflict creates a serious hazard in the workplace turning worker against worker."

But in Florida, Daytona Beach New-Journal editors could approve the decision of the city fathers in neighboring Ormond that accommodation is preferable to laws.

"Instead of going overboard to kill such laws," wrote the Daytona Beach Evening News, "sensible people will work with each other to resolve smoking disputes amicably and to do so without bringing in government, the police or the courts."

Smokers and nonsmokers, we hope, will continue living and working together as they have for generations, without laws. They know that life is a matter of give and take.

And a smoker knows when it is appropriate to light up. Most are courteous enough to refrain voluntarily when it's obvious they might be bothering others. Most smokers will be accommodating and reasonable.

After all, consideration of the other fellow underlies all our interaction, at work or at play. Or it *should.*

Common Sense, Above All

Common sense tells us not to raise our voices in a restaurant or a busy office. It tells us not to bathe in heavy perfume or overdo the garlic before going to the movies, not to let our kids run up and down supermarket aisles.

Common sense tell us that cooperation and mutual understanding—respect for the preferences and sensitivities of others—are the simplest and least intrusive means by which smokers and nonsmokers can continue to get along.

Common sense about public smoking is for the common good. Like the Golden Rule. And it might even assure that no one will have to ride *outside* the plane.

Analyzing Cigarette Advertising

Every one of us is bombarded daily with advertising messages telling us what products to use, what we should be consuming, and how these products can improve our everyday life. Many ads also attempt to convince us that the product advertised can make us glamorous, sexy, worldly, and otherwise perfect. One of the products frequently advertised in this manner is cigarettes. The cigarette advertisement on the opposite page depicts the glamorous qualities cigarette companies would like us to think smoking their product can bring out in us. This activity will help you analyze the messages conveyed both directly and indirectly in cigarette ads and how these messages compare to reality.

Instructions:

Step 1. After breaking into groups of 4 to 6 students, each small group should examine the ad pictured on the opposite page. Discuss what messages the ad conveys about cigarette smokers.

Step 2. How, according to the ad, will cigarette smoking influence:

1) your relationships with others?
2) how you cope with the everyday problems of life?
3) your spare time?

Write some statements expressing the messages that are conveyed in the ad. Example: 1. Smoking is glamorous. 2. Smoking can make women more appealing to men. Then, compare these statements to what you know to be true about the effects of cigarette smoking. Are the messages realistic? Come to a group consensus on this issue before moving on to step 3.

It's More you.

It's long.
It's slim.
It's elegant.

20 CLASS A
CIGARETTES

More

FILTER CIGARETTES

120'

Warning: The Surgeon General Has Determined
That Cigarette Smoking Is Dangerous to Your Health.

17 mg. "tar", 1.3 mg. nicotine av. per cigarette by FTC method.

Step 3.   Try to separate the messages conveyed in the ad from the product. Is the product itself, in this case cigarettes, useful to you and others in your group? Why or why not?

Step 4.   The class should come together and each small group should share its conclusions. The class as a whole should then attempt to come to a consensus on how advertising affects your lives. Do you buy products in some part because of the way they are advertised? Do you think cigarette advertising is 1) the same as other advertising; 2) Worse or better than other advertising? Why or why not?

Periodical Bibliography

The following list of periodical articles deals with the subject matter of this chapter.

Jack Alexander   "Alcoholics Anonymous," *The Saturday Evening Post*, January/February 1983.

Bennett H. Beach   "Is the Party Finally Over?" *Time*, April 26, 1982.

Julia Cameron   "Drugs, Alcohol, and Stress," *Mademoiselle*, May 1985.

John Duka   "Elizabeth Taylor: Journal of a Recovery," *The New York Times*, Feburary 4, 1985.

William Price Fox   "Whiskey-making Gets in Genes," *USA Today*, March 22, 1985.

Kenneth S. Kantzer   "Drunken Driving: Are We Angry Enough to Stop It?" *Christianity Today*, August 5, 1983.

John Leo   "That's Your Last Drink, Buddy," *Time*, August 20, 1984.

Allan Luks   "Uncorking Neo-Prohibition," *Commonweal*, August 12, 1983.

J.D. Reed   "Water, Water Everywhere," *Time*, May 20, 1985.

Ronald Schiller   "Why Americans Are Drinking Less," *Reader's Digest*, January 1985.

Michael Specter   "Are Drunk-Driving Laws Driving Up the Suicide Rate in Jails?" *The Washington Post National Weekly Edition*, March 11, 1985.

Robert Joe Stout   "Alcoholism: The Disease That Does Not Exist," *America*, September 17, 1983.

USA Today   "Effects of Women's New Roles," February 1985.

Should Drug-Related Laws Be Reformed?

"I applaud the administration for promoting a mandatory legal age of 21."

The National Drinking Age Should Be Raised

Clifford D. Peterson

Clifford D. Peterson is a free-lance writer who lives in Arlington, Virginia. He approves of the proposed legislation for raising the national legal drinking age to 21. In the following viewpoint, Mr. Peterson claims that the maturation process would help young adults to make wiser choices concerning their drinking patterns.

As you read, consider the following questions:

1. The author thinks that the same qualities that make an 18-year-old a good soldier also make him a poor drinker. Why?
2. What does Mr. Peterson think is the correlation between the legal drinking age and alcoholism? Do you agree?
3. What is the role of government and family in promoting healthy drinking behavior, according to the author?

Clifford D. Peterson, "Drinking Age Jury Still Out: Not What Reagan Promised Us . . . But a Good Place to Begin," *The Washington Times,* July 11, 1984. Reprinted with the author's permission.

Several months ago, the Virginia Legislature denied an attempt to raise the legal drinking age to 21. The liquor lobby, combined with college students, helped to defeat the measure, and one of the arguments was the association between the legal drinking age and the 18-year figure which is the age at which young people can enlist in the uniformed services without parental consent. This figure was also the draft age when Selective Service was in effect. Simply stated: if you are old enough to fight, you are old enough to drink.

This argument has been presented before. I remember, as a youth, when it came up in the early '40s. It was used then as a justification to change the voting age from 21 to 18. "If you are old enough to fight for your country, you are old enough to vote." At the age of 10, when I first heard my mother make that statement, it sounded completely reasonable. Later, when we did change the voting age to 18, I opposed the move because I felt the argument was spurious. Simply stated: the very reasons that made 18-year-olds good soldiers argued against their enfranchisement.

18-Year-Old Daredevils

The average 18-year-old makes a good soldier because he is immature, prone to make rash decisions, a daredevil, and easily broken down and remolded into a new person with loyalties to his buddies, his unit and his leadership (sometimes referred to as his country). These are hardly the qualifications which would suggest good citizenship in a Democracy or a Republic. Fortunately, the intoxicating qualities of politics are relatively benign and seem to have little effect on any but the most involved and, one would assume, more mature young people. Even though the basic argument was spurious, there is no apparent damage in having enfranchised the multitudes in order to allow the participation of the few interested enough to get involved in the political scene.

The qualities that make the average 18-year-old a good soldier are exactly those that make him or her a lousy driver, pot smoker, or any controlled-substance user. Intoxication amplifies immaturity. In the case of the drinking youth, the effects are malignant and the spurious argument becomes extremely serious.

More Mature at 21

Some readers probably will assume that the author is a teetotaling prohibitionist. Nothing could be farther from the truth. I have been drinking alcoholic beverages for more than 20 years and I enjoy them very much. As a matter of fact, I would not enjoy having to stop drinking. I believe that one reason that I can still enjoy good wine, brandy, cocktails, and beer is that I did not start using alcohol until I was well over 21 and at least somewhat more mature than I was at 18. A very good friend, who happens to be an alcoholic, says, half-seriously, that we all have so much alcohol

Ed Gamble, *Florida-Times Union*. Reprinted with permission.

that we can drink in one lifetime and that he merely drank his share up early.

Those who lobby for "drinking rights" for youngsters might do well to remember my friend's statement. We'll all be better off, even the sellers, if we take a little more time to use up our quota. There is certainly no reason to start a race early, when the object is endurance.

A First Step

I applaud the administration for promoting a mandatory legal age of 21. That's a first step. Then if parents will enforce the law at home and the public will help the law to enforce it in the streets, we will have taken a big step toward reducing the effects of this gigantic problem called alcoholism. It might even ease the drinking-and-driving problem.

"The solution I would prefer (is) a national law lowering the drinking age to 18."

The National Drinking Age Should Be Lowered

TRB from Washington

TRB from Washington is a regular column published anonymously in *The New Republic* magazine. This particular article was written by Michael Kinsley, an editor of *The New Republic*. A former editor of *Harper's* magazine, he is also a contributing editor of *The Washington Monthly*. Mr. Kinsley attended Magdalen College, Oxford, as well as Harvard Law School and is a member of the District of Columbia bar. In the following viewpoint, Mr. Kinsley claims that a national lowering of the drinking age is being used as a scapegoat by politicians.

As you read, consider the following questions:

1. Why does the author think that a law raising the drinking age to 21 would be ineffective in lowering traffic fatalities?
2. According to the author, what would be the most effective way to lower traffic fatalities?
3. How does the author explain the tendency of politicians to rally for higher drinking age legislation?

In one of his recent Saturday radio chats, President Reagan declared that drunk driving is as great a threat to America as a foreign enemy. Drunk driving makes a nearly ideal political issue. There aren't many ways a politician can please so many and offend so few without even proposing to spend a lot of money. The opposition lacks a constituency. As the final report of the President's Commission on Drunk Driving put it, "No one is in favor of drunk driving, not even drunk drivers."

But drunk driving is not a social problem terribly amenable to political solutions. What can we do about it? The President's Commission has many sound but unexciting suggestions for better law enforcement. Changing public attitudes is the best hope, and it seemed to me over the Christmas holidays that all the recent publicity really has made drivers more careful. But you can't legislate attitudes. Looking for something you *can* legislate, the sobriety lobby has zeroed in on raising the drinking age to 21.

A Federal Problem

President Reagan supports this proposal but, typically, opposes federal government action because he feels it is a matter that should be left to the states. The Presidential Commission, hypocritically, opposes a national drinking age on federalist grounds, but urges a cutoff of federal highway funds to any state that doesn't go along. In fact, the drinking age is a classic example of something that should *not* be left to the states, since lack of uniformity is a large part of the problem. Right now drinking ages vary, in no particular pattern, between 18 and 21. Twenty-year-olds will drive a long way, if necessary, to a state where they can drink. Trouble is, then they have to drive home. But this problem could be addressed as well by the solution I would prefer: a national law lowering the drinking age to 18.

It would be silly to present this as a civil rights issue, involving fundamental questions of either discrimination or freedom. Most people under 21 become people over 21, and even more would do so if they were forbidden to drink. Apart from libertarian extremists, we're all willing to tolerate restrictions on freedom for the public good, even for the paternalistic purpose of protecting people from themselves. Young drivers, both drunk and sober, kill themselves and others (though mostly themselves) in disproportionate numbers. The National Safety Council estimates that 730 lives a year could be saved with a national drinking age of 21.

Traffic Deaths and Recession

On the other hand, it's equally silly to be absolutist in the other direction and say that any burden on freedom is justified if it will save 730 lives. Far more than 730 traffic deaths were avoided in 1982 by the recession, which led to less driving, but nobody would say we should therefore avoid prosperity.

A national mandatory seat-belt law would save thirteen thousand lives a year, but somehow that proposal gets people's libertarian juices flowing in a way the higher drinking age does not. Why the difference? Obviously one reason is that drunken drivers endanger others besides themselves (though the fatality figures would be far less alarming if they only counted innocent victims). But there are two other reasons. First is a failure of empathy. Most people won't be affected by a higher drinking age. Second, there's a sense that drinking has no positive value, and freedom to drink needn't be weighed in any social cost-benefit analysis.

Ineffective Prohibition

It is self-evident that, in a nation fairly awash in alcohol, no law is going to keep young people sober.

Prohibition for children is merely the easy approach because, among those above age 21, near-unanimity exists that no one more callow should drink. But if we are really serious about reducing traffic deaths, this is no way to go about it. . . .

William P. Cheshire, *The Washington Times*, June 25, 1984.

A Gallup Poll shows that 77 percent of the population favor a uniform drinking age of 21. Not surprisingly, the majority increases with age. But even a 54 percent majority of 18-to-21-year-olds say they favor raising the drinking age to 21. How can this be, when other polls show that the vast majority of high school seniors do drink occasionally, if not to excess? Do they plan to stop if the law is changed? Unlikely. The answer, I think, is that teenagers, like other people, switch into an artificial civic mode of thought when engaged in public policy questions. They become intoxicated with high-mindedness—drunk on sobriety—and their judgment is not to be trusted.

Drinking in Moderation

The National Safety Council, for example, passes out a speech for business executives to give in their local communities which begins, "The world probably would be a better place if no one drank alcoholic beverages." Oh, please. Drinking in moderation—which is what most people, even teenagers, do—is one of life's pleasures. Sensible public policy in a free society takes the positive value of pleasure into account, even a minor pleasure with no civic benefit. Prohibition was a mistake not just because it was unenforceable, but because it was wrong on principle.

Prohibition for 18-to-21-year-olds is an easier case to make than prohibition in general. The imposition on individual freedom is only temporary, and the potential social benefit is disproportionately large. But even so, that imposition deserves some consideration in the cost-benefit analysis.

After all, about 99.4 percent of 18-to-21-year-olds are *not* involved in alcohol-related traffic accidents every year. If the United States Congress compiled the same record, there would be fewer than three drunken accidents a year involving members of Congress, a standard the national legislature would be hard pressed to meet.

Law Restricts Freedom

Promoters of age-21 laws say they really don't aspire to prevent younger people from drinking; they just want to discourage it. Indeed, their most optimistic forecasts are that only about a fifth of drink-related traffic deaths in the 18-to-21 age group would be avoided by making drinking by this group illegal. The fact that a law will be widely disobeyed doesn't make it wrong. On the other hand, it's no defense of a law restricting freedom to say that most people will ignore it.

Many states lowered their drinking age during the Vietnam War, on the theory that if you're old enough to fight and die for your country, you're old enough to drink. This argument still strikes me as hard to answer, especially these days when young Americans are dying for their country again, at President Reagan's behest. Maybe we make an exception for soldiers. But what about policemen, Olympic athletes, garbagemen, even college students—it's ridiculous to tell these people they shouldn't have a beer or two on Saturday night.

"I was and am in favor of the legalization of marijuana."

Marijuana Should Be Legalized

Richard C. Cowan

Richard C. Cowan bases his argument for the legalization of marijuana on the premise that marijuana is dangerous, but that legalization would permit distribution channels to be more closely regulated. Mr. Cowan, a Texas-based investor, argues in the following viewpoint that legalization would curb marijuana's profit to the underworld and reduce the amount of law enforcement funds that now go toward narcotics control.

As you read, consider the following questions:
1. According to Mr. Cowan, how does marijuana rate in addictiveness to other drugs in this culture?
2. What is the basis for Mr. Cowan's argument that marijuana should be legalized?
3. Mr. Cowan calls the narcotics police an "enormous, corrupt international bureaucracy." Do you agree? Why or why not?

Richard C. Cowan, "Is Decriminalization Advisable-Yes," excerpted from pages 492-495, *National Review*, April 29, 1983. Reprinted with permission from National Review Inc., 150 East 35th Street, New York, NY 10016.

I was and am in favor of the legalization of marijuana, but not because I think that it is "harmless." Nothing is harmless to everyone or at every dosage level. Neither I nor the National Organization for the Reform of Marijuana Laws (NORML) claims that marijuana is harmless, nor have we *ever* based our arguments for "decriminalization" or legalization on that premise. . . .

Of course marijuana is "habit-forming," or, if one must sound sinister, "psychologically addictive." Amost everything pleasant is habit-forming. Television, for example. . . .

In practice, an experienced smoker does not require massive doses to get high, and tolerance does not always lead to dependence. Indeed, there are many poisons and allergens to which people may develop "tolerance," but certainly not dependence. . . .

The 1982 NAS [National Academy of Sciences/Institute of Medicine, *Marijuana and Health*] report says: "Cannabis dependence does not mean the same thing as cannabis addiction. Dependence means only that a withdrawal syndrome can occur when drug-taking is stopped. Addiction implies compulsive behavior to acquire the drug." In fact almost any activity, e.g., hand-washing, can become the object of compulsive behavior, but, in terms of "addiction" marijuana doesn't compare with heroin, or the barbiturates. Incidentally, it also does not compare with either alcohol or tobacco. . . .

The NAS report says, "The use of marijuana follows that of alcohol and tobacco. It is preceded by acceptance of a cluster of beliefs and values that often reflect disavowal of many standards upheld by adults." The behavioral deterioration commonly associated with drug abuse often *precedes* the drug abuse, but of course is aggravated by it.

So why do we say that a life of drug abuse begins with marijuana and not alcohol? Because that is where we arbitrarily draw the line that makes both marijuana and heroin illegal. The law creates the only real connection: both are on Schedule One of the Controlled Substances Act. That is another story, but I do detect certain elements of cause and effect.

The fact that no one has ever died from a marijuana overdose was perhaps more important in 1972 than today, but it does indicate the low toxicity of the drug. Thousands of people die every year from overdoses of aspirin, Darvon, alcohol and of course tranquilizers, as well as heroin and cocaine. . . .

No Physical or Mental Problems

Marijuana used in moderation *causes no identifiable physical or mental problems for individuals who are otherwise healthy.*

At the risk of appearing "irresponsible," I think that this is still generally true, with the important qualification that some individuals may be sensitive to substances in doses that are innocuous to most. Some people should abstain from even the smallest doses

133

of any psychoactive drug. . . .

Now, if I may, I would like to explain what I consider to be the principal dangers of marijuana for children and adults.

First, for children there may be greater physical dangers than for adults. For example, around the time of puberty any disturbance in hormone levels could have serious consequences. Some studies have indicated that moderately heavy smoking can reduce testosterone levels temporarily to a low/normal level. This would be of little importance to *most* adults, but for *some* children it might have permanent consequences, which, given the different rates of maturation, might not be immediately apparent. This is not to say that one joint and Junior is a permanent soprano, or Susie will grow a beard. Whatever the risk may be it is dose-related. The more the child smokes, the greater the risk.

Pot's Economic Potential

Obviously, legalizing marijuana could be a powerful jolt to the U.S. economy. It may not get us out of OPEC's clutches and it wouldn't cure inflation. But legal pot would mean new jobs, new careers, new corporate profits and new Government taxes.

Chris Barnett, *Playboy,* March 1980.

Obviously, with heavy smoking there might be some immediately apparent, and probably reversible, respiratory problems, but generally speaking, I would be more concerned about the development of the child's mental processes. A person under the influence of marijuana can still think and deal with the real world. However, marijuana does alter consciousness in such a way as to encourage non-linear thought. If a person has a good understanding of the real world, if he is mature, experienced, educated, and skilled at linear thought, this state may not be dangerous. In fact it may be useful. It offers the possibility of new perspectives—which should subsequently be analyzed when not stoned.

Being stoned may also reduce the critical faculties, in the sense that one is apt to be more enthusiastic about things than when "straight." Since much humor is based on incongruity, things may seem very funny, especially to the inexperienced user.

It should be obvious that while there is nothing terribly sinister about all of this, it could pose serious problems for children, for the immature of all ages, and for people who just do not think very well. The effect is again dose-related. The more one smokes, the greater the effect. The longer one stays stoned, the less frequently one can align oneself with the linear real world.

Smoking, . . . is also used to escape the pain of the real world, especially the problems of growing up. Children certainly need to learn to deal with life's problems without sedation, and being stoned may very well make things worse. Still, as a teacher of troubled children said to me once, "If I had all of their problems I might get stoned, too." It is often rightly observed that drug abuse causes problems in the schools, but the degree to which problems in the schools cause drug abuse is seldom appreciated. However, it is easier to blame drugs than to confront the more basic problems....

If we were to take the resources wasted on keeping marijuana from adults and redirect them toward keeping it from children, legalization might even reduce the availability of pot in the schools....

Reasons for Legalization

The reasons why marijuana should be legalized, with conservative leadership, are fairly simple and straightforward. And they have nothing to do with marijuana's being "harmless."

Conservatives generally understand, as liberals often do not, that laws can have an effect opposite to that which is intended. Price controls can aggravate inflation. Busing for racial balance has caused more segregation. Legislated equality creates greater inequality. Similarly, because of its prohibition, marijuana—the most popular illicit drug by far—is thrown into the same distribution channels and cultural milieu as other, much more dangerous substances. The finite resources devoted to suppressing marijuana are hence not available for the suppression of these more dangerous substances, or for just keeping all drugs away from children, who are supposedly our primary concern. (Although, in fact, marijuana use by children seems to have reached the saturation point and started declining—in spite of, rather than because of, prohibition.) Contraband marijuana will always be of uncertain potency and purity, especially by the time it reaches children, the least sophisticated buyers.

At the same time, the profits from the marijuana traffic are an important contribution to the underworld. The enforcement of the marijuana laws is a substantial burden on the criminal-justice system and a major source of police corruption. A large number of people have been drawn into an illegal industry, and more than twenty million people regularly do business with them. This must undermine their respect for the law in general.

Medical Purpose

Meanwhile, marijuana is more easily acquired by a 16-year-old who should not use it than by a sixty-year-old cancer or glaucoma patient who needs it. Marijuana is not perfect in its therapeutic applications, but for many people it is the only thing that will stave off blindness, agony, even death. Nothing so clearly demonstrates the limited vision of some anti-marijuana crusaders than the legal and bureaucratic interference with its medical use. There are specific legislative remedies for this problem, but they are opposed by the supporters of prohibition for ideological reasons. Conservatives should, at the very least, endorse the use of marijuana for medical reasons, instead of attacking it as "the back door to legalization."

In general, the politicization of drug research undermines the credibility of valid drug information. In the short run, untrue but frightening reports about the dire effects of pot may result in reduced consumption. In the long run, these reports will be seen to be false, and users will, in reaction, disbelieve even the reports that are true. Even worse, warnings about the effects of other drugs also lose credibility, with most unfortunate consequences. Statements such as "marijuana is the most dangerous drug," are not just harmless hyperbole—they necessarily imply that angel dust, speed, and heroin are "safer."

The Libertarian Philosophy

Marijuana and other "pleasure" drugs are outlawed completely under federal statutes, and banned by virtually every state as well. . . .

It is not likely that excessive use of marijuana does fog the brain and cause other harm, as its detractors claim. . . .

But, this is not the crucial point. The key point is that if you accept the Libertarian premise that your life is your own, and not the State's, the government has no business telling you what you can and cannot do, except for prohibiting you from using force and fraud against others.

The Libertarian Party, Position Paper No. 6.

Some supporters of marijuana prohibition argue that the legalization of sale or cultivation, or even the decriminalization of simple possession, will convey the message, especially to children, that marijuana is "harmless." These people, carried away by their own polemics, have thus attributed a meaning to changing the marijuana laws that in the contemporary American context is unique, with legality implying both safety and sanctity, not only for adults but also *especially for children*.

Questioning the Dangers of Marijuana

The first thing to understand is that while questioning the validity of reports on the dangers of marijuana does not imply that marijuana is "harmless," it must raise questions about the veracity of the anti-marijuana crusaders at some level.

Consider the implications of what I am saying, if I am correct. The narcotics police are an enormous, corrupt international bureaucracy with billion-dollar budgets, and multibillion-dollar graft opportunities. They have lied to us for fifty years about the effects of marijuana and now fund a coterie of researchers who provide them with "scientific" support. Some of these people are fanatics who distort the legitimate research of others for propaganda purposes.

I realize that this is much more extreme than saying that marijuana is harmless, which, again, it is not. If I am right, then the anti-marijuana propaganda campaign is a cancerous tissue of lies undermining law enforcement, aggravating the drug problem, depriving the sick of needed help, and suckering in well-intentioned conservatives and countless frightened parents.

I conclude with a challenge to all the supporters of marijuana prohibition for a full-scale debate of the real issues involved here. First, of course, is what are the real effects, and dangers, of marijuana? But also, what are the lies that have been and are being told about it, and why are they being told? Also we must discuss the overall drug problem, including alcoholism. And last but not least, we must discuss the effects of prohibition on law enforcement, the corruption of the narcotics police, and the intrinsically immoral methods that are routinely, and necessarily, used to enforce the laws.

"Illegality may not stop the use of marijuana, but it may serve to hold the line while people are educated as to its dangers."

Marijuana Should Not Be Legalized

Stuart M. Butler

Stuart M. Butler directs one of the Heritage Foundation's research teams. Until 1982, Mr. Butler was a Schultz fellow in health and urban affairs at the Foundation. An adjunct fellow at the National Center for Neighborhood Enterprise, he holds a Ph.D. in economic history from St. Andrews College in Scotland and has taught at Hillsdale College in Michigan. In the following viewpoint, Mr. Butler contends that legalizing marijuana would be a mistake.

As you read, consider the following questions:
1. Does the author believe that the criminalization of marijuana hampers individual freedom? Do you agree?
2. How does the marijuana user compare to the alcohol user when behind the wheel of a car, according to the author?
3. What does Dr. Robert DuPont say is the major danger of decriminalizing marijuana?

Stuart M. Butler, "The Marijuana Epidemic," *Backgrounder*, May 4, 1981. Reprinted with permission.

The inescapable conclusion from the scientific evidence now available is that marijuana is a dangerous substance. The increase in potency in recent years means that we are now dealing with a very different problem than the once faced in the 1960s. The evidence also shows that THC is quite different from alcohol in the way that it lodges in certain organs and causes damage to them in a short period of time.

There are really four aspects to this question, and each raises important philosophical and practical issues:

1. To what extent should society interfere with the individual's decision to pursue a dangerous activity?
2. Is there harm, or a cost, to non-users?
3. Does society have the right to enforce some collective lifestyle on the individual to preserve some notion of "culture" or "way of life"?
4. Is an effective law possible, given a resolution of the other issues?

Taking each of these questions in turn:

Marijuana and Individual Freedom

It has always been a tenet of the idea of liberty that the individual has the right to pursue a dangerous activity, or to knowingly damage his own health. If it were otherwise, we should ban everything from hang-gliding to eating candy.

On the other hand, it has usually been conceded that there may be another justifiable position in the case of certain segments of society. When a person does not *realize* the consequences of an action, it is reasonable to warn him, and perhaps to physically prevent him from undertaking it. Most smokers of marijuana have very little understanding of the likely consequences of taking the drug. It would seem quite appropriate to embark on a program of education, particularly in schools, to reduce this ignorance. In addition, a policy aimed at making the drug less available, by presenting obstacles to supply, would reduce the likelihood of casual access by the ill-informed—while the determined user would still be able to obtain supplies.

Drugs do, of course, involve a complication when considering the ability of the user to judge the consequences of his actions. We recognize that children should be protected from many things because inexperience and poor judgment can lead to unforeseen results. But some drugs actually cause reduction in the power of reasoning, or the ability to cease using the substance. This is one reason why we ban heroin but not hang-gliding. Whether there is a sufficient observable effect on the processes of the brain for us to class marijuana with heroin rather than hang-gliding is open to serious question. Yet there is probably sufficient evidence available to suggest that THC does affect motivation and the will to resist higher doses, and other drugs, to justify a policy of active discouragement.

When a drunk decides to drive his automobile, he poses a physical threat to others, and so it is reasonable for society to impose heavy penalties on such actions for the protection of innocent parties. There is plenty of evidence for us to conclude that the use of marijuana interferes with the reactions and skills of people who drive or fly, and that this is hazardous to other people. In addition, the effects of marijuana usually last longer than those due to alcohol. It is quite reasonable, therefore, for society to punish marijuana users who drive or fly under the influence of the drug. Sophisticated laboratory techniques are now available to enable the level of THC in the body to be known with reasonable accuracy, and routine detection equipment should soon be operational. So it will be possible to provide clear guidelines, and penalties, to deal with the smoker-driver.

Marijuana's Psychological Costs

Heavy pot use has been blamed for serious psychological problems, including psychosis, criminal behavior and impaired intellectual function. Dr. Robert Heath of Tulane University, New Orleans, gave monkeys cannabis and produced abnormal brain-wave patterns and pathological changes in brain cells. Dr. Louis J. West and William H. McGlothlin of UCLA described what they called "amotivational syndrome" among pot smokers. It is characterized by apathy, impaired concentration and a diminished ability to stick to complex tasks. . . .

The full dangers posed by marijuana probably will not be known for years. But the implication that the drug is no worse—and perhaps even better—than alcohol hardly justifies approving its use with abandon. "One of the major costs of alcohol to society has been psychological," says Dr. Reese Jones of the University of California in San Francisco. "Marriages are destroyed, kids are messed up, jobs are lost. The psychological costs of marijuana are also going to be great."

Matt Clark, *Newsweek*, January 7, 1980.

The idea of cost is not so simple. If the brilliant scholar becomes a heavy smoker, quits college, and goes on welfare, he is taking from society rather than contributing to it. Yet only a small minority of users could be said to impose costs such as this. Active discouragement would seem to be the most practical way of dealing with the situation.

The Imposition of Society's Standards

This is in many respects the most difficult issue of all, and marks a clear difference of opinion between the libertarian and the conservative. If one believes that "society" is simply a collection of individuals, it is difficult to argue that the spreading use of a drug is detrimental to society in any sense, assuming individuals other than the users are not harmed. On the other hand, if one feels that the strength of a society, and the benefits that it can provide to its members, depends on the broad acceptance of certain obligations and customs—and that the individual is hurt when these customs are eroded—then it could be legitimate to discourage certain activities.

It is at least arguable that the widespread use of marijuana, leading to a decline in motivation, educational achievement and health, may reduce the benefits of society for us all. If this is so, then it would provide an additional reason for active discouragement.

Just and Effective Law

It has been argued by many that we are in a form of "prohibition era" with respect to marijuana. The drug is illegal, but the law is openly and widely flouted, just as it was when alcohol was made illegal. The law is held in disrespect and the punishment of marijuana users is deeply resented. According to this argument, otherwise law-abiding people find themselves dealing with criminals, and only complete legalization will restore faith in the law and get the business of marijuana out of the hands of criminals.

While this argument does have a surface plausibility to it, it is fraught with dangerous implications. In the first place, the almost universal public ignorance of the harmful consequences of marijuana use lies at the heart of the discontent with the law. If the drug were to be legalized, making it available at the corner drugstore, it would confirm the general belief that marijuana was fairly harmless. If the drug were freely available, with the consent of government, it would be virtually impossible to persuade users that they face real dangers. How could one justify a situation where marijuana was made legal when every attempt had been made to ban saccharine?

Illegality may not stop the use of marijuana, but it may serve to hold the line while people are educated as to its dangers. To remove the legal restrictions on its use could also remove any chance of reversing the trend.

Decriminalization of Marijuana

There is, of course, a distinction between the issues of legalization and decriminalization. In the one case we are considering making the distribution and consumption of a drug a legal activity; while on the other we are talking about reducing the penalties for taking the drug.

It is a little difficult to justify putting someone in jail when they are probably ignorant of the consequences of taking marijuana. Even if they are fully aware of the possible damage, it does seem unreasonable to apply harsh criminal penalties when no other person is affected. While full legalization would undoubtedly lead to

141

an explosion of use, non-criminal penalties for the possession or use of small quantities of marijuana, together with criminal sanctions for the possession of large quantities or supplying marijuana to children, would be a more just and acceptable position.

A Grievous Error

There are, however, many experts who feel that even decriminalization would be a grievous error. This view has been put forward very cogently by Dr. Robert DuPont, the former NIDA director:

For many years, while I was in government, I supported decriminalization of marijuana and was actively publicized by the marijuana lobbying organizations as one of their chief advocates or supporters. I was never this, but I did for some years favor decriminalization of marijuana. I have changed my mind completely on that point and I now strongly oppose decriminalization. I am persuaded that we, as a nation, are dealing with a massive epidemic

"Irreversible brain damage, damage to the respiratory system—
pass me my scotch and cigarettes—personality changes..."

with grave consequences for our society, and that decriminalization is a signal in this political debate that, however much one might feel that it is not a good idea to put people in prison for possession of small amounts of marijuana, support for decriminalization is seen as support for marijuana. We all need to recognize that the battle lines are drawn and that decriminalization is the major line that is drawn across the political landscape right now.

The argument surrounding the decriminalization issue is thus not so much one of principle as one of practical politics. If removing criminal penalties for the possession of small quantities of marijuana (while maintaining criminal sanctions for distribution) would not lead to a significant increase in use, or to overwhelming pressure for legalization, then decriminalization would have the support of many people who nevertheless consider the drug as very damaging.

Access and Supply

A policy of active discouragement and education may be pursued in several ways. A number of states, for instance, have banned so-called headshops, where drug-related equipment is sold. The determined user can still find ways of obtaining paraphernalia, but open encouragement to the non-user is reduced by such a measure.

A much more effective form of discouragement, however, would be to actually reduce the level of supplies reaching this country. Enormous quantities of marijuana reach the United States from the Caribbean and South America. It is a multi-billion dollar traffic that involves radio warning planes, large cargo ships, high-speed pickup boats, secret landing strips, and large payoffs to local police. It is not uncommon for seizures of ships to reveal loads of marijuana worth up to $40 million at street prices.

The Coast Guard has been overwhelmed by the volume of the trade, and the tenacity and equipment of the smugglers. Seizures now account for probably less than 15 percent of the total—making but a small dent in massive profits. If anything is to be done to contain the staggering increase in the quantity of marijuana reaching this country, there must be a significant boost in the resources made available to the Coast Guard, the Drug Enforcement Administration, and other services involved with drug interception. Only by driving up the risks faced by smugglers do we stand much chance of reducing the drug flow.

Marijuana and Hard Drugs

Some argue that reducing the availability of marijuana in this country might actually be counterproductive. If you deny people marijuana, they claim, they will merely turn to something more dangerous. This is a spurious argument. For the heavy user with psychiatric problems, marijuana is generally only a stepping stone to hard drugs, or a means of enhancing the effect of other substances. If these people are denied marijuana it would make little difference to the damage they will inflict on themselves. Far more important is the person who tries marijuana because it is inexpensive and freely available, and who then becomes a chronic user or moves on to hard drugs. A reduction in the supply of marijuana would lessen the chances of a casual introduction to the drug. Even among existing users, a switch to alcohol or tobacco is far more probable than hard drugs.

Undesirable Effects

Increased hunger, increased thirst, dry mouth and throat, sense of slowed time, laughing and giggling, drowsiness, red eyes, poor concentration, and silly behavior are reported as common undesirable effects [of marijuana]. Other undesirable effects have been reported less frequently; they include anxiety, headache, aggressive feelings, irritability, crying, suicidal thoughts, nausea, amnesia, and apathy.

Symptoms of psychosis such as depersonalization, micropsia, macropsia, auditory hallucinations, and visual hallucinations are occasionally reported.

Ronald A. Weller, *Medical Aspects of Human Sexuality*, March 1985.

Of course, the marijuana reaching this country has to come from somewhere, and that can present sensitive policy issues. In certain countries, the cultivation of marijuana for export to the United States has become a significant part of the domestic economy, and a major source of foreign exchange. There have been cases of the United States supporting the actions of foreign governments seeking to reduce cultivation, such as Mexico, but this kind of cooperation is rare and not very effective.

The Drug Trade

Jamaica is a good example of the kind of problem faced by the United States. The country is a major supplier of marijuana to America. The trade is worth well over $1 billion a year, equal to Jamaica's entire foreign debt, and greater than all other exports combined. Jamaica is also unstable and bankrupt, and is a target of Cuban penetration.

When the Jamaican government changed hands in 1980, the United States found itself in a very delicate situation regarding the drug business. The new Prime Minister, Edward Seaga, is a friend of the West, and so the United States is understandably hesitant to undermine what is left of the island's economy. But marijuana is crucial to the economy. As Seaga pointed out recently, "The ganja (i.e., marijuana) trade in the last several months was virtually what was keeping the economy alive." According to him, the trade is "here to stay," and the question is not whether it should be wiped out but whether it should be completely legalized:

> so as to bring the flow of several hundred million dollars in this parallel market through the official channels, and therefore have it count as part of our foreign exchange—which would mean an extremely big boost to our foreign exchange....

Mr. Seaga's tidy, businesslike approach to the drug trade is complemented by a convenient interpretation of the scientific evidence. Medical reports, he states with authority, "seem to suggest there's no conclusive evidence that ganja is harmful...." Mr. Seaga would be well advised to talk to some of Jamaica's leading psychiatrists at Kingston Hospital, who seem to have reached somewhat different conclusions regarding the effects of marijuana.

A Solution

While the situation in Jamaica may be outrageous, dealing with it presents many problems. It would be easy to drift into the feeling that really nothing can be done without damaging the fabric of the country. But if the government of Jamaica (or any other country) condones the cultivation and exportation of a drug that is harmful to the people of the United States, it has only itself to blame for the consequences. It is an absurd form of foreign aid for the U.S. Government to stand idly by while a country encourages the supply of a dangerous drug to America, simply because that country needs foreign exchange!

In the interests of its own citizens, the U.S. government should state clearly that marijuana is dangerous and a threat to the American population; that it is an unfriendly act for any government to condone it and that policies will be adopted to dissuade such tacit support. The idea that Jamaica can only survive if marijuana cultivation is allowed to continue is ridiculous. The reason that the industry is now so important to Jamaica is that it is highly profitable. If the incentives were altered, other industries would develop. It should therefore be the goal of U.S. policy to apply penalties against Jamaica and similar countries if they continue to allow the trade to flourish, while offering American assistance to develop other industries. Tolerating the present state of affairs is an abrogation of responsibility by Washington. How can we justify putting our citizens in jail for using marijuana when we refuse to deal effectively with the chief suppliers of the drug?

"The street sale of drugs must be stopped, no matter what the cost to the government, because the cost to society is so great."

The US Should Strengthen the War on Drugs

Daniel Patrick Moynihan

Daniel Patrick Moynihan is a Democrat senator from New York. A long-time social and political leader, Senator Moynihan was graduated with a Ph.D. from Tufts University and was a Fulbright scholar. In the following viewpoint, Senator Moynihan claims that increasing anti-drug enforcement funds and personnel is the best way to fight the drug war. He argues that "any display of official tolerance or indifference" to drug abuse "is disastrous."

As you read, consider the following questions:

1. Why does Senator Moynihan think that there is a link between supply and demand of illegal drugs?
2. What are some of the historical examples that the author gives to demonstrate the danger of removing drug restrictions?
3. Senator Moynihan believes that the fight against drug abuse needs to include the restriction of drug production in other countries. Why?

Daniel Patrick Moynihan, in an address before the Albert Einstein College of Medicine of Yeshiva University in New York on May 31, 1985.

As truly self-destructive behavior, nothing is more startling than the epidemic of drug use among young people and, increasingly, older people also.

Heavy heroin use began in the mid-1960s. Since then there have been successive onslaughts of new substances—narcotics, hallucinogens and stimulants, with cocaine being the most recent.

The abuse of drugs or liquor is one of the effects technology has had on our society, even though we do not often think of it as such.

The Art of Distillation

The art of distillation was discovered ages ago. ("Alcohol" is an Arab term; "whiskey" is a Celtic one.) But there was never a surplus of grain and therefore never an abundance of hard drink. Folks made do with beer or wine, mild intoxicants.

The agricultural innovations of the 18th century, however, produced a grain surplus. These technologies crossed to America where the availability of new land compounded the potential for making a mess of things, and we promptly did.

Soon it emerged that the most economical way to transport grain back over the mountains to the Eastern Seaboard was as whiskey, and transport it we did. Next we proceeded to protect it from foreign competition. The first law passed by Congress prescribes the oath of office to be taken by officials of the new republic. The second imposed a 10-cent-a-gallon duty on rum. In no time at all, alcohol consumption in the United States was staggering.

Irresistible Stimulant

Drug abuse, as we encounter it today, is very similar to alcohol abuse a century ago when whiskey was first widely produced. People had no experience with the widespread availability of such a powerful stimulant, and to North Europeans it was at first irresistible. It felt good and was thought to be good for you.

It became routine to drink at breakfast and to go on drinking all day. Laborers digging the Erie Canal were allotted a quart of whiskey a day, in eight 4-ounce portions commencing at 6 a.m. Only slowly did it sink in that such a regimen was ruinous to health and a risk to society. When it did, society responded.

Apart only from the movement to abolish slavery, the most popular and influential social movement of 19th-century America concerned the effort to limit or prohibit the use of alcohol. The former brought about three amendments to the Constitution, the latter two.

Alcohol abuse continues to be a major health problem. But at least the dangers are understood far better than in the past.

Natural Drugs

The use of what might be termed high-proof drugs appeared roughly a century later than the use of high-proof alcoholic drink.

C.P. Houston, *Houston Chronicle*. Reprinted with permission.

Just as beer and wine are naturally fermented products of grain and grapes, narcotics and stimulants appear in nature as elements of the poppy, the coca plant or whatever.

In the 19th century's first half, morphine was produced from opium. In combination with the hypodermic needle, it was widely used in Civil War medicine, giving rise to a form of addiction that was popularly called "soldier's disease."

A generation later, heroin, a "distillation" of morphine, was developed by the Bayer Pharmaceutical company in Germany. (When tested on employees, it was found to make them feel heroic—hence its trade name.)

In like manner, cocaine, the active ingredient of the coca leaf, was isolated before 1880. Its early use was medical.

Federal Prohibition

Along with alcohol, these substances came under federal prohibition early in this century. Alcohol prohibition was a convulsive event that led to the creation of a criminal underworld of exceptional influence. There was always a certain amount of drug trafficking in that underworld, and it continued at modest levels until the epidemic outbreak of heroin use in the 1960s. It then provided the model on which the large-scale import and distribution of drugs commenced in the 1960s.

In 1969 I became assistant to the President for urban affairs. I resolved to use my authority on a short list of critical matters. The first was welfare reform; the second was drug abuse.

In the late summer of 1969, I was sent by the President on a mission to Turkey and France. Our purpose was to break the "French connection," the trail from the poppy fields of Afyon Province in Turkey to heroin laboratories in Marseilles to the streets of New York. With the cooperation of the French and Turkish governments, we succeeded. In fairly short order heroin became scarce and hugely expensive.

In that period, the federal government was reorganized to deal with this issue at much higher levels of executive energy. The State and Justice departments and the Public Health Service set up special major units to handle narcotics.

Yet 15 years after these events we seem to have made little progress on heroin use, while acquiring a massive problem with cocaine.

What happened?

Nothing that wasn't to be expected. We have a large population that is disposed to drug abuse. So long as there is such demand, there will be some supply. We understood perfectly well in 1969 that if we broke the French connection, the drug traffickers would soon establish another, which they did in Mexico. Mexico was closed down, and they turned to Pakistan. If Pakistan can be closed down, they will turn to some other source.

Supply and Demand

Cocaine follows the same pattern. What we can do is disrupt the traffic. This has solid effect here at home. When supply goes down the prices go up, the number of new users or casual users declines. Disrupting street sales appears to have the same effect.

But nothing will have a final effect until our population changes its mind about drug use.

At least two things must be done. First, any display of official tolerance must be furiously suppressed. The street sale of drugs must be stopped, no matter what the cost to the government, because the cost to society is so great.

Similarly, any open production of drugs in another country for the purpose of sale here must be made a priority issue of foreign policy. The State Department won't do this on its own. It must be forced: no arms, no aid, no loan rescheduling, no anything to countries that remain indifferent to drug traffic. We cannot ask others to perform miracles that we cannot perform ourselves. Our experience with Turkey and France and Mexico shows that this can be done, and that it has effects *here*.

But again, any display of official tolerance or indifference is disasterous. An example. The U.S. Customs Service is authorized to employ 13,370 persons in Fiscal Year 1984. This Spring—as an economy measure!—the Administration requested that this number be reduced by 923 positions, and that the overall budget of the Customs Service be cut $23.5 million. Most of the positions the Administration asked to cut are in the area termed "inspection and control," which is to say intercepting contraband, including drugs. The Senate Finance Committee and the House Committee on Ways and Means would have none of this. But what kind of signal did it send to, let us say, Colombia?

I think back to a luncheon some fifteen years ago at the residence of the American Ambassador in Paris. Our guest was the head of the French National Police, the *Surete.* He listened in silence as I recounted the social wreckage that heroin had brought to our cities, heroin produced in France. After a point, he became incredulous: was it *possible* we were just now telling this to the French Government? It was clear something would have to be done, even if it meant taking on Marseilles, something French policemen do not relish. But the question obviously nagged at him: what had taken us so long? Luncheon over, we said our farewells; I helped him with his coat. Whereupon he turned, looked me in the eye, and asked: "What kind of people are you?"

I hope we care enough about each other, and about our institutions to fight this plague until it is no more.

"America's war on drugs has many losers and no victors. . . . It's time to end the war."

The US Should End Its War on Drugs

Doug Bandow

Doug Bandow is a syndicated columnist with Copley News Service and is a senior fellow at the CATO Institute. Mr. Bandow, who received a J.D. degree from the Stanford School of Law, was a policy analyst for the Reagan administration and an editor of *Inquiry* magazine. In the following viewpoint, Mr. Bandow claims that by legalizing all drugs, America's drug war would end. He does not believe that drug use should be encouraged, but rather that legalization would stop the robbing and murdering caused by addicts who must pay a high price for illegal street drugs.

As you read, consider the following questions:

1. According to the author, what is the prime danger of using heroin?
2. What does Mr. Bandow believe is the relationship between illegal drugs and crime?
3. According to the author, what kinds of civil rights are violated because of drug laws?

Doug Bandow, "Let's Stop the War on Drugs," *St. Louis Globe-Democrat*, June 16-17, 1984. Reprinted with the author's permission.

I'm scared of the war on drugs. In Washington, D.C., I work across the street from an apartment complex, Potomac Gardens, where four people have been murdered the past year, all in connection with drug dealing.

Calling the police is no answer. All they can do is push the dealers somewhere else. In fact, Potomac Gardens didn't become the center of drug trafficking until the police cracked down in some other neighborhoods last year. Anyway, the district can't handle more drug cases: law enforcement officers admit that drug enforcement already is overloading the legal system.

But I'm not only scared; I'm angry, too. Angry over the damage done to the careers, reputations and lives of drug users, from the famous to the unknown, the thousands arrested every year across the county.

In fact, the drug laws are used to enforce social conformity, not to prevent physical harm. One pharmacological text admits that the phrase drug abuse "conveys the notion of social disapproval, and is not necessarily descriptive of any...adverse consequences."

Legal Drugs

The illegal substances are not benign, but most are not significantly more dangerous than legal "drugs," like cigarettes and alcohol, used by millions of Americans today. Marijuana, for example, has been linked to a number of physical ailments, but Dr. Norman Zinberg of Harvard Medical School says that aside from damaging the lungs and harming those with heart problems, there is "enough evidence to follow up, but there is nothing definitive."

And neoconservative sociologist James Q. Wilson has admitted that "there are apparently no specific pathologies—serious illnesses or physiological deterioration—that are known to result from heroin use per se."

Instead, the prime danger of using heroin comes from drug prohibition: street heroin is impure, varies in concentration and is taken in unsanitary conditions.

This doesn't mean drug use should be encouraged; I don't use drugs just as I don't smoke or drink. But consenting adults should be free to balance the potential dangers and pleasures of snorting cocaine just as they can chew tobacco and hang-glide.

Punishing Drug Use

Only where drug use threatens others—driving while under the influence, for example—should it be punished. (Drug use by children deserves special attention, but banning drugs for everyone makes as much sense as returning to Prohibition to keep alcohol out of the hands of minors.)

Drug users and sellers aren't the only victims of the war on drugs.

Drug Glossary

Distributed by Heritage Features Syndicate

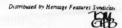

Pusher **Joint** **Dope**

Reprinted with permission of Heritage Features Syndicate.

According to D.C. Police Chief Maurice Turner, "Addicts rob, burglarize, steal and sometimes murder to support their habits." The harm wrought by these violent predators is immense: The Drug Enforcement Agency estimates that one out of every five property crimes is committed by heroin addicts.

Drug users rob, burglarize, steal and sometimes murder because drugs are illegal, which makes them so expensive. Turner says that many addicts use $100 to $125 worth of heroin a day, and with "that type of habit, they're going to have to steal approximately six times that much to sell on the open market."

A government study in Detroit found that as the drug laws were more strictly enforced, drug prices rose and the number of other crimes committed increased.

Yet, according to analyst Roy Childs of the Cato Institute, the actual cost of the raw materials for even a $200 daily fix of heroin, or an equivalent dose of morphine, is just dollars a day. How many addicts would rob, burglarize, steal and sometimes murder for a few dollars a day?

Moreover, it is drug prohibition that has pushed the drug business—unlike the cigar market—into the hands of those who murder each other and who push drugs on kids. We should learn from history: The mob dropped bootlegging once the government dropped alcohol prohibition.

The victims of other crimes also are suffering because we waste as much as 40 percent of local police resources, 25 percent of prison space and similar proportions of prosecution efforts and court time on drug enforcement. Prison overcrowding, early release of violent criminals and corruption among vice squad cops are the inevitable results.

Finally, victims of the drug war include people whose civil liberties are violated as the government uses ever-more draconian weapons to enforce the majority's mores. For example, last year the Supreme Court OK'd warrantless searches and seizures on boats and the head of the DEA has boasted of a 242 percent increase in federal wiretaps. The New York City police once even arrested all 375 patrons of the Gotham Disco and led them away in chains, charging them with "loitering for the purpose of using drugs."

I'm a non-combatant in this war, but I am still a victim. And I'm more scared of the government's efforts to control drug use than the activities of drug users and sellers.

America's war on drugs has many losers and no victors. Until we admit that it is an immoral and unwinnable war, the body counts will continue to rise, with all of us the victims.

It's time to end the war.

Distinguishing Between Fact and Opinion

This activity is designed to help develop the basic reading and thinking skill of distinguishing between fact and opinion. Consider the following statement as an example. "Several thousand people are killed on the nation's highways every year by drunk drivers." This statement is a fact which no historian, political commentator, or citizen of any age would deny. But consider a statement which links education to highway fatalities. "If people who habitually drive while intoxicated were better educated regarding the effects of alcohol upon their bodies, there would be far fewer highway fatalities." Such a statement is clearly an expressed opinion. The remedies for drunk driving depend on one's point of view.

When investigating controversial issues it is important that one be able to distinguish between statements of fact and statements of opinion.

The following statements are taken from the viewpoints in this chapter. Consider each statement carefully. *Mark O for any statement you feel is an opinion or interpretation of facts. Mark F for any statement you believe is a fact.*

If you are doing this activity as a member of a class or group compare your answers with those of other class or group members. Be able to defend your answers. You may discover that others will come to different conclusions than you. Listening to the reasons others present for their answers may give you valuable insights in distinguishing between fact and opinion.

If you are reading this book alone, ask others if they agree with your answers. You too will find this interaction very valuable.

> O = *opinion*
> F = *fact*
> U = *impossible to judge*

1. The National Safety Council estimates that 730 lives a year could be saved with a national drinking age of 21.

2. About 99.4 percent of 18-to-21-year-olds are *not* involved in alcohol-related traffic accidents every year.

3. A national mandatory seat-belt law would save thirteen-thousand lives a year.

4. If you are old enough to fight, you are old enough to drink.

5. Intoxication amplifies immaturity.

6. Nothing is harmless to everyone or at every dosage level.

7. The use of marijuana follows that of alcohol and tobacco.

8. Marijuana used in moderation causes no identifiable physical or mental problems for individuals who are otherwise healthy.

9. Marijuana laws are held in disrespect and the punishment of marijuana users is deeply resented.

10. The US Coast Guard has been overwhelmed by the volume of the marijuana trade, and the tenacity and equipment of the smugglers.

11. As truly self-destructive behavior, nothing is more startling than the epidemic of drug use among young people.

12. In the 19th century's first half, morphine was produced from opium.

13. Drug laws are used to enforce social conformity, not to prevent physical harm.

14. The prime danger of using heroin comes from drug prohibition: street heroin is impure, varies in concentration and is taken in unsanitary conditions.

15. Addicts rob, burglarize, steal and sometimes murder to support their habits.

Periodical Bibliography

The following list of periodical articles deals with the subject matter of this chapter.

Steve Chapple — "A Myopic Approach to Marijuana," *The New York Times*, November 9, 1984.

Christian Science Monitor — "Drugs and Drinking: Preserving Safety in the Skies," January 28, 1985.

Mathea Falco — "The Big Business of Illicit Drugs," *The New York Times Magazine*, December 11, 1983.

Ashbel Green — "Myopia on Teen-Age Drinking," *The New York Times*, June 28, 1984.

Louis Lasagna and Gardner Lindzey — "Marijuana Policy and Drug Mythology," *Society*, January/February 1983.

Flora Lewis — "Tall Is Not High," *The New York Times*, March 22, 1985.

Courtland Milloy and Linda Wheeler — "Washington's Other Industry: Heroin," *The Washington Post National Weekly Edition*, April 8, 1985.

The New York Times — "Don't Export Unapproved Drugs," September 12, 1984.

Rex R. Reed — "Prohibition for the Younger Set?" *Reason*, May 1984.

The New Republic — "Heroin and Cowardice," February 25, 1985.

Boyce Rensberger — "Designer Drugs," *The Washington Post National Weekly Edition*, April 1, 1985.

Jeff Riggenbach — "Marijuana: Freedom Is the Issue," *The Libertarian Review*, July 1980.

Richard Vigilante — "Pot-Talk: Is Decriminalization Advisable?" *National Review*, April 29, 1983.

George F. Will — "Is the ACLU Being Reasonable?," *Newsweek*, January 31, 1983.

Is Drug Addiction
Exaggerated?

"The combined costs imposed on society by the daily heroin users. . . totaled about $55,000 annually per offender."

Drug Addiction Is a Major Problem

Bernard A. Gropper

Bernard A. Gropper, Ph.D., is a manager at the National Institute of Justice. Dr. Gropper, an experimental psychologist, heads the research on the relationship of drug addiction and alcoholism to crime. In the following viewpoint, he writes about the links between drugs and crime and some of the associated costs to society.

As you read, consider the following questions:

1. List some of the evidence the author cites to substantiate his claim that drug addicts impose a high cost on society?
2. According to Dr. Gropper, how are drug abuse and crime linked?
3. What does Dr. Gropper say are some of the other costs exacted by drug abuse?

Bernard A. Gropper, "Probing the Links Between Drugs and Crime," *NIJ Reports,* November 1984. This article is reprinted with the permission of the National Institute of Justice, US Department of Justice. The points of view or opinions in this article do not necessarily represent the official position or policies of the National Institute or the US Department of Justice.

Recently completed National Institute of Justice-supported studies of career criminals by researchers at the Rand Corporation (Chaiken and Chaiken, 1982) found that a majority of the most serious offenders (the "violent predators") among the inmates in prisons and jails of three states had histories of heroin use, frequently in combination with alcohol and other drugs. Such a history of drug abuse, in fact, proved to be one of the best "predictors" of serious career criminality.

Other National Institute-funded research (Wish, 1982: Johnson, Wish, Strug, and Chaiken, 1983) indicates that narcotics abusers engage in violence more often than earlier studies would lead us to believe. Recent studies have shown that heroin-using offenders are just as likely as their non-drug-using or non-heroin-using counterparts to commit violent crimes (such as homicide, sexual assault, and arson)—and even more likely to commit robbery and weapons offenses.

High Risk for Violence

Data being developed by researchers at the Interdisciplinary Research Center on the Relations of Drugs and Alcohol to Crime (RC) lend further support to the growing body of evidence suggesting that drug abusers are a high risk for violence. Reports from several cities indicate that a quarter or more of homicides are related to drug trafficking (Goldstein, 1982; McBribe, 1983).

Perhaps even more disturbing is the finding that 75 percent of all robberies reported by the national sample of youth, and 50 percent of the felony assaults, were due to a small but highly criminal group. This was the sub-sample, comprising less than 3 percent of all youth, who had committed three or more index offenses and were pill or cocaine/heroin users (Johnson, Wish, and Huizinga, 1983).

Robberies or assaults, in fact, are proving to be rare among criminally active youths who are not also involved in illicit drug use. While such data cannot show whether drug abuse is necessarily the primary or only "cause" of these behaviors, they show that it is very much a characteristic of serious and violent offenders.

Changes in Crime with Changes in Drug Use

Among the most compelling evidence of the impacts of hard drug use on crime are the findings reported by teams of researchers in Baltimore (Ball, Shaffer, and Nuroc, 1983) and at UCLA (McGlothin et al., 1978); Anglin and Speckart, 1984). These Institute-supported studies clearly confirm one of the major assumptions of drug treatment—that reducing the level of drug usage can reduce the level of criminal activity, even among relatively hard-core drug users.

The Baltimore team analyzed background factors and long-term patterns of crime for 354 black and white male heroin addicts. The

C.P. Houston, *Houston Chronicle*. Reprinted with permission.

sample was drawn from more than 7,500 known opiate users arrested (or identified) by Baltimore police between 1952 and 1976 so as to be representative of the addict population at large.

The results show how the intensity of the criminal behavior—especially property crime—of such addicts tends to be directly related to their current drug use status. During a 9-year period at risk, their crime rates dropped to relatively low levels during periods when they had little or no narcotic use. While they were actively addicted, however, their criminality was typically about four to six times higher. Overall, they averaged 2,000 crime-days (defined as any day on which they committed one or more crimes) per addict. For those who had several periods of addiction and reduction or cessation of narcotics use, the levels of criminality clearly tended to rise and fall with drug usage....

Crime Levels During Active Drug Abuse Periods

Over the course of approximately 9.5 years, the Baltimore addicts committed a total of nearly 750,000 offenses! Theft made up the greatest part of their criminal activity totaling 829 crimes per addict. Drug-distribution offenses accounted for 581 crimes; forgeries, 172; robberies and assaults, 46; and gambling, pimping, fencing, con games, etc., another 561.

During their periods of active addiction, the Baltimore users committed thefts (burglary, shoplifting, auto theft, and other larcenies) 35 percent of the time; engaged in drug dealing 25 percent of the time; and committed other types of crimes on 33 percent of their days at risk. Even excluding their drug-dealing offenses, while actively addicted they averaged more than 150 "crime-days-per-at-risk" involving theft, violence, confidence games, or other crimes—with approximately a third of these days involving the commission of two or more types of offenses on the same day.

Other studies have shown similar offense patterns, although not on so grand a scale. A study of a sample of 573 male and female heroin abusers in Miami (Inciardi, 1979), for example, also revealed a higher rate of addict crime, averaging 375 offenses per addict over the course of 1 year. High levels of crime by street-level heroin abusers were also found by a research team working in New York City (Johnson et al., 1985).

For the California treatment sample, over their active addiction careers (the period from first daily use to last daily use) official arrests and self-reported criminal behaviors increased directly with levels of drug usage. At the highest rate of use (three or more "fixes" per day), arrest rates were 2.5 to 3.5 times the rates at the lowest level of use (one fix or less per month), and crime-days were 10 to 20 times more frequent. For example, white addicts reported 157 crime-days at their highest use levels, versus 12 crime-days at their lowest, and Hispanic addicts reported 149 versus 7.

Lower Crime Rates

In contrast to their high levels of criminal activity while actively addicted, the addicts in each of these studies showed significantly reduced criminality during periods of reduced use or non-addictions to narcotics. For example, the high crime rate of the Baltimore heroin users (255 crime-days per year) while active fell to an average of 65 crime-days per year when not addicted.

While the absolute level of property crime involvement was greater for the California addicts (perhaps reflecting both geographical and ethnic differences in the population samples), they too showed substantially reduced crime rates when not actively addicted. Their self-reported property crime rates were four to seven times lower during non-addictive periods, and their arrest rates were cut in half.

Multiple-Drug Use

One point to be considered in all these studies, however, is that heroin addicts are also typically multiple-drug abusers. They use other drugs, such as alcohol, marijuana, or cocaine, either in addition to heroin or as temporary substitutes.

Record-High Drug Use

A UN report found international drug use at a record high. It concluded that almost 50 tons of cocaine is smuggled into the US every year. Not only is the United States affected. So, too, are Western European nations where many drug users live, and Latin American and Asian nations where the growth or production of drugs is big business and, through corruption, threatens the integrity of some governments.

In addition, law enforcement authorities warn that the No. 1 cause of crime in the United States is the desire of drug users to obtain money to purchase illegal drugs. Crimping the drug flow, they say, is essential to reduce crime.

The Christian Science Monitor, March 14, 1985.

Thus, in all the studies discussed here, periods of "non-addiction" do not necessarily mean that the subjects were totally drug-free during those times. Despite this, these finds strongly suggest that heroin use markedly elevates offense rates, and that eliminating or reducing such costly drug usage, even to some other levels or types of drug use (Collins et al., 1984), does tend to reduce criminal behavior significantly.

Costs of Street-Level

Another recent study, under National Institute co-sponsoring with the National Institute on Drug Abuse, explored the behaviors and economic impacts of street-level opiate users (Johnson et al., 1985). Its findings indicate that, although they are able to obtain drugs and survive through many methods, criminality is very common among street heroin abusers and clearly related to their levels and patterns of drug usage.

The research team, from the IRC at the New York State Division of Substance Abuse Services, gathered data from 201 heroin users who were recruited directly from their Central and East Harlem Neighborhoods. The subjects provided 11,417 person-days of self-reported data during 1980-1982 on their day-to-day drug usage and on how they supported themselves.

The study classifed users according to their frequency of drug use: daily (6 to 7 days per week), regular (3 to 5 days per week), or irregular (2 days or less per week). The findings provide a far more detailed picture of the street-level economics of drug usage and crime than has previously been available.

Patterns of Drug Use and Crime

Like the Baltimore addicts, most of the Harlem heroin abusers committed a large number of non-drug crimes and an even larger number of drug distribution offenses. Daily heroin users reported the highest crime rates. They averaged 316 drug sales per year and participated in 564 more drug distribution offenses through "steering" (directing customers to sources of supply), "touting" (promoting a particular dealer's drugs), or "copping" (conveying drugs and money between buyers and sellers, who may not actually meet). Daily heroin users also committed more violent crimes (i.e., robberies), a quarter or more of which were committed against other drug users or dealers, drunks, and other street people.

Almost all tended to use a variety of other drugs in addition to heroin; 90 percent also used cocaine and alcohol, and 73 percent used marijuana. Some drug use occurred on 85 percent of the days—heroin on 54 percent of the days, alcohol on 51 percent, cocaine on 27 percent, and illicit methadone on 10 percent.

The daily heroin users each consumed more than $17,000 worth of drugs per year compared to about $5,000 for the irregular users, with non-cash arrangements covering about a third of their consumption. Daily heroin users also committed about twice as many robberies and burglaries as regular users, and about five time as many as the irregular users.

However, the daily users did not tend to commit more crimes per day than the other groups. Most of them had more criminal cash income during a year only because they were criminally active on more days (209 non-drug crimes per year, compared with 162 among regular and 116 among irregular users). The daily users did not tend to have significantly higher arrest or incarceration rates than the less intensive users, and may thus be considered more "successful" as criminals since they committed more crimes and used more drugs than the less regular users.

Relatively Modest Returns Per Crime

The returns per crime proved to be relatively small, though they tended to be somewhat greater for the daily users ($41 per crime) than the $25 per crime netted by the irregular users). The average returns from robbery ($80) and burglary ($81) were modest compared with the risks. The typical drug sale or distribution offense provided $5 or less cash income.

The average daily heroin user gained more than $11,000 per year cash income from crime. This rose to more than $18,000 when the economic value of the drugs received without cash payment is included. In comparison, an irregular user netted only $6,000 total.

Economic Impact on Society

These figures do not, of course, represent the full range of economic consequences that heroin users imposed upon other persons and society. To provide a somewhat more extensive picture,

GETTING BIGGER

© Pierott/Rothco

Johnson et al. (1985) developed estimates of 33 different types of economic harm imposed by such street heroin abusers. Among them were:

- **Non-Drug Crime.** The average street opiate user committed non-drug crimes (including burglary, robbery, and theft) from which victims suffered an economic loss of almost $14,000 annually, based on the retail value of stolen goods. The toll from such non-drug crimes by daily heroin users was nearly four times (amost $23,000) that due to the irregular users (almost $6,000).

- **Freeloading.** The public and relatives or friends of daily heroin users contributed more than $7,000 annually to them in the form of public transfer payments, evasion of taxes, cash "loans," and provision of shelter and meals.

- **Drug Distribution Crimes.** Street-level heroin abusers contribute substantially to the underground economy. In addition to being drug consumers, they function as low-level drug dealers and distributors. In this New York sample, the average daily heroin user distributed approximately $26,000 per year in illegal drugs. From this, they received about 40 percent in cash or drug "wages," while 60 percent went to higher-level dealers and others in the illegal drug distribution system.

The combined costs imposed on society by the daily heroin users in this study totaled about $55,000 annually per offender. Regular heroin users cost society about $32,000, and irregular users about $15,000 each per year. These costs are in addition to those due to other economic factors typically addressed by prior research on social costs—such as foregone productivity of legitimate work; criminal justice system expenses for police, courts, corrections, and probation and parole; treatment costs; private crime prevention costs; and less tangible costs due to fear of crime and the suffering of victims.

"The estimated number of addicts is one of a class of 'mythical numbers' that is becoming the routine product of government agencies."

Drug Addiction Is Exaggerated

Peter Reuter

Peter Reuter is a senior economist at the Rand Corporation in Washington, DC. In the following viewpoint, he argues that numbers estimating the number of drug addicts are often grossly exaggerated in order to justify government narcotics control funds. Mr. Reuter describes discrepancies in the reporting procedures that lead him to believe the figures are inaccurate.

As you read, consider the following questions:

1. What, according to the author, is the discrepancy between the estimated number of heroin addicts and property crimes?
2. What does Mr. Reuter give as a reason for the "inflated" figures of drug abuse?
3. Which three factors does the author give to explain why estimates of heroin addicts are allowed "to circulate without criticism?"

Peter Reuter, "The (continued) Vitality of Mythical Numbers." Reprinted with permission of the author from: THE PUBLIC INTEREST, No. 75 (Spring, 1984), pp. 135-147. ⓒ 1984 by National Affairs, Inc.

Thirteen years ago in these pages Max Singer dealt with the following puzzle. Heroin addicts were believed to commit numerous crimes, particularly burglary and shoplifting, to support habits that then cost $30 per day and made addicts unable to function in regular jobs. There were estimated to be 200,000 addicts in New York City. Even with adjustments for addict time in prison and estimates of their non-criminal incomes, these figures jointly implied that addicts stole almost ten times as much as was estimated actually to have been stolen in New York. Singer argued that the number of addicts in New York may be overestimated; it was more likely to be 70,000 than 200,000.

Much has changed since Singer's article appeared. The continued importance of the heroin crime problem over the last decade has led to some major studies of the criminal activities of heroin addicts. Addicts in those studies appear to commit extraordinary numbers of crimes when not in prison. We have learned a modest amount about the paths to addiction and the possibility, not considered in 1971, that many heroin users are not addicts. The number of heroin addicts is no longer estimated simply by adding up the numbers on registers maintained by various local police departments and applying an essentially arbitrary "fudge factor." It is now the product of a complex statistical formula established by social scientists.

Yet we are still left with the same puzzle. The number of addicts nationally is estimated to be about 500,000 (which supposedly does not include non-addicted users). If we use the estimates, generated in various academic studies, of the number of crimes committed by addicts, we find once again that the addict population alone seems to commit more of certain kinds of property crime than actually occurs.

I believe that the problem still lies with the estimates of the number of addicts. Behind the complex estimating formula is some very questionable, but unquestioned, data collection. There is a strong interest in keeping the number high and none in keeping it correct. In that respect the estimated number of addicts is one of a class of "mythical numbers" that is becoming the routine product of government agencies. These numbers are generated by the demand that the government appear to know a great deal more than it actually does. They are often, as in the case of the number of addicts, protected from criticism partly by the one-sided interest in keeping them high and partly by their near irrelevance, at least so far, to policy-making. . . .

The Illegal Drug Market

A new set of numbers has further enhanced the devil image of drugs. These are the estimates of total income from illegal drug sales. For the years 1978 to 1980 an entity with a curious name, the National Narcotics Intelligence Consumers Committee (NNICC), consisting of representatives of eleven federal agencies, published estimates of total income from the sale of heroin, cocaine, marijuana, and "dangerous drugs." The estimates rose from about $50 billion in 1978 to about $80 billion in 1980.

These figures have been enthusiastically received. They have been quoted by Democrats and Republicans alike. Then-Attorney General Smith used them in October 1982 to bolster his argument for an increased federal drug enforcement effort. They are routinely cited in the stories on drugs that magazines and newspapers publish on dreary "no news" days. They have even entered into the margins of academic literature, though it is fair to say that respectable academics, who might well be able to use the estimate of drug income in discussing crime in America, have had the good sense to ignore them.

Drug Disinformation

I do not think it an exaggeration to say that the government policy toward mind-changing drugs since 1966 has been unscientific and hysterical. . . . The unhappy fact is that almost everything that is written in the popular press or broadcast in the electronic media about drugs is wartime disinformation, noisily disseminated by those whose livelihood benefits from an inflammatory, one-sided approach to an extraordinarily complex phenomenon.

Timothy Leary, *USA Today*, November 28, 1984.

But no one has criticized them. The Internal Revenue Service, a member of NNICC, has raised some doubts, expressed with admirable honesty in a dissent printed in the 1980 NNICC report. Otherwise the numbers stand unchallenged.

In fact, they are without plausible foundation. The data on which they are based do not support them, and are themselves of dubious origin. Again, that is not to say that the estimates are wrong, but the government's claim to have even a rough estimate of the level of expenditures on illicit drugs is simply unreasonable.

Consider the number for annual marijuana expenditures, which NNICC estimated at $18.3 billion to $26.8 billion in 1980 (the estimated quantity consumed was 10,200 to 15,000 metric tons). Given that the possession of small quantities of the drug is not subject to criminal sanction for about one-third of the population, and that there is truly a mass market for marijuana, household survey data may provide a reasonable base for estimating the amount of marijuana consumed. Together with price data, surely obtainable since the police arrest about 400,000 persons annually for marijuana possession or sale, one might then have a rough estimate of the total expenditures for marijuana.

Reconstructing the Estimate

It is extremely difficult to reconstruct the method used by NNICC to produce its estimate. The detail provided in the published documents is inadequate. I have relied on a draft of a forthcoming publication sponsored by one of the agencies represented on NNICC. The NNICC estimate is based on a national household survey carried out about every second year. That survey provides little detail about marijuana use beyond very broad categorizations of frequency of use. However, an annual survey of high school seniors, conducted by the University of Michigan, provides much more detailed information about marijuana use by respondents. With only mildly heroic assumptions, it is possible to use the high school senior data together with household survey data to produce an estimate of total marijuana consumption. The result of doing that produces an estimate of total consumption of about 4,200 metric tons for 1982, barely 40 percent of the bottom of the official estimate range. The revenue yielded by this quantity is estimated at about $4.9 billion, about 25 percent of the lower end of the official estimate.

The differences between the survey estimate and the official figures arise mainly from assumptions about the amount of marijuana in a cigarette and the price paid by regular heavy users. The government assumes that the amount of marijuana in a cigarette has remained constant over a long period, during which the average potency of marijuana has risen very rapidly. The best available data (which are not very good) show that the weight of marijuana in each joint has in fact declined by about 2 percent in the period 1976 to 1982. The government also assumes that heavy users pay the full retail price, though it is likely that heavy users, by buying in quantity (four or more ounces at a time), are able to buy at a substantially lower price.

The $4.9 billion estimate from the survey data should not be taken too seriously. Analyses of self-report data on consumption of substances about whose use people are sensitive, such as alcohol and tobacco, indicate that non-response, underreporting, and the like lead to substantial underestimates of total consumption from survey data. The figure may be closer to $7 billion or $8 billion; it is surely not as high as $20 billion.

Sales and Purity

The estimate for cocaine, the largest item in the 1980 NNICC revenue estimates, at $29 billion, assumes that cocaine is sold at 30 percent purity. In fact, as the IRS pointed out in its dissent, that is the wholesale purity; at retail, purity is closer to 12 percent. Given the method used by NNICC for making its estimates, this error alone raises the estimate 150 percent above its plausible value. A number of other assumptions identified by the IRS in its dissent from the 1980 estimate show that the NNICC figure is again almost four times its plausible value.

The heroin figure starts with the assumption of 500,000 addicts, which I have already suggested is almost certainly much too high. The estimated consumption levels for individual addicts, divided into three classes, seem too high. According to the NNICC numbers there are almost 150,000 addicts who, during the two-thirds of the time they are on the street, spend $100 per day on heroin. The theft requirement to support that habit is highly implausible.

'Street Value' Estimates Considered Unreliable

When a law enforcement agency puts a dollar value on the amount of drugs seized in narcotics raids, how good are the numbers? Discussions with law enforcement officials—including those who put out these numbers—indicate that they should be treated with extreme skepticism. This is especially true when the "street value" is given for contraband confiscated in bulk quantities.

"Street value" is someone's computation of what the drugs theoretically would be worth once broken down into retail units. By the time various levels of profiteering and drug-cutting are factored in, a $10,000 transaction at the wholesale level may be reported by authorities as having a street value of $300,000 or more.

Criminal Justice Newsletter, April 15, 1985.

Singer noted in his original article that mythical numbers seemed to be characteristic of the study of crime, mentioning the wholly artificial figure for illegal gambling revenues cited by the Kefauver Committee in 1951. As in the case of heroin addict estimates, there have been refinements of the official estimates for gambling income. Though more elaborate, these figures are, alas, quite as unsound as the transparent guesses they replace. My own favorite mythical number is the figure for the number of compulsive gamblers, a number that circulated in several official documents during the late 1960s and early 1970s. The figure, ten million, seems to have been based on a late-night phone call to a Gamblers Anonymous hotline, made by a desperate government official who needed a number to fill out a table on the social costs of various behavioral disorders. The number disappeared after a while for lack of documentable provenance, but it did enjoy modest celebrity for a few years.

No doubt there have always been mythical numbers in the world, numbers that satisfy some deep-seated urge to be able to fix the size of the "enemy," internal or external. Greek citizens may really have believed that Xerxes had an army of one million when he invaded their country, even if modern scholarship has shown that this would have been far beyond his logistical capacity. But it is surely not too much to ask that the myth-making be kept an activity of the informal sector and that the government stick to providing estimates only when it has some reasonable basis and need for doing so.

Absence of Criticism

Why are numbers like estimates of the heroin addict population allowed to circulate without criticism? I think at least three factors help explain this phenomenon. First, there is no constituency for keeping the numbers accurate, while there is a large constituency for keeping them high. The broad concensus that the drug traffic is evil simply exacerbates the problem, even when people disagree on the best approach for overcoming that evil. For example, some feel that the answer is legalization, at least of marijuana. Nonetheless it is in their interest to see that the numbers on current traffic stay high, since the numbers bolster their argument by suggesting the immensity of the existing problem. For the much larger groups who want more rigorous law enforcement or more treatment and prevention programs, the high income figures are additional evidence of the seriousness of the situation and the need for further efforts. It is hard to identify an organized constituency, apart from drug dealers, who might benefit from a lower estimate. The agency members of NNICC, who might at least seek to give the estimates a downward trend in order to show success, seem more satisfied to have a high number to justify their budgets. The Internal Revenue Service's recent enthusiasm for getting the numbers down, closer to the true value, may be explained, in part, by the fact that its budget is little affected by the size of the drug problem.

Data Is Scarce

The second factor explaining the wide circulation of these estimates is the lack of any systematic scholarly interest in the whole issue. The literature on drug dealing, as opposed to drug use and the relationship between drug use and crime, is extremely slender. There are few outside the federal government who have involved themselves in the estimation problems associated with drug markets. The agencies have not been very willing to provide data. Indeed, DEA has discontinued publication of some of its major series, making research even more difficult. The Associate Attorney General's claim that the South Florida Task Force had managed to raise the price of cocaine was refuted when an innocent DEA official unwittingly released data showing that the price seemed to have dropped. This price series used to be published openly; now it is obtainable only through the indiscretion of government officials.

The third factor is the most fundamental. The numbers have almost no policy consequence. It is certainly hard to identify any policy measure that rests on the estimate that the marijuana market generates $20 billion rather than $7 billion. The size of the government's expenditures on drug treatment or law enforcement is certainly not driven by such numbers. Nowhere is there evidence that calculations are made of the marginal return from investing additional government resources on drug problems, in terms of the effect of expenditures on the scale of drug market incomes.

But movements in these numbers do have some significance. A rise in the official estimate of the number of addicts has often been a major tool in pressing for expanded drug treatment programs. The announcement that drug market incomes have increased by over one-third is a rallying point for those seeking additional funds for drug law enforcement. It is impressive that in December 1982, during a period of great budgetary austerity, President Reagan was able to obtain an additional appropriation of $127 million for new regional drug task forces. These task forces are almost certain to make most of their cases against marijuana and cocaine dealers, rather than heroin dealers, and the purported increase in the income generated by these markets in recent years certainly played a role in mobilizing Congressional support for the request.

The Perceived Drug Problem

NNICC is sufficiently concerned about the quality of its earlier drug revenue estimates that, in preparing a report on 1981, it decided to omit dollar estimates, though not quantity estimates, until a more serious analysis could be carried out. It will be interesting to see the consequences of a substantial downward revision in the numbers, which is the likely outcome of a more serious effort. My own guess is that the major agencies involved in preparation of the estimates will be embarrassed but that there will be no substantive change in law or policy. The drug problem is perceived as big; its actual size is irrelevant to the government's response to it.

This may be taken as further evidence for the proposition that the quality of official data is largely a function of its importance to those who use it. The actual size of the heroin addict population and of drug market incomes is simply not important either to the agencies that prepare the estimates or to any other organized group. Numbers without purpose are numbers without quality.

173

"All you've read and heard about in the peanut-gallery media is the monumental and heroic efforts of the Colombian government to chase all the cocaine mafiosi out of their country."

Cocaine Use Is Sensationalized

Dean Latimer

Dean Latimer is executive editor of *High Times,* a monthly magazine devoted to relaxing public attitudes toward drug use. Latimer claims that the media and government attitudes toward cocaine are misinformed and misdirected. In the following viewpoint, Mr. Latimer holds that the media is deliberately exaggerating cocaine's dangers to rally support for the government's international drug wars.

As you read, consider the following questions:

1. According to the author, what is the "real" danger of cocaine?
2. What does the author believe is the political dilemma of cocaine-producing countries?
3. Does Mr. Latimer portray all cocaine users as potential addicts?

Dean Latimer, "Cocaine '85: The Pleasures and Perils of 'the All-American Drug,'" *High Times,* March 1985. Reprinted with permission.

Here's Dr. Donald Ian Macdonald, newly nominated by President Reagan to head up the entire federal Alcohol, Drug Abuse and Mental Health Administration (ADAMHA), addressing the annual convention of the National Federation of Parents for Drug-Free Youth in Washington late last year:

"All over the country, I hear the cocaine story. What's happening with this drug? I don't think we know. We do know that more people are showing up in the emergency room. We do know that more people are dying.

"What we have begun to think is that it takes about five years after a person begins using cocaine before that person shows up in the emergency room. Cocaine usually is preceded by marijuana use.

"If that's what is happening, maybe things will get better, because we are now five or six years beyond that 1978 marijuana peak [among high-school seniors]. The price of cocaine has gone down, and now it is going up again. It's being sold now in capsules. We do need to know more about cocaine."

Knowledge Needed

Dr. Macdonald, who is a pediatrician from Clearwater, Florida, will be administering the funds and directing the research of all the federal goverment's "abuse" services for the next four years, pending his rubber-stamp confirmation in the Senate this spring. He pretty obviously *does* need to learn a great deal about cocaine, if he believes there's something especially menacing about cocaine appearing on the street in deceptive, pharmaceutical-looking capsules, for oral ingestion. (Nobody swallows cocaine in capsules, Dr. Macdonald; absorption of cocaine through the gastrointestinal tract is lousy, erratic and undependable. The capsules are busted *open*, y'see, and then the coke is *snorted,* like usual.) He also obviously believes that marijuana-smoking leads to cocaine-snorting, so that if we can just keep the kids off pot, the coke trade will dry up and blow away. And he assumes automatically that anyone who uses this mysterious drug is doomed to experience a sudden life-threatening crisis of some sort within five years after initiation.

Dr. Macdonald makes a good audience, then. He is exactly as ignorant as most other people in the world about cocaine, and exactly as puzzled when he hears all these horror stories in the cocaine-crazed popular media. There obviously does really and truly exist a Grave Problem in our country today, involving more people than ever before doing more cocaine than ever before, and doing it in ways that are bad for their health. This is a very legitimate focus of public concern. Since the new ADAMHA director is now learning about cocaine from absolute scratch—from a little *less* than absolute scratch—just like everyone else in the land, I hope he will find the following analysis useful for his inquiries.

But I have to warn him, cocaine's really *not* like marijuana at all. In this case, the truth behind the media scare campaign is just about as frightening as the scare stories themselves. As Paul Krassner said once, "The truth does not necessarily make you free."

The Cocaine Glut

There used to be a myth—assiduously promulgated for years and years by all the best official sources, from NIDA to the DEA—that the cocaine-yielding coca plant grew only at remote, restrictive altitudes in the Andes. *Coca erythroxylon* and *novogranatense* were mountain shrubs, not tropical plants, we were all told. If we merely watch those Andean countries closely—Peru, Bolivia, Colombia—we can control cocaine production.

We were being lied to, by golly.

Cocaine Deaths Are Rare

Sigmund Freud was among many creative individuals to shout the praises of cocaine. The drug, he and others have said, produces a sense of intense stimulation, psychic and physical well being and reduced fatigue. Over the past century, cocaine has been used not only for the above effects but also for medical, mainly anesthetic, purposes as well....

Data from several nationwide surveys shows that among persons 12 years old and up, 3 to 4 percent said they had tried cocaine and fewer than 1 percent said they had taken the drug within the month prior to the survey. In the 18 to 25-year-old group, the peak age group for all illicit drug use, 13.4 percent said they had tried cocaine, 2 percent within a month of the survey. Cocaine figured only rarely in cases of drug-related deaths and was seen infrequently in emergency room drug cases.

Science News, July 16, 1977.

Coca grows just fine down in the South American jungles, and just about everywhere else in the world. That was discovered in the late '70s, when wholesale Bolivian coca agriculture spread down out of the mountains to the desolate lowlands of Beni Department, the Amazonian watershed on the eastern border with Brazil. The new Beni producers, such as celebrated neofascist Roberto Suarez, made so much money that they took over the whole Bolivian government in 1980 for two years of fascist terror and global dope-dealing. And now coca's being grown all over Brazil, and Venezuela and Argentina too, according to the State Department's Bureau of International Narcotics Matters (the only trustworthy narco outfit in the whole government, ADAMHA not exluded).

Sure, sure—all you've read and heard about in the peanut-gallery media is the monumental and heroic efforts of the Colombian government to chase all the cocaine mafiosi out of their country. This is true, and it's a genuinely historical achievement for Colombia. But the advantage to the United States is minimal, because of all this new coca husbandry in Brazil and Argentina, nations which, like Bolivia, are so impossibly in eternal debt to global institutions like the International Monetary Fund that illegal dope money is the only money that can be made and *kept* there.

The result is more cocaine in the world than ever before. In the process of chasing out those narco-mafiosi last spring, Colombian authorities discovered a coke-lab complex along the Yari River that was stockpiling 13.5 *tons* of finished cocaine hydrochloride. That was more coke in one bust than the total of all cocaine seizures in previous law-enforcement history. And even though the whole 13.5 tons was diligently destroyed, it did not *nudge* the price of coke on the street in the United States. More coke than ever before has been coming in, all year long. Rural Louisiana is currently the preferred drop zone for all these tons of reinforcing contraband; parish sheriffs there report that while they were lucky to bust an occasional gram of coke just a couple of years ago, nowadays they're snaring it by multiples of kilos. It is possible that all this portends broad new changes in patterns of individual cocaine use.

Getting High

Dr. Mitch Rosenthal, director of the Phoenix House detox-and-rehab center in New York City (funded only partially through ADAMHA), has the handle on it already. "Today, more than 36 percent of the population has used an illicit drug," says Dr. Rosenthal. "It is no longer a phenomenon of the minority poor, the underclass. Over 20 years, there has been a de facto decriminalization of drug use. Our culture, in effect, has said, if you want to get high, then get high."

That's true, Dr. Macdonald, we did say that. We still say it, too.

Dr. Arnold Washton of Regent Hospital in New York, co-proprietor of the famous 800-COCAINE "helpline," has the handle on it himself: "What we have is the baby boom of World War Two that has shifted from marijuana to cocaine."

Even *women,* who traditionally have stayed shy of hard-core drug stuff (in white North American society, anyhow), are into this cocaine nastiness, Washton recently advised an appalled President's Commission on Organized Crime. "Women are being introduced to cocaine through courtships," Dr. Washton told the Commission. "Instead of candy or roses, men bring cocaine as a gift." That's a top New York City *psychiatrist* talking there, Dr. Macdonald! And he says the percentage of women calling his "helpline" has risen from one-third to almost one-half *in just one year.*

Benjamin Ward, police commissioner of the selfsame city—

177

where all historic drug trends seem still to originate, even before they manifest in Miami—is *getting* the handle on it. The price of cocaine at the wholesale level in New York totally caved in between 1981 and 1984, from nearly $100,000 a kilogram to barely $40,000. Although the city's established rich and trendy "end consumers" are still, as always, paying around $100 per aggregate gram, a gram today is nearly 40 percent cocaine, whereas four years ago it was barely 10 percent coke. (The rest is called "the step" or "the cut," Dr. Macdonald: mannitol, procaine, inositol or phenylpropanolamine, with just a *trace* of Borax for that tell-tale cocaine odor.) This means that the sort of cocaine which was formerly available strictly to well-heeled high-society types in rich and trendy circles is now equally available to every cabdriver, bistro waitress, housewife, and—yes—school kid in town. And if that's happening in New York this year, Dr. Macdonald, then in four more years it'll be happening in Sioux Falls and Pocatello—white kids on freebase, Dr. Macdonald! Police Commissioner Benjamin Ward's reaction?

Street Drugs

"New York City does not produce the drugs that are sold on its streets," he says. "The coca plant does not grow in Brooklyn. The opium poppy does not grow in the Bronx. There are no fields of marijuana in Central Park. If the federal government had used its enormous power to prevail on those countries that cultivate drug crops, cities like New York would not have to combat these drugs on the street."

A Calm Analysis

Cocaine use is likened to an epidemic, prompting calls for tougher laws—though we already have the world's toughest drug laws.

It is time for some calm analysis. Cocaine madness, like "reefer madness," is based on misunderstanding.

This is not to say that cocaine cannot be dangerous. It, and many other things, including salt, coffee, tobacco and alcohol, can be dangerous if misused. But each can be used in moderation.

Sheldon L. Richman, *USA Today,* June 7, 1984.

There it is, Dr. Macdonald: the Police Commissioner of New York City (a Democratic Party fief) wants to know, implicity, how Ronald Reagan let the price of coke drop through the floor during his first term, and what the feds propose to do about it before the '88 elections. This is exactly the sort of complicated headache which ADAMHA directors have to grapple with all the time.

It gets just unmercifully complicated, too. You can't blithely call for sending the United States Marine Corps into those cocaine-producing countries—although that approach has many powerful political adherents—because they're all on our side, traditionally, against the Communist Menace. Although Peru and Bolivia have nominally "socialist" governments at the moment, they were elected by the democratic process, and they shun Moscow and Peking and Cuba religiously. As for Colombia, it's our staunchest and most effective ally in that whole part of the world. But all these governments are pretty shaky, because their economies are all shot to hell, and have been that way for as long as anyone there can remember. Sending in *Yanqui* troops for any reason would only guarantee violent revolution, and wouldn't Dr. Castro in Havana just love *that?*

Crop Substitution

If the ol' send-in-the-Marines ploy isn't the answer—and it obviously isn't, not even for the war-mongering Reaganauts—then what *can* be done to eliminate cocaine at the source? Well, "crop substitution" is a popular dodge, in which US AID funds are used to introduce coca-growing peasants to alternative forms of legal tillage: soybeans, cotton, peanuts, corn and so on. The reason coca can be so profitably grown 'way back in the boonies, y'see, is because the coca leaf-paste is wonderfully compact and transportable. Immensely profitable bundles of it can be easily flown, mule-trained, or canoed out of the bush to the final refining labs. You can't do that with soybeans or cotton or anything else that's nutritious and legal, because it's just too bulky. So we not only have to teach the *campesinos* how to grow all this new legal herbiage, but we have to put in roads and fuel depots and airstrips back in the bush there. (And the *narcotraficantes* move dope on these new roads.) But the *real* job comes when we finally have to persuade the country's established, traditional commodities marketers—the *haciendado* clans who run the corn and peanut and cotton companies—to accept free-market competition from these upstart bush peasants. At that point, overnight, the country's most trusted media invariably expose US AID's crop-sub programs as a big subversive Communist plot.

The current "socialist" government of Hernan Siles Zuazo in La Paz, Bolivia for instance, currently repudiates crop-substitution money from the United States. Siles Zuazo has developed an understandably jaundiced view of U.S. antinarcotics initiatives ever since last summer, when a gang of DEA-trained civilian narcs called "Los Leopardos" kidnapped him out of his own palace one early morning, as part of a botched right-wing coup attempt. The DEA's thinking had been that since Bolivian cops only make around $25 a month, they're useless against well-heeled snort movers, unless they can be "motivated" properly. So the DEA put together this crack, crisply-uniformed squad of incorruptible young stormtroopers, trained by all the best behavior-modification methods, and set them to kicking down doors and roughing people up around the upland growing region. Los Leopardos did less than nothing about coke kingpin Roberto Suarez and his private army down in the *Yungas,* harvesting untold tons of coca leaves four times a year, year in and year out; but these snappy young goosesteppers sure *looked* like they were doing something important, and the pop media back in the USA just loved them to pieces. Then one morning last July they kidnapped the 70-year-old president of *their own country,* and broke one of his ribs in the process, and held him for a whole agonizing day with a gun at his head, until U.S. Ambassador Edwin Corr negotiated his release and turned off the coup. So the Bolivians aren't even accepting our useless crop-sub money, for the time being.

Cash Crop

Meanwhile, Roberto Suarez still has most of the Beni—and now a good deal of the upland *Chepare* region—under coca, plucking four multi-billion-dollar harvests every single year. Jaime Paz Zamora, Siles' vice-president, gloomily tells *The New York Times:* "Basic logic indicates that half our foreign exchange comes from the coca. The real central bank of Bolivia isn't in La Paz. It's in the *Chepare.*"

The Media and Cocaine

The responsibility of the media and academics is more straightforward: to tell as much of the truth as possible to whoever will listen. The truth is that, on balance, our enemies are no deeper in the [cocaine] drug trade than are our friends, and the whole thing doesn't matter nearly as much as some people think it does.

Mark Kleiman, The *Wall Street Journal,* April 9, 1985.

Siles and Paz Zamora last year briefly floated this rather complicated idea: suppose the La Paz government were to buy up all the coca from Suarez some harvest season, and simply *burn* nearly all of it? Thus, most of the coca in the world would be eradicated, no? The little they would spare could be infused into low-proof, quality-controlled coca beverages, like the original Coca-Cola or Vin Mariani wine. Since that would then be virtually *all* the cocaine in the whole world, the revenues it would generate on the international gourmet-beverage market could be used to buy up Roberto Suarez' *next* coca crop. And so on, yes? No. *The New York Times* itself reacted with righteous horror to this suggestion that any "legal" form of coca should ever be suffered to desecrate the free marketplace. (Think of the children, Dr. Macdonald!) Also, the socialist La Paz parliament officially voted to censure President Siles for even thinking of *talking* to that murdering fascist Suarez. Siles went on a public hunger strike to protest the censure, and another coke-stopping scheme went down the tubes....

The New Cocaine Addict

You hear about these new cocaine addicts everywhere, even in HIGH TIMES last month: "Among cocaine users, it is estimated that roughly ten percent will become cocaine addicts." (Dr. David Smith and Richard Seymour, "Addiction In The '80s," HIGH TIMES *Abuse Folio*, February, 1985.)

Of course, Smith and Seymour of the Haight-Ashbury Free Medical Clinic were good enough to explain, in the same piece, how this term "addiction" has been radically altered in its official definition over just the last five years, so that it now conveniently comprises any conceivable sort of repetitive "bad" behavior, from alcoholism to gambling to enema fetishism. A cocaine "addict" is not the same thing as your traditional skag junkie, and the problem is not the same problem. However, although the word's definition has radically altered, its mass-media *connotations* are the same as ever. An "addict" is a sick, pathetic, evil, cunning, worthless, threatening, contemptible, murdering, thieving, swindling, suffering, hopeless automaton: a *golem* nightmare figure conjured up to evoke all your deepest childhood fears and hatreds. The only new thing about it is that cocaine has now been elected to serve, with heroin, as the magic drug instrument which transmutes worthwhile human beings into social Frankensteins. In fact, cocaine is now being touted as a *better* instrument for this purpose than heroin ever was. Some influential researchers and government spokespersons are already telling coffee-time news anchorwomen that cocaine does this awful thing to people *whether they want to be addicts or not!*

The Danger of Freebasing

As coke gets cheaper and more widely available, people everywhere are tempted to go for the hard-core high of freebasing or shooting up. *Everything* changes after that.

In the 1977 NIDA report on cocaine, otherwise-thoughtful researchers rashly insinuated that there might be sort of a built-in safety factor to snorting little pinches of expensive and highly-adulterated cocaine. You can't get a whole lot of coke into your bloodstream all at once by insufflating it through the limited absorption surface provided by the tiny blood vesicles in your nasal mucosa. Thus you enjoy nothing close to the true intravenous or freebase *rush* (what passes for a "rush" after snorting is a relatively gentle escalation of mood), which qualifies as the instantest gratification possible. And just so, there's no instant, post-snort rollercoaster down into depression and aggravated drug-craving ("The Cocaine Blues") to further reinforce instant and incessant self-administration. Snorting, then, is a comparatively safe, and even relatively elegant way to self-administer this drug. If you're going to try it once, you could do worse than to try it in this fashion, and *never* in any other fashion.

Freebasing is something else again. As we have stated repeatedly in *High Times,* Dr. Macdonald, freebasing is a really splendid way to overdose dead on cocaine. Freebase, y'see, is simply ordinary snortable salt cocaine (cocaine hydrochloride) which has been converted into a sort of confectioner-sugar texture by simple chemical processes. This flaky freebase, being burnable, is put into a metal pipe, which is heated with a blowtorch, and the abuser inhales the fumes. The volatilized cocaine is taken into the bloodstream through yards and yards of alveolar lung tissue, and goes directly up to the brain, where it makes users just *intensely* high; in fact, it's called a "rush." This "rush" only lasts about 20 seconds, though, and is instantly followed by such a rapid dump-down of spirits that—well, real sophisticated, civilized people can get pretty *embarrassing* behind freebase, grappling for the pipe, begging for it, promising obscene sexual favors for another hit. . . .

So in the final analysis, cocaine compulsion may after all qualify as a less spurious type of "addiction" than enema fetishism. This whole aggravated syndrome of coke tolerance and withdrawal symptoms has only appeared in a few extremely well-heeled freebasers and toot-shooters so far, to be sure; people who can afford to *fress* up multiples of grams of pure coke every day, at contemporary cocaine prices.

"Only in recent months have many health officials and scores of thousands of users been forced to face up to the true deceptive and enslaving nature of cocaine."

Cocaine Use Is Not Sensationalized

Donald D. Schroeder

Donald D. Schroeder is a senior writer in news research and analysis at *The Plain Truth* magazine, a monthly religious magazaine of conservative opinion. He has been a staff member since 1959. In the following viewpoint, Mr. Schroeder claims that the number of deaths from cocaine is steadily growing because the use of cocaine is spreading.

As you read, consider the following questions:
1. The author claims that cocaine is the most dangerous drug in use. Upon what does he place this claim?
2. According to the author, how do cocaine users die from using the drug?
3. What are some well-known examples of cocaine addiction that Mr. Schroeder illustrates?

A great human tragedy is in the making!

For the second time within a century, cocaine—the white powder crystallized from coca leaves—has exploded into a major social and public health crisis in human affairs. . . .

Early Drug Experiments

The first popularizing of the drug began in the 1880s. The psychoanalyst Sigmund Freud experimented with cocaine. He praised it for the euphoric feelings of vigor, sense of power and confidence it gave him. Other prominent physicians and popular personalities promoted it. (Later, Freud publicly admitted cocaine injections produced rapid physical and mental deterioration, paranoia and hallucinations.)

By the turn of the century, cocaine's aura of innocence was gone. What was the effect on the many who had indulged? In 1924, Dr. Louis Lewin wrote: "I have seen among men of science frightful symptoms due to the craving for cocaine. Those who believe they can enter the temple of happiness through this gate of pleasure purchase their momentary delights at the cost of body and soul. They speedily pass through the gate of unhappiness into the night of the abyss" (Cocaine Papers—Sigmund Freud, by R. Byck, 1974).

Early in this century, after numerous cocaine tragedies, the drug was prohibited by law in many nations, except for medical use. Various other addicting opiate drugs were also prohibited.

But humanity, inundated by the do-your-own-thing philosophy and drug culture of the post-World War II era, failed to remember the tragic drug errors of the past, or even recent human experience.

A Pattern of Use

Again in the last few decades, cocaine use—as also marijuana— has followed the pattern of the earlier introduction. Cocaine has been widely proclaimed to be a relatively safe recreational drug in moderate use, even by some medical and scientific personnel.

Cocaine (in street terms also called coke, snow, flake or toot) is most commonly snorted through the nostrils to achieve a euphoric high, but it can also be eaten, smoked or injected.

Until recent months, cocaine advocates told us (and some still do) that coke is a relatively risk-free drug. "A snort in each nostril and you're up and away for 30 minutes or so. No hang-over. No physical addiction. No lung cancer. No holes in the arm or burned out cells in the brain," they said. Instead users were guaranteed drive, sparkle, energy.

But the truth is far different! Only in recent months have many health officials and scores of thousands of users been forced to face up to the true deceptive and enslaving nature of cocaine. This is a drug that causes a craving dependency and addiction more severe than heroin and other addicting drugs.

Cocaine is now regarded by many drug experts as the most subtle and dangerous drug ever to enslave and destroy human lives!

"It [cocaine] probably produces the most tenacious dependency of all the chemicals on this planet that you can give the human brain," says Ron Siegel, a University of California at Los Angeles psychopharmacologist and one of the nation's leading cocaine researchers.

Cocaine is now considered by Dr. Siegel and many other drug experts as the *most addictive* of drugs in terms of its psychological and, in many advanced cases, physical grip on hooked users.

Dr. Mark S. Gold, medical director of the National Cocaine Hotline, strongly refutes the common erroneous belief that cocaine is nonaddicting and nonthreatening to life and health.

The Third Time Around

The irony of the cocaine story in the 1980s is that this is the third time around for cocaine in America. This is the third time Americans have undertaken a disastrous flirtation with this drug. Now, apparently forgetting those earlier unhappy experiences, a whole new generation of Americans is discovering cocaine and repeating the same old tragedies: the lost hopes, the broken lives, the deaths. In 1982, more than 22 million Americans had used cocaine at least once, and more than four million had used the drug during the month before the survey.

Robert L. DuPont Jr., *Getting Tough on Gateway Drugs*, 1984.

Says Dr. Gold, "The popular view today is that cocaine is a chic, safe drug, unlike heroin, that can be used without fear of addiction. But callers to our help line tell us they cannot stop even though they recognize that it is destroying their lives."

Cocaine Is a Killer

Contrary to popular belief among many users, cocaine is a killer, says Dr. Gold. Death can occur rapidly from convulsions, lung failure, stroke and even drowning in one's own internal secretions. "What's so devastating . . . is that we have found that there is a huge chunk of high functioning people who are getting into something they don't understand," says Dr. Gold. "They have acquired through repeated use a lifelong, debilitating, chronic illness for which there is treatment through remission and abstinence, but no known cure."

What has deceived many cocaine users is that *in early stages of repeated use* when one is deprived of the drug *it does not cause the classic withdrawal symptoms* of many addictive drugs—cramps, nausea or convulsions.

However, as the cocaine habit grows, the psychological addiction becomes so strong, the user's ability becomes so minimal, that the resulting damaging addictive cravings are equal to or worse than those caused by heroin or other addictive drugs. In long-term heavy users, classic physical withdrawal symptoms do occur.

Cocaine is now known to cause fatal convulsions, respiratory failure and cardiac collapse, even at moderate doses, in new or seasoned users. At high levels of use, or dependency levels, cocaine can induce psychosis and paranoia and suicidal desperation. Addiction and death can come from any method of use, but the danger is greatest with smoking (free-basing) or injection.

New Addicts

In recent years cocaine first became the popular drug-of-choice in upper and more affluent middle-class society—among doctors, lawyers, accountants, architects, entertainers, athletes and others with comfortable incomes.

Until recently, high cost (formerly more than $100 a gram) was a factor in limiting its use. It was a status drug only the near-rich and successful could afford. It was called the champagne of drugs because it was believed to be physically nonaddictive and harmless to health in moderate use.

Cocaine appealed to active and progressive middle- and upper-class moods and values. In sporadic use it didn't have the depressant or sedating effects of marijuana, the popular drug of the turned-off, dropped-out generation of rebellious youths. Nor the characteristics of heroin or hallucinogens, the opiates of social losers.

A Stimulant

Cocaine was a stimulant that brought almost instant euphoria from a simple snort or two through the nose, an intense feeling of energy, power and control. It seemed to magically create euphoric feelings of creativity, confidence, invincibility and also in some users give heightened erotic excitement.

Cocaine seemed the ideal drug to tune you into what is supposed to make success and happiness in modern affluent society. It seemed as if highly esteemed qualities of stamina, emotion and character could be achieved through the use of a harmless white powder used moderately.

Cocaine's effects lasted only from five to 30 minutes, sometimes a little longer, rather than hours like many other street or medical drugs. The initial short-term euphoria seemed something one could control. Many therefore reasoned, if for five minutes why not forever?

Snorters started out using cocaine recreationally at parties, celebrations, or privately for its quick euphoric "rush." Others started to use it occupationally—to keep up alertness, energy levels, and "creativeness" in their jobs. They felt they had to have something extra to give them an edge in competition with others in demanding or high-pressure jobs.

Short-Term Effect

But the short-term euphoric lift from a few brief snorts, the feeling of being confident and on the top of things, is quickly over. This

C.P. Houston, *Houston Chronicle.* Reprinted with permission.

high is often followed by a letdown and depression that can only be relieved by more snorts of cocaine. The stronger the stimulation the more pronounced the crash.

Once succumbing to the desire for continued euphoric high feelings, users wanted them more and more. Said one initiate, "After one hit of cocaine I feel like a new man. The only problem is, the first thing the new man wants is another hit."

Many cocaine users believe as long as they use coke they will have superlative sexual experiences. The facts are, repeated cocaine use eventually causes sexual dysfunction and impotence and other serious health problems.

Growing Female Addiction

In many Western nations, women are the largest users of licit drugs for personal and health reasons. Middle-class women haven't been, for the most part, attracted to illicit street drugs. But many women, aware of dangers with such drugs and also popular tranquilizers, have been captivated by the status appeal and false propaganda about cocaine. Middle-class women are now estimated to be around half of all cocaine addicts.

One professional woman with a successful career tearfully revealed how she had a loving husband, a beautiful daughter and a marvelous home. But she found her work and life filled with pressure. She was told by a friend that coke would help her face the world, so why not take advantage of it.

"Within four years, cocaine cost me my job, my husband, my self-respect, even my daughter," she confessed. "When my habit grew so I could no longer get enough from friends, I found a part-time dealer where I worked....One day I just exploded and walked away from everything."

Addicted in 30 Seconds

Another woman said after her first use of coke, "I was filled with the most incredible feeling I have ever known. It was absolute euphoria. I felt beautiful, sexy, important, totally in control and at the top of my world. What I didn't realize is that I had become addicted in those 30 seconds. From that moment on, my entire life was focused on cocaine."

A TV producer said, "I needed something to increase my physical endurance. But once you're hooked, you find all sorts of reasons for using it. You need coke to be more creative. Soon, you begin to develop this hip superiority. Everything you do is terrific."

But is the work really terrific? Medical authorities now confirm through controlled tests that cocaine is a *destroyer* of talent—not an enhancer. "Coke just gives users the *perception* of being more creative," says one famous Hollywood star. "The users think they are doing their best work, but they are literally giving you gibberish."

So widespread is cocaine use among TV and movie producers and actors that insiders say it is one reason for so many poor quality programs.

Coming Down

Coming down from a cocaine high commonly causes such deep gloom in many regular users that they feel impelled to use more cocaine as a remedy. Bigger doses often follow, and soon the urge becomes a total obsession. Medical personnel now report increasing numbers of cocaine addicts are turning to free-basing (smoking a purified form of cocaine) or intravenous injection in attempts to recapture some former euphoric high.

Cocaine addiction can happen quickly or take some time. Many users believe they can handle the drug if they use it sparingly and infrequently. But the catch is there is no way to know for sure who will become quickly addicted. Differences in individual constitutional chemistry can cause one person to become more rapidly addicted and crave the drug (or any drug) than another person using it similarly. And individual mind-set at time of use is very, very critical.

Surfacing Cocaine Dangers

The scope of the cocaine problem in terms of nonfatal overdoses, accidents, and other violent deaths is just beginning to surface. Cocaine was outlawed at the turn of the century because of the problems associated with its unrestricted use. History now repeats itself as we again realize its dangers.

Roger E. Mittleman and Charles V. Wetli, *Medical Aspects of Human Sexuality,* March 1985.

These persons often lack a background of proper adult example or training in control of emotions and alcohol or drugs. They automatically grab for and abuse any chemical substance that temporarily gives them a high and relieves them of their problems. Others lose control by using drugs or alcohol a little more and more.

Male cocaine addicts often turn to embezzlement and women addicts to prostitution. One woman says she would have done anything for cocaine—even killed for it.

Road to Financial Disaster

Accounts of financial ruination among successful people hooked on cocaine are numerous. Many middle-class and millionaire addicts have been reduced to ruin.

One middle-class woman secretly drew out thousands of dollars from the children's college educational fund to support her craving for cocaine, nearly ruining the children's educational opportunities.

An upper-middle-class businessman spent $1,200 a week on cocaine, but lost his business after five months. "I started having a lot of problems with people, yelling at customers.... I was taking my profits, selling my merchandise, selling my equipment, selling everything to buy coke. I've literally blown a fortune."

One rock star squandered millions of dollars on cocaine. It was "all smoked up," said a friend. A movie starlet spent a million dollars on cocaine before breaking her habit. By the time she sought help her body was wasted to less than a hundred pounds.

Another hooked female co-star of a popular TV situation comedy couldn't remember her lines or stand throughout a simple scene. She became like a cadaver and had to be fired....

Adulterants and Disease

Virtually all street cocaine is not pure. It is cut and adulterated many times over as it passes from dealer to dealer in order to increase profits. A user cannot possibly know what he or she is taking without elaborate tests. Dealer-users on the street often themselves cut their supplies (with who knows what) in order to finance their own drug habit. Frequently used to cut cocaine concentration is the simple sugar lactose.

Also commonly used as cheaper adulterants are lidocaine, procaine, caffeine, amphetamines (pep pills) and other drugs that give sensations similar to cocaine, but which can cause their own specific damages to human tissues and organs. "Injecting street cocaine is absolutely crazy," wrote one cocaine connoisseur.

The chronic cocaine sniffer is easy prey for bacterial infections in the nose and throat. This is because the cilia, the tiny hairlike filaments of the nose and respiratory organs, are paralyzed, inhibiting the proper flow of protective mucus to membranes. Many coke users seem to have perpetual colds, nagging infections or respiratory problems.

Cocaine also constricts the blood vessels that supply oxygen to living tissues. This constriction commonly causes an ulcer that wears through the cartilage between the nostrils, causing a large hole. Without cartilage the nose becomes misshapen. Sometimes the nose bridge of a coke addict becomes so weakened it collapses under pressure and has to be restored surgically.

A Racing Metabolism

Cocaine increases the heart and blood pressure. Persons with heart problems or high blood pressure, especially those who don't realize they have such conditions, could kill themselves by using cocaine. Coke races the metabolism. It rapidly burns energy and depletes critical vitamin and mineral reserves.

Heavy cocaine users risk cardiac arrest or convulsions, the latter a form of internal suffocation, because the victim cannot breathe fast enough to replace the oxygen being used up by the body.

Cocaine addicts often desperately try to reduce the comedown crash after use of the drug. Some combine it with sedating drugs like heroin (called speed-balling). This roller-coaster effect was the ride that killed John Belushi, the well-known American actor. Others try to escape the grip of cocaine by using alcohol cr other drugs, but instead become hooked on them.

Mixing cocaine with alcohol is particularly dangerous. Police report some heavy drinkers use cocaine to keep awake while they drive home. Unfortunately the coke often wears off midway home, causing the high alcohol content of the blood to suddenly produce a blackout and an accident.

Don't Make Others' Mistake

There is a reason why drug tragedy after drug tragedy hits our modern world! We live in a drug-inundated world. We have been bombarded by modern advertising, taught by social, perhaps even parental and peer examples to look to drugs to solve our mental and personal distresses. We have been led to believe that somewhere there is a magical pill or powder that will relieve us of all our pain and discomfort and make us happy again.

Drug after drug—illicit but also frequently licit—is ballyhooed as an effective way to cope with life—only to turn out after a period of use to be something that injures, afflicts with undesirable or tragic side effects, or even kills.

"I worry that in our zeal to protect some people from drug abuse we aren't damaging others who need tranquilizers desperately."

Tranquilizer Addiction Is Exaggerated

Seymour Rosenblatt and Reynolds Dodson

Seymour Rosenblatt is professor of psychiatry at Mount Sinai Hospital and chief of that institution's Affective Disorders and Lithium Clinic. He is in private practice in New York. Reynolds Dodson, a former magazine editor, has written articles that have appeared in many national periodicals. In the following viewpoint, Dr. Rosenblatt and Mr. Dodson justify the role of tranquilizers in drug therapy. They link the use of these drugs to a reduction in the number of hospitalized psychiatric patients.

As you read, consider the following questions:

1. According to the authors, what are the benefits of using tranquilizers such as Valium?
2. How do the authors explain the drop in Valium sales?
3. Do the authors think that tranquilizer abuse or alcohol abuse is a greater problem in society?

Seymour Rosenblatt and Reynolds Dodson, *Beyond Valium.* New York: G.P. Putnam's Sons, 1981. Reprinted with permission.

In the next twenty years humanity will witness one of the greatest revolutions in the history of medicine. Indeed, in many ways the revolution is already upon us. Television and newspapers worry about "Valiumania"; best-selling books denounce us as a "pill-popping culture"; feminists suggest the existence of a "conspiracy" in which tranquilizers are employed to perpetuate male "control."

As a psychopharmacologist—a "drug doctor," if you will—my life has been touched by much of this controversy. The first important psychoactive drug was discovered at about the time I began my career, and I have spent the last thirty years intimately involved in all phases of psychiatric drug treatment and research. It has been an exciting period. I have watched with satisfaction as countless millions have been released from hellholes of despair. I have seen men and women, their lives in shambles, miraculously rise from the ashes of depression. I have seen schizophrenics learn to communicate sensibly and manic-depressives put away thoughts of suicide. I have seen the emotionally disturbed begin to be treated like humans, admitted to hospitals instead of interned behind gray walls somewhere. It has been one of the most satisfying careers a person could follow.

Damaging Myths

But there has been a more negative, misunderstood side of my work, too. I have shared the public's alarm about drug abuse. I have watched mildly anxious people turn into addicts. I have seen legitimate drugs become perverted by our culture, turned into holy grails of euphoria which they were never intended to be. And I have felt frustrated. I have seen intelligent reporters, who should know better, spread the most damaging myths about drugs and their function; I have seen the half-baked notions of faddists and junkies become accepted as fact by an uneducated populace.

In view of this criticism and its effect upon my profession, I feel the time has come to set the record straight—to explain to people how drugs really work and the implications they have for the future. This will not be easy, for it is a very complex subject, an issue fraught with prejudice and emotionalism. I feel a little like the man explaining nuclear fission to the people living around Three Mile Island....

There is an impression that psychiatrists are "pill happy," that drugs, being unnatural, are inherently evil, that even the most benign of tranquilizers can weaken one's will or erode a user's spirit. There is a suspicion of doctors, a suspicion of drug companies, a suspicion of people who use tranquilizers to "cope" and, finally, a suspicion of America itself, whose culture is thought to have created this phenomenon.

Some of the charges are even more specific. Valium, the most

popular target, has been charged with everything from creating psychosis to destroying fetuses to being the equivalent of arsenic. There have been reports linking Valium to fatalities....Suffice it for now to say that they are not true, and they serve no useful purpose beyond scaring the wits out of people.

This is not to say that drugs are panaceas or that their widespread use is not a dangerous phenomenon. Indeed, they are dangerous, because people abuse them, and until recently we have had very little real knowledge of them. Betty Ford was right to warn women about pill dependency. Editorialists are correct to deplore the sale of "street drugs." I'll also admit that there are those in my profession who prescribe drugs too frequently and without proper knowledge of them....

In 1950, before the advent of psychoactive drugs, our state and county mental hospitals were filled to overflowing. We had 512,501 patients locked behind bars on a full-time basis. By 1975 this number had dropped to 193,436. That's a net reduction of about 62 percent, despite the increase in our population.

Within the same period deaths in those hospitals dropped from 41,280 to 13,401—a reduction of almost 67 percent. What makes these figures even more dramatic is that admissions were up almost two and a half times—from 152,286 to 376,156. This indicates that more people were being reached, if only on a short-term or revolving-door basis. This wouldn't have been possible without drug therapy, and certainly not through traditional analysis.

Simultaneously we are in the process of correcting our excesses, particularly in our usage of the so-called minor tranquilizers. We have seen a dramatic drop-off in both prescription rates and refills of these drugs, including Valium and Librium. According to Dr. Mitchell Balter, dean of statistics for the National Institute of Mental Health, overall sales of Valium-like substances have fallen almost 40 percent since the early seventies. Roche Laboratories, which produces Valium, reports a similar decline in the sale of their product—from a 1975 high of 61.3 million prescriptions to a 1979 low of 38.5 million.

This indicates a healthy trend—and perhaps an anticipatory response to the recent criticism. In other words, by the time the media got around to worrying about it, the tranquilizer fad had already subsided. . . .

Lost to Therapy

As a practicing psychiatrist, I worry that in our zeal to protect some people from drug abuse we aren't damaging others who need tranquilizers desperately. I have had anxious and depressed people come into my office who, if I took away their tranquilizers, would be lost to all therapy. They might steal tranquilizers, or they might take to alcohol, or they might lose their jobs, their families, their dignity. It is the same dilemma we faced with alcohol during Prohibition. And alcohol abuse in America today is a far bigger problem than our dependence on tranquilizers.

So even if Valium has some imperfect aspects, its positive effects remain a worthy objective. We need to understand anxiety better, and we need a substance that will ameliorate its ravages.

"Valium and its chemical relations are not at all the safe tension-relievers the drug-company promotional wizards would have us believe."

Tranquilizer Addiction Is Not Exaggerated

Public Citizen Health Research Group

Eve Bargmann, Signey M. Wolfe, Joan Levin and the staff of the Public Citizen Health Research Group are the authors of *Stopping Valium*, the book from which this viewpoint is excerpted. The authors seek to enlighten the public on what they perceive to be the addictiveness and overuse of Valium and other tranquilizers. In the following viewpoint, the authors warn of Valium's side effects and describe why they think that doctors overprescribe tranquilizers.

As you read, consider the following questions:

1. According to the authors, what is the most widely prescribed drug in the US?
2. The authors state their reasons for believing Valium is addicting. What are those reasons?
3. What do the authors claim are some of the side effects of taking Valium?

Stopping Valium, Washington, DC: The Public Citizen Health Research Group, 1982. Reprinted by permission.

Each day millions of white, yellow and blue Valium pills are pulled from American pockets, handbags, and medicine chests.

Each year from 1972 until 1980 (the last year for which reliable figures are available), Valium has been the most widely prescribed drug in the United States.

Sales of Valium and its chemical cousins, the benzodiazepines, have soared to phenomenal heights over the past 15 years, fueled by massive promotional efforts.

So successful have these campaigns been that today more than 10 million Americans are taking Valium or one of its chemical cousins. According to the Food and Drug Administration, 1.5 million people have taken these drugs long enough to be in serious danger of addiction.

Addiction? Yes! Because what few people know—though the word is getting out—is that Valium and its chemical relations are not at all the safe tension-relievers the drug-company promotional wizards would have us believe.

Tranquilizer Addiction

Addiction to Valium and similar drugs is a major problem in this country. Over 8,000 emergency room visits a year result from such addiction. And every year, 4,500 people who have taken Valium and similar drugs continuously for over 4 months may be addicted, but they may not know it because they have not stopped taking these drugs and therefore have not developed withdrawal symptoms. Many others have been treated by private doctors rather than by drug-treatment centers; and many who know or suspect that they are addicted may not yet have sought help.

If you told your doctor that you were anxious and he or she recommended that you treat it by drinking a pint of whiskey a day for the next six months, you would probably be shocked. Yet Valium and all benzodiazepines, like alcohol, are addicting drugs—and a prescription, especially one with refills, may give you enough to result in addiction.

Many people—including many doctors—do not realize that taking the *usually prescribed doses* of Valium and like drugs can result in addiction. Stopping Valium or any benzodiazepine abruptly after a few months or less of continuous use may result in withdrawal symptoms that range in severity from anxiety and inability to sleep to hallucinations and seizures.

Prescription for Addiction

Often a prescription for Valium amounts to a prescription for addiction. On the average, it contins 55 pills, enough for 20 days; in many cases, it can be refilled 5 times. This provides a 4-month supply of 330 pills—a potentially addicting dose. And just a phone call to the doctor can secure another 4 months' worth.

Addiction is just one of the dangers you face when you take Valium or any benzodiazepine. You need to know about these dangers if you take these drugs—or if you are even thinking about taking them.

A few of the costs of taking Valium and other benzodiazepines are:

• **Mental impairment:** Mental and physical abilities decline measurably in the majority of people who use Valium-type drugs. Memory and learning ability become predictably worse in people who have taken these drugs. Drowsiness, decreased coordination, and slowed reaction times are other frequent effects.

Overprescribing Tranquilizers

Abuse starts when a user continues to take the drugs regularly and indefinitely. Some doctors overprescribe the tranquilizers. They may be trying to help patients who suffer from complaints for which there is no simple medical cure. Or they may just be giving in to a patient's insistence on a supply of the drug. Some patients go to several physicians with the same complaint in order to obtain additional drugs. Others also find black market, illegal sources of the drugs.

In an average year an estimated one in every ten adults in the United States takes Valium or Librium. More than half, about 68 percent, are women. No one knows if this is because women have the greater need or because doctors are more inclined to prescribe tranquilizers for women than for men.

Gilda Berger, *Addiction: Its Causes, Problems, and Treatments,* 1982.

• **Impaired Driving:** Driving skills, such as braking ability, are significantly impaired after taking Valium-like drugs. People who have taken Valium or similar drugs are also more likely to have traffic accidents.

• **Confusion, hallucinations, paradoxical rage:** Some people have severe mental reactions due to Valium and other benzodiazepines. These are unusual, but they are also dangerous.

• **Addiction:** As already discussed, people taking prescribed doses of Valium or similar drugs can become physically, as well as psychologically, addicted.

• **Death:** Valium causes over 800 deaths a year. Over 300 of these are accidental overdoses, generally caused by taking Valium along with other drugs or alcohol....

Skillful Marketing

The high levels of stress and tension that Americans face have certainly helped the sales of anxiety-reducing drugs. But much of the success of these drugs, and especially the phenomenal success of Valium, is also the product of years of intense and skillful promotion. . . .

Aggressive marketing—including not only advertisements but also gifts to doctors, "medical education" of doctors by drug companies, and detailmen, the door-to-door salesmen of drug companies—has paid off handsomely for Valium's manufacturer. From 1972 on, Valium has been the top-selling prescription drug in America.

Coping Through Chemicals

> As things now stand, the tranquillizers may prevent some people from giving enough trouble, not only to their rulers, but even to themselves. Too much tension is a disease; but so it too little. There are certain occasions when we ought to be tense, when an excess of tranquillity (and especially of tranquillity imposed from the outside by a chemical) is entirely inappropriate.
>
> —Aldous Huxley, *Brave New World Revisited*

Tension is a symptom. Feeling anxious is a sign that something is wrong, either within you or in your situation. Prescribing Valium or any tranquilizer for a situational problem is like giving a man with a broken leg morphine for his pain and telling him to keep walking.

a critical thinking skill

Distinguishing Primary from Secondary Sources

A critical thinker must always question his or her source of knowledge. One way to critically evaluate information is to be able to distinguish between *primary sources* (a "firsthand" or eyewitness account from personal letters, documents, or speeches, etc.) and *secondary sources* (a "secondhand" account usually based upon a "firsthand" account and possibly appearing in newspapers, encyclopedias, or other similar types of publications). A diary about the Civil War written by a Civil War veteran is an example of a primary source. A history of the Civil War written many years after the war and relying, in part, upon that diary for information is an example of a secondary source.

However, it must be noted that interpretation and/or point of view also play a role when dealing with primary and secondary sources. For example, the historian writing about the Civil War not only will quote from the veteran's diary but also will interpret it. It is certainly a possibility that his or her interpretation may be incorrect. Even the diary or primary source must be questioned as to interpretation and point of view. The veteran may have been a militarist who stressed the glory of warfare rather than the human suffering involved.

This activity is designed to test your skill in evaluating sources of information. Pretend that you are writing a research paper on drug abuse. You decide to include an equal number of primary and secondary sources. Listed below are a number of sources which may be useful in your research. Carefully evaluate each of them. First, place a *P* next to those descriptions you feel would serve as primary sources. Second, rank the primary sources assigning the number (1) to the most objective and accurate primary source, number (2) to the next accurate and so on until the ranking is finished. Repeat the entire procedure, this time placing an *S* next to those descriptions you feel would serve as secondary sources and then ranking them.

If you are doing this activity as a member of a class or group, discuss and compare your evaluation with other members of the group. If you are reading this book alone, you may want to ask others if they agree with your evaluation. Either way, you will find the interaction very valuable.

1. A study of career criminals by researchers at the Rand Corporation.

2. A TV documentary about drug abuse in the nation's cities.

3. An estimate by the National Narcotics Intelligence Consumers Committee for total income from illegal drug sales.

4. A feature story in *Time* magazine concerning drug addiction.

5. A poem describing cocaine paranoia written by a cocaine addict.

6. Pulitzer-prize winning articles by a newspaper reporter describing the horrors of heroin addiction in children.

7. A book by a pediatrician in charge of the federal Alcohol, Drug Abuse, and Mental Health Administration in which he warns about the dangers of cocaine addiction.

8. An eyewitness account of drug addicts and crime by a city policeman.

9. Papers by Sigmund Freud in the 1880s about his experiments with cocaine.

10. Viewpoint five in this chapter.

11. The autobiography of television journalist Barbara Gordon describing her addiction to valium.

Periodical Bibliography

The following list of periodical articles deals with the subject matter of this chapter.

Joel Brinkley	"The War on Narcotics: Can it Be Won?" *The New York Times,* September 14, 1984.
Jane E. Brody	"Personal Health," *The New York Times,* May 23, 1984.
Jean Cobb	"Heroin in Hospitals," *Common Cause Magazine,* November/December 1984.
Department of State Bulletin	"International Narcotics Control," October 1984.
Pico Iyer	"Fighting the Cocaine Wars," *Time,* February 25, 1985.
Edward I. Koch	"Needed: Federal Antidrug Aid," *The New York Times,* April 27, 1984.
John E. LeMoult	"Legalize Drugs," *The New York Times,* June 15, 1984.
Peggy Mann	"Danger: Drugged Drivers," *Reader's Digest,* October 1984.
Gina Maranto	"Coke: The Random Killer," *Discover,* March 1985.
John McCaslin	"Search for a Solution Goes On, but U.S. Drug Traffic Worsens," *Washington Times,* March 7, 1985.
The New Republic	"The Dope Dilemma," April 15, 1985.
Craig Pyes and Laurie Becklund	"Inside Dope in El Salvador," *The New Republic,* April 15, 1985..
Charles B. Rangel	"Drug Traffic Can—and Must—Be Curbed," *USA Today,* May 1984.
Richard M. Ritter	"PPA: Diet Drug Under Fire," *Psychology Today,* December 1984.
Jack Shafer	"Designer Drugs," *Science '85,* March 1985.
Elaine Shannon	"The Asian Connection," *Newsweek,* June 25, 1984.
Anastasia Toufexis	"Linking Drugs to the Dinner Table," *Time,* September 24, 1984.
Claudia Wallis	"Heroin, a Doctor's Dilemma," *Time,* June 11, 1984.

CHAPTER

6

How Should Drug Addiction Be Treated?

CHEMICAL DEPEN- DENCY

"(Cocaine users) would benefit greatly from a substantially increased fear of punishment."

Cocaine Users Should Be Punished

Jody Powell

Jody Powell, former press secretary for the Carter administration, is a syndicated columnist in Washington. His knowledge of how the press and the power structure work brings a unique perspective to his writing. In the following viewpoint, Mr. Powell claims that severe punishment for cocaine *suppliers* and not for cocaine *users* has allowed cocaine addiction to spread dramatically in the US.

As you read, consider the following questions:

1. According to the author, what are some of the effects of fighting the cocaine drug war at the source?
2. Where does Mr. Powell suggest that the drug war be fought?
3. How does the author explain the cocaine user's criminal role?

Jody Powell, "End the Immunity for Cocaine Users," Jody Powell, © 1985, Dallas Times Herald. Reprinted with permission, Los Angeles Times Syndicate.

The news magazines have made it official, as they did with AIDS, herpes, the deficit and the Beatles—our society is facing a crisis. This time it is called cocaine.

As many as 10 million Americans use the powerfully addictive drug at least once a month, and 5,000 use it for the first time each and every day. We now purchase in excess of 80 tons of cocaine every year, and the figure is climbing.

Attempts to halt the flow have produced friction with our neighbors in that already troubled region to the south and turmoil in already less-than-stable governments. There are reliable reports that the Marxist government in Nicaragua and conservative officers of the Panamanian defense forces have become involved in the unbelievably lucrative trade. American drug enforcement agents and their Latin American allies have been assassinated and kidnaped. Drug dealers in Bolivia have put out a $500,000 contract on the life of our ambassador to that country, Edwin G. Corr.

Supply Is Increasing

Still, the vicious white powder flows across our porous borders, despite rapidly increasing expenditures for enforcement and an unprecedented level of drug seizures and arrests. The supply in this country has risen so rapidly that the price is being driven down drastically, thus encouraging new users and increased consumption by those already involved with the drug.

In all the voluminous news reports and analyses of what can and should be done, ranging from advertising campaigns to massive use of U.S. military forces, one question seems always to receive short shrift, if it is mentioned at all: What about the users?

Traditionally our approach has been to go after the pusher and not worry about the purchaser. That approach is based in part on practicality and efficiency: The closer one gets to the source of supply, the greater the return in drugs intercepted and disruption of future production and distribution. It is also based on a sense of fairness. Aren't the suppliers of drugs much more culpable than the users?

Some law enforcement officials are now suggesting that it may be time for us to rethink those assumptions. One is U.S. Attorney Charles Lewis, head of the federal drug task force for the Gulf Coast region. He advocates no diminution of pressure on suppliers, but he suggests putting more pressure on users.

Fear of Punishment

On the efficiency issue he argues that the war "has to be fought in the minds of the citizens of our country." He and others feel that those minds would benefit greatly from a substantially increased fear of punishment.

On the question of what is right and fair, Lewis notes that American users of cocaine "are paying for bribery, murder and cor-

205

ruption."

The man has a point.

Experience suggests that we will never come close to choking off the flow of drugs into this country, short of a horribly expensive and intrusive sealing of our borders. Nor are we likely to approach the elimination of production, given the reluctance of foreign governments to cooperate and the tremendous financial reward for those involved in or offering protection to the trade.

Compelling Moral Issue

The moral issue is even more compelling. Are middle- and upper-middle-class American users, who know full well the implication of their drug purchases, somehow less deserving of punishment than uneducated Latin American peasants who see the coca leaf as the only way out of poverty and despair? How do we justify demanding that miserably paid policemen in Mexico or Colombia or Bolivia risk their lives to solve our problems when coke-snorting American athletes and entertainers, who earn more per minute than these people do per year, are coddled, excused and winked at?

Putting Pressure on the Purchasers

Some experts believe that the only way to win the cocaine battle is to put pressure on the purchasers. "This war has to be fought in the minds of citizens of our country—it's they who spend billions of dollars consuming these drugs," says U.S. Attorney Lewis. "They're paying for bribery, murder and corruption." And that's too steep a price for any kind of high."

Melinda Beck, *Newsweek*, February 25, 1985.

There are, to be sure, problems associated with putting pressure on the purchasers: laws to be toughened, resistance from local police who fear that such an approach would be wasteful of limited resources, and, no doubt, political pressures, since significant numbers of "good citizens" are faced with the prospect of some time in the slammer.

But these problems are not insurmountable, particularly if we are willing to allocate more resources.

We can't get them all, but we can get some of them, and I find myself in total agreement with those who think it's time we got started.

"Because cocaine abusers pose special problems and have special problems, new forms of treatment are needed."

Cocaine Users Should Be Treated

Mitchell S. Rosenthal

Mitchell S. Rosenthal is a psychiatrist and president of the Phoenix House Foundation, which provides services to prevent and treat cocaine and other types of drug abuse. His position provides him with a knowledgeable perspective on cocaine addiction. In the following viewpoint, Dr. Rosenthal argues that more widely available treatment programs and increased funding from the government would curb the cocaine epidemic.

As you read, consider the following questions:

1. How does Dr. Rosenthal compare cocaine trafficking to a giant corporation?
2. In the author's opinion, what is the most frightening aspect of cocaine use?
3. What is the first step that Dr. Rosenthal believes should be implemented in cocaine treatment programs?

Mitchell S. Rosenthal, "To Fight Growing Use of Cocaine in New York," *The New York Times,* December 31, 1983. Copyright © 1983 by The New York Times Company. Reprinted by permission.

After the snow and cold of this December are long forgotten, many Americans will still be caught in a blizzard of sorts. Use of cocaine—"snow"—is spreading throughout the nation at a terrible cost to society.

If there were one corporation marketing cocaine today in the United States, its $30 billion annual revenues would place it seventh among the Fortune 500 corporations—between the Gulf Oil Corporation and the Ford Motor Company.

According to recent estimates, users in the United States consume 40 to 48 metric tons of cocaine annually. In 1977, cocaine was not among the top 20 drugs directly related to death statistics. By 1978, cocaine ranked 16th. And by 1980, it was ninth.

No. 1 Drug Problem

At a recent hearing on cocaine abuse before the New York State Senate Investigations Committee, Senator Roy M. Goodman described cocaine addiction as the No. 1 drug problem in the state. At a meeting sponsored by the National Institute on Drug Abuse in December 1982, representatives from cities across the country almost universally noted with alarm the continued growth in popularity of cocaine.

The most frightening aspect of cocaine use is its infiltration of all levels of American society. Once a limited-access drug for a privileged few, cocaine is now the all-American drug, running rampant throughout the mainstream of the establishment. From the executive suite to the courtroom, coke is influencing the behavior of millions of upwardly mobile and otherwise conventional middleclass Americans. The use of cocaine by athletes, corporate executives and other successful members of society sends a signal that all illicit drug use is socially acceptable.

The cocaine crisis is alarming not only for its seduction of an escalating number of people in the nation's financial and industrial network but also for its far-reaching social and economic impact as well. It represents a growing proportion of the $26 billion a year that drugs cost the American economy.

New Forms of Treatment Needed

There are a number of ways that we can—and must—respond to the cocaine crisis in New York. Because cocaine abusers pose special problems and have special problems, new forms of treatment are needed. But New York drug abuse service agencies are already doing all that can be done with the present level of government support. They are hard-pressed to develop new programs for cocaine abusers. There must be special funding that will allow them to fund new programs without reducing services to abusers of other drugs.

A first step would be health insurance that offers coverage for treatment of drug abuse. Many cocaine abusers hold down respon-

sible jobs yet cannot obtain the care they need without masquer-
ading as emotionally ill or alcoholic. Legislation has already been
passed that requires providers of health insurance to offer the option of treatment for alcohol abuse. Similar legislation for drug
abuse would not only allow more men and women to seek the treatment they need but also would give employers an alternative—
other than dismissal—to offer employees.

Public Information Campaign

While treatment can help today's cocaine abusers end their dependency, it will not by itself keep the epidemic from spreading.
A large-scale, sophisticated public-information campaign is needed to spell out the risks and costs of the use of cocaine.

The Cokeaholic

A Cokeaholic has lost all control. He cannot break his addiction
without professional help. At the root of cokeaholism is cocaine's
extraordinarily reinforcing high: euphoria, omnipotence, power,
strength, control, joyousness, ecstasy. The cocaine high is one of
the most, if not the most, powerful chemical reinforcers.

Daniel Kagan, Nannette Stone, and Marlene Fromme, *Cocaine: Seduction and Solution,*
1984.

Private industry must seek out and help abusers so as to help
prevent the further spread of cocaine use. Employers, from owners of professional sports teams to small-business proprietors,
should make it clear that they will not hire drug users and should
insist that drug-using employees cannot remain on the job without
accepting treatment. Professional associations must also deal
realistically with the use of cocaine by providing drug-abusing
members with education, counseling and referral programs.

By failing to address the problem of drug abuse, corporate,
professional and public officials in effect take a neutral position,
thereby passively licensing drug abuse.

What is needed is an aggressive and concerted stand, not only
by parents and drug-abuse professionals but by leaders in all areas
of society as well.

"Faced with an incurable disease, alcoholics have only one reliable way of bringing the disease under control: swearing off alcohol for good."

Alcoholism Should Be Treated As a Disease

Changing Times

An intrinsic part of the debate on alcohol treatment is whether or not alcoholism should be considered a disease. *Changing Times,* a monthly consumer magazine based in Washington, D.C., published the following viewpoint on the characteristics of alcoholism. In the viewpoint, the author claims that alcoholics have an incurable disease which can only be brought under control through abstinence.

As you read, consider the following questions:

1. Why does the author think that alcoholics should never drink alcoholic beverages?
2. In the author's opinion, do underlying personality problems cause alcoholism or does alcoholism cause personality problems?
3. Does the author believe that alcoholism can be cured?

First came his arrest for drunk driving, which made the local papers and television. Then he confronted the chilling reality of being passed over for promotion; and finally, an ultimatum from the boss: Either seek help for alcoholism or be fired. After years of drinking uncontrollably, Tom, badly frightened, finally checked into an alcoholism treatment center.

Earlier he had sought help from Alcoholics Anonymous, which didn't work for him. This time an advertisement for Parkview-Westchester in Yorktown Heights, N.Y., suggested an approach that appealed to him. Following an evaluation by the center's professional staff, Tom, a police officer, began a 30-day period of intensive treatment in which he learned how alcoholism was not only destroying his life but also wrecking the lives of those around him.

Parkview, a freestanding residential rehabilitation center, enrolls clients who agree to spend about a month living at the center while undergoing intensive treatment for their alcoholism.

Denial of Alcoholism

Tom began each day at 7 A.M. with breakfast, followed by a group meeting with other patients, whose influence ultimately turned out to be crucial to his recovery. "We all denied our alcoholism at first," Tom says, "but then we came to admit it, which is the first step in recovery."

Afternoons spent with therapists helped convince him that his drinking problem was a disease for which abstinence was the only control. Evening visits by volunteers from AA reinforced the lessons of the day. Along the way, Tom's wife and daughter spent a week in a separate wing of Parkview, which stressed the importance of educating other family members about the nature of alcoholism. The program gave Tom the discipline he had been unable to develop himself.

Fortunately for Tom, most of the $250-a-day cost of treatment was covered by insurance. A year later he has not touched a drop.

Chemical Dependency Can Kill

For 32-year-old Jack, a similar career of misery ended in a Washington, D.C., clinic. By age 17 he was abusing alcohol, but outright dependence didn't show up until his mid twenties. He vainly tried nearly anything, including AA, to help him stop. The light dawned when Jack seriously injured himself falling from his car while drunk. He decided to go to Seton House, an alcohol recovery center at Providence Hospital. "Therapists there convinced me I had a chemical dependence that would eventually kill me unless I gave it up," Jack recalls.

After years of addiction, he accepted the discipline and structure of the 28-day, hospital-based residential treatment program with its 90-day follow-up. He returned to college to finish work

211

on a long-neglected undergraduate degree and now works as a counselor to other alcoholics at Seton House.

Not all stories of recovery are so dramatic. Nor does every alcoholic need such extreme treatment. But the cases show how even advanced alcoholism can be brought under control if the victim finds appropriate therapy and is able to take advantage of it in time. The tragedy is that a vast majority of the country's nearly 15 million alcoholics deny that they have a problem, fail to recognize the seriousness of their dependency until it's too late or resist offers of help because they believe all is lost. It needn't be that way.

Early Signs of Trouble

Alcoholism can't be cured, but it can be arrested and its victims restored to a more normal life. Budding alcoholism can be detected and interrupted before it reaches a severe stage. Early signs of trouble, though, are more likely to be picked up by family, friends or the boss than by a doctor.

Reducing the Stigma

"A disease model lessens the stigma attached to alcoholism so that individuals no longer need to deny that they cannot control their drinking behavior. With this defensive need removed, many of the most severe pathological symptoms, such as paranoia and hostility, disappear."

Stephanie Brown, *The Stanford Magazine,* Summer 1982.

If there is a true "alcoholic personality," researchers have been unable to settle on a consistent definition. Many authorities depict the alcoholic as depressed, insecure, compulsive, tense or fearful, and burdened with a sense of guilt and isolation. Because drink seems to blunt fear and anxiety and impart a feeling of confidence and acceptance, the theory goes, the drinker tends to use alcohol increasingly as a defense and to depend on it for fabricated esteem. Over time it takes more and more alcohol to achieve the effect.

Problems Are Result, Not Cause

However, those theories are based on observations of alcoholics already deeply in trouble. When several large groups of men were studied prospectively (that is, before and after they became addicted) over a period of 40 years, Harvard alcoholism authority George Vaillant writes in *The Natural History of Alcoholism,* personality quirks more often appeared to have been the result rather than the cause of alcoholism.

So-called problem drinking doesn't always progress to the worst stages of alcoholism. More telling is a person's compulsion for alcohol, increasing dependency on its effects and a gradual advance from occasional to frequent drinking. Most authorities agree that alcoholism is a complex disorder that is influenced by a combination of physiological, psychological and environmental factors. Says the National Council on Alcoholism: "The person with alcoholism cannot consistently predict on any drinking occasion the duration of the episode or the quantity that will be consumed."

The Search for Treatment

Faced with an incurable disease, alcoholics have only one reliable way of bringing the disease under control: swearing off alcohol for good. Most therapists believe the evidence is too shaky to justify adopting moderate drinking habits as a general goal of treatment. These are the main techniques currently used to treat alcoholism.

Inpatient Treatment

No matter where the treatment is sought, an alcoholic who is intoxicated will probably receive medical care in the form of hospitalization and steps to eliminate alcohol from the blood. If, after the patient is detoxified, the decision is for hospital rehabilitation, antidepressants and vitamin supplements may be prescribed to overcome withdrawal symptoms and malnutrition. Personnel will continuously monitor vital signs. According to Boston University's Dr. Leonard Saxe, who has analyzed the cost and effectiveness of alcoholism treatment for the federal government's Office of Technology Assessment, alcoholics admitted to a hospital program (which lasts three or four weeks) usually have relatively stable social backgrounds and fewer years of hard drinking behind them.

Private psychiatric hospitals also treat a sizable number of people who abuse alcohol, although alcoholism might not be the primary diagnosis. Treatment in a psychiatric facility is likely to include individual and group therapy, alcohol education and sometimes the use of Antabuse, a drug that makes you sick if you try to drink alcohol after taking it.

Inpatient treatment is also available at freestanding clinics associated with a hospital, like Seton House, or in facilities like Parkview that are not part of a hospital. Freestanding residential rehabilitation typically consists of group counseling, in which a leader conducts sessions that try to change the pattern of the drinker's behavior or get at the root cause. Family involvement is often crucial, as is the association with self-help groups like AA, and the fellowship of men and women who help each other stay sober by sharing their experiences and encouraging each other to remember that "we are powerless over alcohol." Treatment at inpatient facilities can cost up to $300 per day.

Probably about 90% of the one million alcoholics under treatment each year are in outpatient therapy. They spend part of the day in a hospital or residential clinic and return home at night. Both hospitals and freestanding centers offer outpatient therapy, which generally resembles inpatient treatment. One advantage of the outpatient approach is that it usually enables workers to stay on the job, at least part-time.

Not a Crime

Alcoholism is an Illness, not a moral weakness or a crime. The alcoholic cannot control his or her drinking and continues to drink too much even though it has caused problems in the past.....

Alcoholics can drink normally early in the illness and are able to hide their symptoms for years. But alcoholism is a progressive disease, and the symptoms always become worse.

Hazelden Foundation, *Learn About Alcoholism,* 1983.

Other sources of outpatient treatment include community mental health centers, which are partly financed by the government, and privately or publicly operated halfway houses, which offer free or inexpensive intermediate care consisting of food, shelter and support. Depending on the extent of treatment, charges in outpatient clinics range from $35 to $50 a day.

Aversion Therapy

Conditioning the alcoholic to abhor the taste, smell and sight of alcohol is the purpose of chemical aversion treatment, which usually requires special hospital facilities. Most such facilities are located in the West and Southwest. A substance called emetine is given just before an alcoholic drink. Nausea caused by the emetine follows, and if the treatment takes, the repeated association leaves the patient with a strong aversion to alcohol. Chemical aversion therapy appears to work best for alcoholics who are strongly motivated to control their disease. Dr. Saxe cautions in his report that, because nausea is repeatedly induced, the technique is potentially hazardous and must be administered under medical supervision. Aversion therapy is expensive, requiring about two weeks of hospitalization, with possible follow-up sessions. Costs range up to $10,000 for a full course of treatment.

Which Treatment When?

Any treatment is better than none. Total abstinence for a year is a popular yardstick for success, and that goal is reached on the average about 60% of the time.

That doesn't mean the alcoholic can enroll in any program and expect success. The alcoholic must want help. The discipline of the live-in setup may be right for some but not for others. Placing teenagers among chronic middle-age drinkers may be inappropriate. Matching patients to specific treatments or predicting favorable outcomes is a risky business; however, here are some guidelines to go by:

• The more affluent and the higher the social standing of the alcoholic, the better the chance of a sober outcome. Being employed and married, having the spouse involved in the treatment, accepting the diagnosis and drinking little or not at all during treatment are favorable signs of recovery, according to alcohol researcher Chad D. Emrick. Negative signs include previous inpatient treatment for alcoholism, aggressiveness, and one or more attempts at suicide.

• Generally speaking, alcoholics seem to respond better to group therapy and combinations of treatment than to a single approach. But the outcome is not influenced much by the length of the treatment or whether it is received on an inpatient or outpatient basis. Debatable, too, is the effectiveness of individual psychotherapy, particularly if the patient continues to drink during treatment.

• An estimated 10% of problem drinkers recover by themselves without treatment. But because nobody can predict who will, it would be a mistake for the alcoholic to forgo intervention.

Alcoholism Treatment

More than 4,200 centers offer alcoholism treatment. Therapy in one form or another is available in every state, either in nonprofit clinics or in one of the growing number of units owned by for-profit health care chains, such as Comprehensive Care and National Medical Enterprises.

Competition for patients and scarce medical dollars is increasing that availability of treatment. That increase also boosts the odds of someone landing in an inappropriate treatment center, a good reason for the alcoholic or any would-be helper to proceed with caution when selecting treatment.

Be wary of extravagant promises that the battle of the bottle will be over at the end of treatment, says Richard Weedman of the National Association of Alcoholism Treatment Programs. Perhaps it will, but getting off alcohol is one thing, staying off is another. Programs that offer follow-up treatment and support have better records than those that let go of patients too soon.

> "Drinking itself, including heavy drinking, is not caused by disease but by learning."

Alcoholism Should Not Be Treated as a Disease

Roger E. Vogler and Wayne R. Bartz

Roger E. Vogler is a professor of psychology at Pomona College and a clinical psychologist at the Center for Behavior Change in Pomona, California. He is a leading researcher of new methods for changing drinking habits and has authored many articles on alcohol abuse for American and European scientific journals. Wayne R. Bartz is a professor of psychology at American River College in Sacramento, California. In the following viewpoint, the authors claim that alcoholics delay getting help because society may view them as being "sick." They support the idea that excessive drinking is a learned behavior that can be unlearned.

As you read, consider the following questions:

1. In the authors' opinion, why do some psychologists insist upon calling the overuse of alcohol a disease?
2. Why do the authors believe that labeling alcoholism a disease prevents alcoholics from seeking treatment?
3. What do the authors think is the solution for alcoholism?

Excessive drinking is a learned pattern of behavior. Yet one of the catchphrases of our time is "alcoholism is a disease." Many "authorities" insist that alcohol abuse is literally an illness that a person either has or does not have. We are all familiar with the term "alcoholic," but you may be surprised to hear that there is no commonly accepted definition. *The Dictionary of Words About Alcohol* has ten pages of definitions of "alcoholism" and "alcoholic." Most alcohol counselors support the disease approach, yet unlike other diseases alcoholism cannot be "caught" through biological means; there is no alcoholism virus, fungus, or germ. Alcoholism is not borne through the air like the cold virus; you cannot sneeze and give someone alcoholism. It is not carried by parasites the way malaria and yellow fever are; no flea or mosquito can bite you and give you alcoholism. You cannot get alcoholism accidentally as you can a broken leg, and you are not born with it as some would claim. If alcoholism were actually a disease, it would be the only disease that is sold conveniently packaged, that produces a huge revenue for the government, that is habit-forming and results in arrests, fines, and even jail sentences. It would be the only disease that is a contributing cause in over half the highway deaths in this country, provokes crime, and is spread by advertising. According to Mark Keller, editor of the *Journal of Studies on Alcohol* and a supporter of the disease definition, it is a disease "of unknown etiology (cause) and unknown site." If we look at the question realistically, we must see that the excessive use of alcohol can and does result in physical disease, and sometimes physical addiction. But drinking itself, including heavy drinking, is not caused by disease but by learning. You must *voluntarily* consume alcohol in fairly large amounts before you have an alcohol problem.

Social Reasons

Why then do some insist upon calling the overuse of alcohol a disease? There are good social reasons for doing so. Over the past century, more and more undesirable behaviors have been redefined by authorities as "sickness' rather than as moral violations or crimes. Murderers, shoplifters, child molesters, or even bored housewives are said to be "sick," victims of "mental illness," and are not held fully responsible for their behavior. While Alcoholics Anonymous has fostered the explanation of a physical difference as the cause of the "disease of alcoholism," medicine, and psychiatry in particular, has unfortunately added the dimension "mental disorder." Alcohol abuse is a relative newcomer to this movement to consider problems in living as mental illness. Only in recent years have the American Medical Association (1968), the National Institute on Alcohol Abuse and Alcoholism (1974), and the World Health Organization (1957) mounted an effort to redefine alcohol abuse as a form of illness. One obvious motive is to decriminalize alcoholic behavior and thereby make it more likely that abusers will seek help on their own. Instead of suffering legal consequences for abusive drinking, the alcoholic may be considered the victim of an illness and therefore treated with kindness and concern. A problem drinker is thereby relieved of the responsibility for uncontrolled drinking, just as most patients are not blamed for their illnesses. However, this change in thinking has simply substituted the negative concept of sickness or mental illness for the negative notions of moral weakness or criminality. In our opinion, the trade-off has not succeeded in encouraging people with a drinking problem to voluntarily do something about it.

Refuting the Disease Theory

The reason I am at such pains to refute the notion that alcoholism is a disease is that such a theory is not helpful to many people—including those whose drinking does not reach the stage of constant intoxication, and those who are not comfortable in the totalitarian atmosphere of Alcoholics Anonymous. What, for example, would we say about a woman who drinks at social gatherings in order to overcome her insecurities? By seeking a physical cause for her "alcoholism," we ignore the real cause of her drinking—a lack of confidence about dealing with other people. Because she doesn't drink to the point of unconsciousness we might refuse to label her an alcoholic. On the other hand, not recognizing the cause of her drinking could readily allow it to grow to more dangerous proportions as the woman fails to come to grips with her sense of inadequacy.

Stanton Peele, *How Much Is Too Much?* 1981.

An additional offshoot of labeling excessive drinking a disease is that alcoholism was brought under the wings of the medical establishment. Only then could Congress legitimately provide funds for a National Institute on Alcohol Abuse and Alcoholism to treat, find cures for, or prevent the "disease." Note that it is unlikely that Congress would or could have funded a National Institute on Bad Habits (which might include smoking, overeating, swearing, excessive drinking, and gambling). Society feels sorry for and wants to help people with a disease, but those with bad habits are expected to take care of their own problems!

Abuse vs. Bad Habits

Why should alcohol abuse alone be called a disease while other abusive behavior such as smoking and overeating are considered bad habits? All are harmful physically. All are economic liabilities and can generate degrees of personal and social difficulty. Physical ailments can indeed be a consequence but are not a cause of any of these behaviors. It is clear that we must look to *social* factors in order to understand why alcohol abuse is the only one of these destructive behaviors generally claimed to be a disease.

Smoking, overeating, and excessive drinking all result from a complex cluster of influences: cultural rules, parental and peer influences, easy availability of the abused substance, desire for a change in mood or feelings, ignorance, inadequacy of social skills, lack of satisfying alternatives, and perhaps to a minor degree some biological predisposition. The two main reasons for giving alcohol abuse special status are: (1) the greater problems caused for others by drinking, and (2) the enthusiastic promotion of the "disease" approach by Alcoholics Anonymous.

Effect on Others

When people overeat or smoke they may influence their own health, but they rarely directly affect others (although we are now concerned about possible hazards in "secondhand" smoke). People who drink too much clearly *do* affect others. They sometimes kill or maim with drunk driving, may go into a rage and attack a loved one, lose their jobs, destroy their families, or abuse their children. Drinking may indeed affect the drinker's entire life pattern and *everybody in it*. Smokers and overeaters rarely have such major direct impact upon the lives of others. They can be ignored, but heavy drinkers often force us to react. Recognizing this, Alcoholics Anonymous has for many years tried to make treatment for alcohol problems more readily available and acceptable. And for *serious* abusers, or alcoholics, AA has probably been the single most valuable source of help. In our opinion, however, fostering the stereotype of the alcohol abuser as a helpless, out-of-control victim of a terrible disease has actually made it *more* difficult for many excessive drinkers to acknowledge their problem until the situation becomes desperate. Generally, the result is that only the most extreme abusers are identified and offered treatment. Nobody wants to admit being "sick," especially mentally, unless the problem is serious. (Imagine a situation where you could not be called overweight or do anything about reducing until you were a hundred pounds above normal, admitted you were "sick," and then the only cure offered was to stop eating—completely!)

Our approach to excessive drinking provides a positive alternative to the historic mistreatment of drinkers as criminals and to the disease approach. We view excessive alcohol consumption as a learned behavior pattern or habit, just like overeating, smoking, or swearing. Habits, whether labeled good or bad, occur in varying degrees and are determined by an individual's entire life experience along with a variety of continuing social and physical consequences. Viewed from this social learning approach, the drinker is not faced with a choice of being or not being an alcoholic; rather, drinking can be measured along a continuous scale from no drinking at all at one extreme to excessive and harmful drinking at the other. If a person's drinking becomes excessive, a host of negative consequences may begin to occur—such as physical ailments, vocational problems, social and marital discord, and legal and economic troubles. These unhappy consequences may themselves increase consumption and thus the problem is com-

"Most doctors say that heavy drinkers don't live long, yet you see more old drunks than old doctors."

pounded.

In contrast, when drinking and its consequences are called an illness, the undesirable label "alcoholic" comes into play and the drinker is often discouraged by the label itself from seeking help. Since smokers and overeaters rarely interfere much with others' happiness, they are not subject to such negative labels and are more willing to seek help. Just look around at the popularity of private clinics and organizations for smokers and overeaters, such as the Schick centers and Weight Watchers, plus the great popularity of fad diets and smoking cures. In contrast, help for the mild alcohol abuser at an early stage (when drinking habits are most easily changed) is usually not available. Even if it were, most would probably avoid being labeled an alcoholic and would therefore not seek out such help. We have all seen the reactions of friends and relatives when someone announces enrollment in a weight-loss class or program. "Great!" "Wonderful!" More power to you!" But what would be the reactions to an announcement like "You'll never guess what course I'm taking at the community college. It's a class on how to drink moderately." The listener might indeed say "Great!" but later would find much to gossip about. "Wait until you hear what Fred told me tonight. He's taking a course in controlling his drinking. He must have a problem with booze. Do you suppose he's an alcoholic?"

Dr. Morris Chafetz, first director of the National Institute on Alcohol Abuse and Alcoholism, writes; "the fundamental problem we face is not the use of alcohol. . . . That is a fact of the human condition we cannot change. The problem is misuse, irresponsible use, of the substance." It is interesting to note that other important members of professions that have traditionally supported the disease approach have begun to acknowledge the learned nature of drinking habits. Dr. Alfred Smith, a psychiatrist who spent fifteen years seeking a biological cause for alcoholism, remarked before the National Safety Congress in Chicago, "It's a terrible disappointment to me to finally face up to the fact that alcoholism is a behavior disorder."

Drinking Sensibly

The simple reality is that most Americans drink, and the great majority drink sensibly. Those who do not drink sensibly are usually afraid to admit it to others or to themselves because of social costs such as possible job loss, rejection by friends and relatives, and reduction in self-esteem. Possibly the most important unfortunate consequence is being treated as a victim of "the disease of alcoholism," with total abstinence offered as the only cure.

> *"Naltrexone taken by itself has no effect on the mind or other functioning of the patient; it is not addicting."*

Naltrexone Is the Best Treatment for Heroin Addicts

Joseph A. Pursch

Joseph A. Pursch, psychiatrist and foremost medical expert in the field of alcohol and drug abuse, has been an advisor to Presidents Ford, Carter, and Reagan. He successfully treated Betty Ford, Senator Herman Talmadge, and astronaut Edwin "Buzz" Aldrin. Dr. Pursch writes a weekly newspaper column analyzing various drug and alcohol-related topics. In the following viewpoint, the author describes why he believes that naltrexone, a recently approved drug by the FDA, may be better than methadone for treating opiate addiction.

As you read, consider the following questions:
1. According to the author, what are the advantages of naltrexone over methadone?
2. On what type of patient does the author believe naltrexone works best?
3. According to Dr. Pursch, what role does therapy have in the treatment of addicts?

Joseph A. Pursch, "A New Testament for Opiate Addiction," *The Los Angeles Times*, March 15, 1985. © 1985, Los Angeles Times Syndicate. Reprinted with permission.

Heroin and other opiate drug addiction has always been a difficult problem to treat. Methadone, the only drug available to clinicians, has not worked satisfactorily for a variety of reasons. Early this year the Food and Drug Administration approved a new drug that so far sounds very promising.

The drug is naltrexone. Marketed as Trexan, it is a synthetic long-acting opioid antagonist or blocking agent. What that means in plain English is that if an addict takes naltrexone and then takes heroin (or any other opiate drug), he will feel no effect no matter how large a dose of opiate he takes and regardless of the method of administration (needle, smoke or swallow). Naltrexone continues to exert this "blocking" effect for as long as 72 hours.

Among the advantages of this new drug are the following: Naltrexone taken by itself has no effect on the mind or other functioning of the patient; it is not addicting, and therefore the patient experiences no effects when the drug is discontinued; it can be given to anybody except those patients who are in liver failure or have acute hepatitis, and a week's supply costs less than $20.

Addict Continues to Work

Naltrexone seems to work best with patients in whom continued addiction would mean that they're going to lose their family, their job or their freedom (jail). It seems especially effective with addicted executives or physicians. Of course naltrexone is not a wonder drug, a complete answer or a painless solution. Although it enables the addict to continue his work or his career, he still has to work on changing his life style and his personality problems, which were at one time alleviated by the use and abuse of narcotics.

A good example is Steve (not his real name), a middle-aged dentist who was addicted to narcotics for 3½ years. He is now on naltrexone. "I consider the drug to be 'insurance' because I'm around drugs all day and I can write myself an illegal prescription for a narcotic at any time. When I first went on naltrexone I took the pill in the presence of my wife. For the first two weeks I encouraged her to look in my mouth and make sure that I had actually swallowed the pill because it made her feel more secure. Since then I have been taking the pill by myself. Although my wife still considers naltrexone as a security blanket for herself, she has also learned in group therapy with me that she really has no control over me or anybody else."

And what has Steve learned in therapy? "I used to say, 'I'm just a dentist,' like some women say, 'I'm just a housewife.' It showed my low self-esteem. I now realize that I've always wanted to be a brain surgeon. I'm slowly becoming confortable with what I am. I've also discovered that in a behavioral sense I'm my wife's fourth child; that I usually don't charge my patients a high enough fee and then hate myself for it; and I'm learning to not let people walk all over me. Most of all I've discovered there is more to life than getting high, and I'm proud because I'm able to accomplish a difficult thing like conquering an addiction."

In some respects naltrexone for narcotic addicts is like Antabuse for alcoholics. One problem with Antabuse has always been that you often wonder if the patient actually swallowed the pill. (You see, addicts quickly figure out that they can "cheek" unwanted drugs: They put the pill between the cheek and the gums, then drink down the water, make a sour face to reassure you, then walk out and spit the pill in the bushes.) With naltrexone there is no such problem. If the pill is kept in the mouth, it becomes very bitter in just a couple of minutes. So, if you keep the patient talking to you for about 15 minutes, you don't have to wonder whether he swallowed the wonder drug.

"(Methadone) is the only program that has large-scale application."

Methadone Is the Best Treatment for Heroin Addicts

Selwyn Raab

Selwyn Raab, an investigative reporter for the *New York Times,* has wide experience in the law enforcement field. He has been a reporter for the *Bridgeport Herald* in Connecticut and has worked for *Newsweek* magazine. In the following viewpoint, Mr. Raab describes the success of methadone programs in enabling addicts to work and conduct reasonably normal lives.

As you read, consider the following questions:

1. How does methadone work in heroin treatment programs?
2. What does the author believe are the benefits of methadone?
3. How does methadone compare to residential drug-free programs, according to the author?

Every business day, dozens of executives and employees in the Wall Street area enter an unmarked suite of offices in a building next to the American Stock Exchange. If they meet at the door, none of the men or women extend any sign of recognition.

The unmarked suite is a clinic, and the clients—former heroin addicts—are there to obtain methadone, a synthetic opiate that blocks their desires for heroin.

Uptown, in a converted tenement in the Bronx, 120 men and women begin each day chanting in unison a 200-word pledge to "rise from the ashes" and to reform themselves. Also former addicts, they are in a Phoenix House center that relies on therapy to overcome drug habits.

The methadone-maintenance clinic and the Phoenix House are two components in a drug-rehabilitation network in New York State that will cost $200 million to operate this year. All of the programs, public and private, residential and nonresidential, have room for 70,000 patients—5 percent of the estimated 1.4 million drug abusers in the state, according to the State Division of Substance Abuse Services.

For two decades, the state has subsidized a variety of drug-rehabilitation efforts. At best, the results have been mixed.

Largest Treatment Method

Methadone maintenance has emerged as the largest treatment method, with 32,000 people in publicly supported and private outpatient clinics. Almost 28,000 are in New York City. About 3,000 patients are in methadone programs on Long Island and in the northern suburbs.

Nationwide, 70,000 people are in methadone treatment.

Methadone works by blocking the desire for heroin without producing the same narcotic high. Its proponents cite two major reasons for its widespread use. It has reduced crime that heroin addicts would normally commit to buy the illegal drug, and, at a cost of $2,200 a year for each outpatient, it is less expensive than drug-free residential care, which costs $8,500 a year a patient.

A state study on drug abuse in 1982 found that "the claims for methadone's capacity to reduce the grim proliferation of heroin use have far less validity than was originally hoped." The report, prepared by Joseph A. Califano Jr., who was special counselor to former Gov. Hugh L. Carey, stressed that methadone had permitted thousands of addicts to work and conduct reasonably normal lives. . . .

Dr. Vincent P. Dole, an internist and researcher at the Rockefeller University who helped develop methadone as a therapy in the 60's, said that "nothing as efficient" had been found to cope with heroin addiction.

"It is the only program that has large-scale application," Dr. Dole said in an interview. "A black market has been created, because there is an unmet demand and because political propaganda and community opposition have made it impossible to open more clinics."

The clinic in the Wall Street area, at 74 Trinity Place, is run by the New York Infirmary-Beekman Hospital. At the clinic, most of the 215 patients appear two or three times a week, where they drink a prescribed dose of bitter-tasting methadone in an orange-flavored concoction. Patients who are considered reliable get take-home supplies for weekends and days when they do not visit the clinic.

Cost-effective Treatment

Our research on methadone maintenance nevertheless indicates that it is the most cost-effective treatment we have today for heroin addiction. The addict receiving this type of treatment is often much better off than on heroin—with respect to both his well-being and ours. That is not to say that this treatment permanently helps all or even a majority of addicts. Probably the figure is closer to 40 percent. Considering all the costs and benefits of the other treatments and punishments at our disposal, this seems to be about as well as we can do.

John Kaplan, *The Hardest Drug: Heroin and Public Policy*, 1983.

Federal law requires that the patients undergo periodic urinalysis to determine if they have lapsed and are using drugs again. Additionally, clinics must provide some type of counseling.

The regimen at the Trinity Place clinic is similar to programs at 95 others in the city. The major difference is that the Wall Street patients are more affluent than in most other programs, and a patient can be charged as much as $40 a week for treatment.

Indefinite Length of Treatment

Many of the patients expressed two principal concerns in interviews. They worried that their careers would be shattered if their employers discovered they were in a methadone program. And, because the treatment is indefinite—perhaps lifelong—they were troubled by the possible physical side effects that might develop.

An assistant vice president at a bank, who asked to be identified only by his first name, Neil, summarized the views of other patients. "If my bosses knew I was on methadone," he said, "it would be the biggest black mark against me. In the straight world, I'm a junkie, someone you may never be able to trust.

"I've met people in business meetings, former junkies who are in this program, and we can't give the slightest nod. It's funny and scary.

Yet, without methadone, I'd be in jail or dead. It saved my life."

Patients said that as former addicts it was easy for them to spot current abusers and that there was widespread use of heroin and cocaine in the financial district.

"Why do they use it?" said Jack, a trader at a brokerage house who is a methadone patient. "They say it's pressure; it's a crutch. There are more junkies on Wall Street than most people realize."

Just Like Medication

Mark, an investment counselor, and his wife, Louise, an executive for a public-relations company, arrive together twice a week for their methadone.

"I know I might have to use it for a long period, or the rest of my life, but that's just like medication for a heart disease," Louise said. "That's how I look at it."

"Methadone offers me stability," her husband said. "I have so many pressures and worries that I can't kick it. I'm not afraid of the physical pain, but the emotional pain of being without it."

Distinguishing Bias from Reason

The subject of drug use often generates great emotional responses in people. When dealing with such a highly controversial subject, many will allow their feelings to dominate their powers of reason. Thus, one of the most important basic thinking skills is the ability to distinguish between opinions based upon emotion or bias and conclusions based upon a rational consideration of the facts.

Most of the following statements are taken from the viewpoints in this chapter. The rest are taken from other sources. Consider each statement carefully. *Mark R for any statement you believe is based on reason or a rational consideration of the facts. Mark B for any statement you believe is based on bias, prejudice or emotion. Mark I for any statement you think is impossible to judge.*

If you are doing this activity as the member of a class or group compare your answers with those of other class or group members. Be able to defend your answers. You may discover that others will come to different conclusions than you. Listening to the rationale others present for their answers may give you valuable insights in distinguishing between bias and reason.

If you are reading this book alone, ask others if they agree with your answers. You too will find this interaction very valuable.

R = a statement based upon reason
B = a statement based on bias
I = a statement impossible to judge

1. Attempts to halt the flow of cocaine have produced friction between the US and its neighbors to the south.

2. We will never come close to choking off the flow of drugs into this country, short of a horribly expensive and intrusive sealing of our borders.

3. The suppliers of drugs are much more culpable than the users.

4. Use of cocaine—"snow"—is spreading throughout the nation at a terrible cost to society.

5. A large-scale, sophisticated public-information campaign is needed to spell out the risks and costs of the use of cocaine.

6. Health care insurance must be expanded to include treatment programs for drug addicted employees.

7. Private industry must seek out and help cocaine abusers so as to help prevent the further spread of cocaine use.

8. The tragedy is that a vast majority of the country's nearly 15 million alcoholics deny that they have a problem.

9. Alcoholism is a complex disorder that is influenced by a combination of physiological, psychological, and environmental factors.

10. Alcoholics are born, not made, so they have no control over their drinking behavior.

11. The person with alcoholism cannot consistently predict on any drinking occasion the duration of the episode or the quantity that will be consumed.

12. Murderers, shoplifters, child molesters, or even bored housewives are said to be "sick," victims of "mental illness," and are not held fully responsible for their behavior.

13. Society feels sorry for and wants to help people with a disease, but those with bad habits are expected to take care of their own problems.

14. The simple reality is that most Americans drink, and the great majority drink sensibly.

15. With a few exceptions, a far more realistic and effective approach to alcoholism is to learn controlled, moderate drinking habits.

16. Methadone programs have reduced crime that heroin addicts would normally commit to buy the illegal drug.

17. Naltrexone for narcotic addicts is like Antabuse for alcoholics.

18. Methadone maintenance has emerged as the largest treatment method for heroin addiction.

Periodical Bibliography

The following list of periodical articles deals with the subject matter of this chapter.

Changing Times	"Help for Those Who Drink Too Much," August 1984.
Consumer Report	"Gum to Help You Stop Smoking," August 1984.
Marla Crockett	"Parent Peer Groups Help Children Say No to Drugs, Alcohol," *The Christian Science Monitor,* August 20, 1984.
Robert E. Johnson	"Natalie Cole Says She Finally Won the Fight Against Drugs," *Jet,* November 5, 1984.
George B. Merry	"Curfews for Teen-agers Gain Support as Curb on Drunk Driving," *The Christian Science Monitor,* July 18, 1984.
Patrick Pacheco	"The Ordeal of an American Family," *Ladies' Home Journal,* October 1984.
Russ Pullman	"Alcoholism: Sin or Sickness?" *Christianity Today,* September 18, 1981.
Selwyn Raab	"The Drug Pipeline: From Europe to New York," *The New York Times,* May 21, 1984.
Society	"Alcoholism Treatment," July/August 1984.
Gloria Steinem	"Betty Ford Today," *Ms.,* April 1984.
USA Today	"New Treatments for Heroin Addicts," February 1985.
Donald M. Vickery and Judith Roman Eichner	"How to Be an Ex-Smoker," *Reader's Digest,* March 1984.

Organizations to Contact

Action on Smoking and Health
2013 H St. NW
Washington, DC 20006
(202) 659-4310

ASH is dedicated to legal action on behalf of the anti-smoking community. Its court victories include winning $200 million in free broadcast time for messages against smoking, a ban on radio and television cigarette commercials, requiring the airlines to provide non-smoking sections on flights, and requiring a warning about smoking to be printed on birth control pill containers. They publish *ASH Smoking and Health Newsletter* and other educational materials.

Al-Anon Family Groups
PO Box 182, Madison Square Station
New York, NY 10159-0182
(212) 683-1771

Al-Anon provides support for families of alcoholics in the belief that alcoholism is a family disease that can hurt all its members. They also offer Alateen groups for teenagers. Their support groups are similar to Alcoholics Anonymous. Al-Anon provides educational books and literature to its members, such as "Alcoholism, the Family Disease," "A Guide for the Family of the Alcoholics," and "Youth and the Alcoholic Parent."

Alcohol Education for Youth (AYE)
1500 Western Ave.
Albany, NY 12203
(518) 456-3800

AYE works to prevent alcoholism by making educational presentations to school, community, and church groups. Their publications include "Responsible Hosts/Hostesses," "So You're Planning a Party," "Counseling Children of Alcoholics at the Elementary School Level," and "Alcoholism, Guide for Ministers and Other Church Leaders." AYE's monthly newsletter is *Action..*

Alcoholics Anonymous
Box 459, Grand Central Station
New York, NY 10017
(212) 686-1100

Alcoholics Anonymous is the primary support group for recovering alcoholics. Most towns have AA chapters which offer support and have brochures available, including "AA—44 Questions and Answers," "Young People and AA," and "Is There an Alcoholic in Your Life?" The AA monthly magazine is *AA Grapevine*. AA books include *Alcoholics Anonymous, Alcoholics Anonymous Comes of Age,* and *Twelve Steps and Twelve Traditions.*

American Atheist Addiction Recovery Group (AAARG)

PO Box 6120
Denver, CO 80206
(303) 758-6686

AAARG is an organization for recovering alcoholic atheists. They disagree with the treatment approach of Alcoholics Anonymous, which asks alcoholics to recognize there is a higher power who can heal them. AAARG publishes a monthly newsletter, *Recovery*.

American Council on Alcoholism (ACA)

Medical Center, Suite 16-B
300 E. Joppa Rd.
Baltimore, MD 21204
(301) 296-5545

ACA is a voluntary organization in contact with thousands of alcoholism programs and agencies. Its four divisions work in industrial alcoholism prevention programs, legislation, public health, and community services. It does not take a position on alcohol, but works against alcoholism. In cooperation with other organizations, it has developed the pamphlets "The Most Frequently Asked Questions About Drinking and Pregnancy" and "The Most Frequently Asked Questions about Alcoholism." The Council developed the "Know Your Limits" campaign on drinking and driving and publishes "A Supervisor's Guide to the Early and Late Warnings of Alcoholism."

American Council on Alcohol Problems

2908 Patricia Drive
Des Moines, IA 50322
(515) 276-7752

The Council promotes abstinence from alcohol, encourages rehabilitation services, and conducts public education programs. It employs research and legislative approaches for the prevention of alcoholism and other alcohol-related problems. It was formerly the National Temperance League. The Council publishes the quarterly *American Issue.*

American Heart Association

7320 Greenville Ave.
Dallas, TX 75231
(214) 750-5300

The Heart Association, one of the anti-smoking campaign leaders, works against smoking by showing the connection between smoking and heart disorders. It publishes several bimonthly periodicals such as *Hypertension, Stroke—a Journal of Cerebral Circulation,* and *Arteriosclerosis,* as well as pamphlets and brochures.

Center of Alcohol Studies
Education and Training Division
Rutgers University
Piscataway, NJ 08854
(201) 932-2190

The Center supports education, training, and laboratory research on alcoholism and is affiliated with Rutgers Summer School of Alcohol Studies. Their library has reference files, abstracts and bibliographies on alcoholism. They publish the *Journal of Studies on Alcohol*.

Children of Alcoholics Foundation
540 Madison Ave., 23rd Floor
New York, NY 10022
(212) 980-5394

The Foundation increases public awareness of the unique problems of children of alcoholics by promoting and disseminating research. They also encourage governmental and private agencies to respond to the special needs of alcoholics' children. The Foundation's publications include articles, papers, and bibliographies.

Committees of Correspondence
PO Box 232
Topsfield, MA 01983
(617) 774-2641

Committees of Correspondence is a national citizens' group that exchanges information on drug abuse issues in an effort to stop the drug abuse epidemic. Their publications include a monthly *Drug Abuse Newsletter* and several pamphlets, including "Cocaine, the Great Addicter," and "Marijuana: More Harmful Than You Think." Reprints available from Committees of Correspondence include "The Marijuana Health Hazard," "Marijuana and the Unborn," "Marijuana and the Brain," and "Papers on Drug Abuse."

Distilled Spirits Council of US
1250 Eye St. NW, Suite 900
Washington, DC 20005
(202) 628-3544

The Council fosters public awareness of alcoholism, drunk driving, and drinking and pregnancy. Their activities include the Healthy Mothers/Healthy Babies program, and the "Friends Don't Let Friends Drive Drunk" advertising campaign. They have a list of publications available, including reprints on alcohol and pregnancy and *Some Thoughts About Drinking for Women in the Workplace*.

Hazelden Prevention Center
1400 Park Ave. So.
Minneapolis, MN 55404
(612) 338-2960

Hazelden advocates preventing health problems by changing chemically addictive lifestyles. They have developed educational programs on chemical dependency for elementary and secondary schools, colleges, businesses, and communities. Their publications are *Student Assistance Program; What, When, and How to Talk to Children About Alcohol and Other Drugs: A Guide for Parents;* and *Crossing the Thin Line Between Social Drinking and Alcoholism.* The toll free number for ordering information from Hazelden Educational Materials is 1-800-328-9000 (outside Minnesota) or 612-257-4010 for Minnesota and outside the continental US.

National Federation of Parents for Drug-Free Youth (NPF)
1820 Franwall Ave., Suite 16
Silver Spring, MD 20902
1-800-554-5437

NPF is a national network of parents working to prevent adolescent drug and alcohol use. Their resource information includes the Nancy Reagan Speakers Bureau and manuals on public speaking, media guidelines, and organizing parent groups. They publish a bimonthly Newsletter and Legislative Update as well as brochures on marijuana, alcohol, and cocaine.

National Organization for the Reform of Marijuana Laws (NORML)
2001 S St. NW, Suite 640
Washington, DC 20009
(202) 483-5500

NORML advocates decriminalizing marijuana and opposes governmental invasion of marijuana users' privacy. They believe the problem of drug abuse cannot be solved through the criminal justice system.

Tobacco Institute
1875 Eye St. NW, Suite 800
Washington, DC 20006
(202) 457-4800

The Tobacco Institute, whose members are manufacturers of tobacco products, lobbies Congress on tobacco-related bills and compiles information on tobacco. It works to show tobacco's contribution to the national economy. The Institute maintains a speakers' bureau and film service. Its publications include the quarterly *Tobacco Observer* and annual *Tobacco Industry Profile.*

Book Bibliography

Alcoholics Anonymous	*Alcoholics Anonymous,* New York: Alcoholics Anonymous World Service, 1976.
The Drug Abuse Council	*The Facts About "Drug Abuse",* New York: The Free Press, 1980.
Constantine Fitz Gibbon	*Drink: A Self-Help Book on Alcoholism,* Garden City, NY: Doubleday and Company, Inc., 1979.
Barbara Gordon	*I'm Dancing as Fast as I Can,* New York: Harper and Row, 1979.
Leonard Gross	*How Much Is Too Much? The Effects of Social Drinking,* New York: Random House, 1983.
James A. Inciardi, editor	*The Drugs-Crime Connection,* Beverly Hills, CA: Sage Publications, 1981.
Brian Inglis	*The Forbidden Game: A Social History of Drugs,* New York: Charles Scribner's Sons, 1975.
Michael Jackson and Bruce Jackson	*Doing Drugs,* New York: St. Martin's Press/Marek, 1983.
Dean Latimer and Jeff Goldberg	*Flowers in the Blood: The Story of Opium,* New York: Franklin Watts, 1981.
Ronald L. Linder with Steven E. Lerner and R. Stanley Burns	*PCP: The Devil's Dust,* Belmont, CA: Wadsworth, 1981.
Hank Messick	*Of Grass and Snow,* Englewood Cliffs, NJ: Prentice-Hall, 1979.
Muriel Nellis	*The Female Fix,* Boston: Houghton Mifflin, 1980.
Beth Polson and Miller Newton	*Not My Kid,* New York: Arbor House, 1984.
Patrick Reilly	*A Private Practice,* New York: Macmillan, 1984.
Roger A. Roffman	*Marijuana as Medicine,* Seattle, WA: Madrona Publishers, 1982.
Larry Sloman	*Reefer Madness: Marijuana in America,* New York: Grove Press, 1979.
Peter Taylor	*The Smoke Ring,* New York: Pantheon Books, 1984.

Index

Hammond, E. Cuyler, 97
Hazeldon Foundation, 214
heroin, 22, 23, 75
  dangers of, 152
  number of users, 171
Hesselbrock, Victor, 35, 37
Hoffman, Helmut, 37
Holden, Constance, 32
Holmes, Oliver Wendell, 18
Huxley, Aldous, 18, 199

Interdisciplinary Research
  Center on the Relations of
    Drugs and Alcohol to Crime,
    160

Jacobson, Michael F., 51
James, William, 18
Jellinek, E.M., 33

Kagan, Daniel, 209
Kaiser-Permanente study, 58
Kannel, William B., 57
Kaplan, John, 227
Kastenbaum, Robert, 59, 60
ketamine, 18
Kinsley, Michael, 128
Klatsky, Arthur L., 55, 56
Kleiman, Mark, 180
Kornegay, Horace R., 87

Lambert, M. Dow, 81
Latimer, Dean, 18, 174
Leary, Timothy, 169
Lester, David, 37
Lilly, John, 18
liquor advertising
  and freedom, 79-82
  promotes alcoholism, 73-78
Lowrey, Alfred, 109, 110
LSD, 18
Macdonald, Donald Ian, 27, 175,
  177, 178, 180, 182
marijuana, 17, 19, 22, 23, 28, 29,
  30
  dangers of, 134, 136-37, 139,
    140, 152
  decriminalization of, 141-143
  effects of, 144
  legalization of
    reasons against, 138-145
    reasons for, 132-137

medical uses, 135, 136
number of users, 169-170
profits from, 135-137, 143-145
McConnell, Frank, 73
Meister, F.A., 58
mescaline, 18
methadone, 22, 225-228
Minnesota Multiphasic
  Personality Inventory (MMPI),
    37
Mittleman, Roger E., 189
moderate drinkers, 55, 56, 57
Moynihan, Daniel Patrick, 146

naltrexone, 222-224
National Association of
  Alcoholism Treatment
    Programs, 215
National Beer Wholesalers
  Association, 81
National Council on Alcoholism,
  74, 213
National Federation of Parents
  for Drug-Free Youth, 175
National Institute of Justice, 160,
  163
National Institute on Alcohol
  Abuse and Alcoholism, 217,
    218, 221
National Institute on Drug
  Abuse, 22, 163, 208
National Narcotics Intelligence
  Consumers Committee
    (NNICC), 169-173
National Organization for the
  Reform of Marijuana Laws
    (NORML), 133
National Safety Council, 129,
  130
Nelson, Harry, 56
nicotine, 110
nitrous oxide, 18
nondrinkers
  and heart attacks, 56, 57

Owen, David, 93

Parsons, Oscar, 35
PCP, 22
Peele, Stanton, 22, 218
Peluso, Micki, 61
Peterson, Clifford D., 125

239